The Political Institutions & Administration

OF NORTHERN INDIA DURING MEDIEVAL TIMES

(*From 750 to 1200 A.D.*)

By

Padma B. Udgaonkar

MOTILAL BANARSIDASS

DELHI :: VARANASI :: PATNA

MOTILAL BANARSIDASS
H. O. Bungalow Road, Jawahar Nagar, Delhi-7.
Branches : Chowk, Varanasi-1 (U.P.)
: Ashok Raj Path, Patna-4 (Bihar)

First Edition 1969

PRINTED IN INDIA

By Shantilal Jain, Shri Jainendra Press, Bungalow Road, Jawahar Nagar, Delhi-7, and published by Sundarlal Jain, Motilal Banarsidass, Bungalow Road, Jawahar Nagar, Delhi-7

Dedicated

to

the memory

of

my parents

Smt. & Dr. A. S. Altekar

INTRODUCTION

In the following pages an attempt has been made to give a comprehensive and authoritative picture of the Political Institutions and Administration of Northern India during *c.* 750 A. D. to 1200 A. D.

We have got monographs on the Mauryan and Gupta administration; the administration of the Rāshṭrakūṭas and the Cholas has been extensively dealt with by Dr. A. S. Altekar and Prof. Nilakantha Sastri in their works dealing with these dynasties. There is also a work by Dr. Mahalingam dealing with the South Indian Polity. Dr. R. S. Tripathi, Dr. D. C. Ganguli and Dr. Beni Prasad have got small sections in their work on the administration of Harsha, the Gurjara Pratīhāras, the Gāhaḍavālas and the Paramāras. But a work giving a comprehensive picture of the Political Institutions and Administration of Northern India as a whole during *c.* 750 to 1200 is still a desideratum.

Northern India during this period was divided into a large number of small kingdoms. Out of these, Kashmir and Kāmarūpa (Assam) led a sheltered life not much influenced by the currents outside their boundaries. Sindh had fallen under the Muslim rule and its Polity had become altogether changed. The history of the Punjab is shrouded in darkness for the greater part of this period. We get some clear picture of the events happening there under the Shāhis and the Tomaras. But our sources, especially epigraphical, are so scanty that we can hardly give any reliable picture of the administration that had developed there.

The Gurjara-Pratīhāras, the Chedis, the Chandellas, the Pālas, the Senas, the Paramāras, the Chaulukyas and the Chāhamānas were ruling over the rest of northern India during this period. They have left us numerous epigraphical records, which throw a lot of light on the administration of the age. Though these kingdoms were separate political entities, their records show that their political institutions and administrative machinary were on the whole of the same pattern. It is therefore quite feasible and reasonable to delineate a picture of the Northern Indian Polity and Administration on the basis of a combined study of their epigraphs. It may also be observed that the records of each dynasty by itself are not copious enough to enable us to have a comprehensive picture of its administration.

The data of the epigraphical records has been supplemented by the information supplied by contemporary works on the political science (*Nīti*) like the *Śukranīti*, the *Kāmandakīya-Nītisāra, the Bārhaspatya-Arthaśāstra* and the Purāṇas, which were most probably northern Indian in their origin, and by the *Rājadharmakāṇḍa* of *Kṛityakalpataru* of Lakshmīdhara and the *Yuktikalpataru* of Bhoja which were certainly north Indian. The evidence from these works has been supplemented by the data of the *Mānasollāsa* of Someśvara and the *Nītivākyāmṛita* of Somadeva, which were written in the Deccan but in contemporary times.

The work deals with the period from *c.* 750 to 1200. A.D. During a part of this period, viz. from *c.* 840 to 950 A. D., greater part of northern India was under the political supremacy of a single dynasty viz. the Pratīhāras. Its epigraphs, however, supply only scanty evidence about its administration. We have, therefore, supplemented this evidence with that supplied by the epigraphs of the Chedis, the Chandellas and the Paramāras, who were once its feudatories, and by those of the Gāhaḍavālas, the Chāhamānas and the Chaulukyas, who ruled over part of the territories once incorporated in the Pratīhāra empire. The Pāla and the Sena dynasties are also included in our survey, because Bengal was usually coming into very close contact with the kingdoms in the Gangetic plane. It may here be pointed out that there was a general uniformity of cultural pattern in Ancient India. And hence the administrative structures of the different dynasties usually did not differ from one another in a striking manner. The account that one obtains from the evidence of a single dynasty is often fragmentary. The study of all the dynasties together gives us a comprehensive and comparative picture; we have therefore offered here a picture based on the records of all the dynasties taken together.

The first chapter deals with the different sources available for reconstructing the picture of the Indian Polity and

Administration of our period. They are mainly literary and epigraphical. In connection with the former, we have taken the opportunity to give a brief synopsis and to make an estimate of the contents of the different *Nīti* works that were composed during our period. The dates of the *Nīti* works as given in the authoritative books on the Dharmaśāstra literature have been generally accepted. In the case of the *Śukranīti*, however, we have discussed its date in great detail and it is hoped that our treatment of this topic will be found to be substantially original.

The second chapter deals with problems connected with the Kingship. It describes in the beginning how the institution of kingship had become hereditary. The reader will find how the Vedic form of coronation disappeared during our period and was replaced by the Paurāṇic one, where emphasis was laid upon the different propitiatory rites, the bath with *Pañchagavya* and the rubbing of the different limbs of the king with the earth collected from different localities. It is hoped that this contrast between the Vedic and Paurāṇic coronation, first pointed out in this work, will be found to be new and interesting. The scope of the king's education was widened in our period; the curriculum now included the study of *Śilpaśāstra*, *Kāmaśāstra*, *Arthaśāstra*, *Astronomy* etc, in addition to the study of *Dharmaśāstra*, *Mīmāṁsā*, *Daṇḍanīti* and *Vārtā*, which were earlier included.

This chapter also deals with the problem of the Divinity of the king and shows how the school of political writers on the one hand was advocating the theory of functional resemblance between some of the deities and the virtuous kings, and how, the school of courtiers on the other hand was declaring the king to be an incarnation of God on the earth. It also describes how only the virtuous king was regarded as a divine incarnation or as people's trustee by our political writers. The position of the junior princes of the royal family has been critically dealt with in the light of contemporary data. How the crown prince was regarded as indispensable in the administration, how younger princes also took prominent part in the Government, how proper provision was made for the maintenance of the queens and the younger princes—all these problems are dealt with in this chapter. The reader may find here much that is new.

In the third chapter, the reader will find a vivid picture of the Ministry based on scores of contemporary inscriptions. Ministers do not figure so prominently in the records of the earlier period as they do in those of our age. The epigraphical material about the ministry is as rich as, if not richer than, the observations of the *Smṛiti* writers. As a consequence, the reader will find the account very realistic. The chapter reveals how the ministers were regarded indispensable for a good government, how their posts had tended to become hereditary and how their secretaries were sometimes eventually promoted to the ministry itself. There is also detailed information about the way in which the business of administration was carried on by the ministry and about the different formulas of approving the order by the ministers. In all this treatment, the reader may find much that is interesting and new.

In the fourth chapter, the reader will find a clear picture of the Central Secretariat and its various departments. How the secretariat used to control the provincial and district administrations through its inspecting staff is indicated by a number of documents. The records also throw light upon the various frauds committed in case of land grants and the steps taken by the state to counteract them. An attempt has been made here to correlate the data of the *Nīti* works and epigraphical records to give a connected account of the working of the different departments.

The fifth chapter deals with Army administration. It is mainly based on the information given by Śukra. It gives us an interesting account of the units, constituents and composition of the army. How soldiers were recruited from all the castes, how they had to maintain discipline, how they had to go through daily exercises, how they were paid regularly and were often rewarded by gifts, how pension was given to the families of dead soldiers—all these problems are dealt with in this chapter. It may be pointed out that most of this information is conspicuous by its absence in other *Nīti* works. The reader will therefore find a good deal of this chapter substantially new.

The sixth chapter deals with Territorial Divisions. The reader will find a variety in the extent and nomenclature of the different territorial and administrative divisions that prevailed in the various kingdoms during our period. The Provincial, District, Town and Village administrations have also been described in this chapter. Here also the information supplied by our inscriptions is checked, compared to and contrasted with the data supplied by the earlier and contemporary inscriptions as well as with that of the works on polity. The reader will not find much information about the provincial and district administrations. The provincial administration was probably carried on old lines. The district administration was apparently not so well organised, as it was in the Gupta period. We do not get any reference to the district council, supervising over the district administration.

As far as the Village Administration is concerned, the reader will find that it was not so well-organised as it was in the contemporary South India. An attempt has, however, been made, as far as possible, to correlate the data scattered over the Nīti works and the contemporary South Indian inscriptions, to give a detailed account of the village administration.

The seventh chapter deals with Revenue and Expenditure. In the beginning, principles of taxation are discussed and then the problem whether the Brāhmaṇas were exempted from taxation has been briefly dealt with. Various aspects of the land tax have been considered in detail and along with it, the question of the ownership of land has been critically examined in the light of the valuable data supplied by the Nīti works and by early and contemporary inscriptions. A number of taxes on ordinary articles of consumption like the tax on leaves, cocoanuts, barley, cattle fodder, cotton fabric, oil, butter, sugar, candied sugar, have come to light. There were also a number of miscellaneous taxes levied upon shops, houses, wells, water wheels, as well as on dancing girls and people indulging in gambling. Different sources of government income have also been critically dealt with. The chapter concludes with a discussion on state expenditure.

The eighth chapter deals with Judicial Administration. The functions and duties of the king as the head of the judicial administration, as well as those of the chief justice and lawyer, have been first dealt with. The fundamental principles followed by Hindu jurisprudence have then been critically discussed. Some light has also been thrown upon the popular courts. The judicial procedure is not dealt with because it belongs to the sphere of judicial and not general administration.

The ninth chapter deals with the relations between the Feudatories and the emperor. In the beginning reasons are given why the principle of non-annexation was followed in Ancient India, leading to the existence of a number of feudatories. Privileges enjoyed by the feudatories of different grades have also been dealt with.

It may be pointed out that continuity and conservatism were the characteristics of Indian polity and therefore the above picture may not appear to be strikingly new. This however cannot be helped. It may be, however, claimed that the book represents a critical study of almost all the available material, both literary and epigraphical, and seeks to give a comprehensive, comparative and critical picture of the nature and the working of the political institutions and administration of Northern India, which has so far not been available.

ABBREVIATIONS

A.V.	Atharvaveda
A. Br.	Aitareya-Brāhmaṇa
A.Ś.	Arthaśāstra of Kauṭilya
A.S.I.W.C.	Archaeological Survey of India, Western circle
A.S.I.A.R.	Archaeological Survey of India, Annual Report
B.D.S.	Baudhāyana Dharmasūtra
B.G.	Bombay Gazetteer
B.I.	Prakrit and Sanskrit Inscriptions of Kathiawar, published by the Bhavanagar Archaeological Department, Bhavanagar
Bārhaspatya	Bārhaspatya-Arthaśāstra
C.I.I.	Corpus Inscriptionum Indicarum
D.K.	Dvyāśrayakāvya
E.I.	Epigraphia Indica
E.C.	Epigraphia Carnatika
Elliot	Elliot and Dowson, History of India as told by her own Historians
G.D.S.	Gautama Dharmasūtra
I.A.	Indian Antiquary
I.B.	Inscriptions from Bengal
I.H.Q.	Indian Historical Quarterly
J.A.S.B.	Journal of the Asiatic Society of Bengal
J.B.B.R.A.S.	Journal of the Bombay Branch of the Royal Asiatic Society.
J.B.O.R.S.	Journal of the Bihar and Orissa Research Society.
J.N.S.I.	Journal of the Numismatic Society of India.
J.R.A.S.	Journal of the Royal Asiatic Society
Kāmandaka	Kāmandakanītisāra
K. ktr.	Rājadharmakāṇḍa of Kṛityakalpataru
M.bh.	Mahābhārata
Manu	Manusmṛiti
Nārada	Nāradasmṛiti
Nvk	Nītivākyāmṛita

Rāj	Rājataraṅgiṇī
R.V.	Ṛigveda
Rāshṭrakūṭas	Rāshṭrakūṭas and their Times
Śukra	Śukranītisāra
Śat. Br.	Śatapatha-Brāhmaṇa
S.I.I.	South Indian Inscriptions
T. Br.	Taittirīya Brāhmaṇa
V.S.	Vājasaneya Saṁhitā
Walters	Walters, on Travels of Yuan Chwang
Yāj	Yājñavalkyasmṛiti

Transliteration

In the transliteration scheme followed in this work, the following are the main points to be noted.

आ	ā	ई	ī	ऊ	ū
ऋ	ṛi	ए	e	ऐ	ai
ओ	o	औ	au	ङ्	ṅ
च्	ch	छ्	chh	ञ	ñ
ट्	ṭ	ठ्	ṭh	ड्	ḍ
ढ्	ḍh	ण्	ṇ	श्	ś
ष्	sh	स्	s		
	Visarga—ḥ		Anusvāra—ṁ		

CONTENTS

Chapter I

ORIGINAL SOURCES

A

Literary Sources, their Time and Nature

The work deals with the political institutions and administration of Northern India during medieval times from c. 750 to 1200 A.D. The sources on which we have to rely are mainly of two categories, literary and epigraphical. A few Muslim travellers visited the country during this period, but their observations on the government of the country are not important. Alberuni, the most famous among them, has written a voluminous account of India and its culture; but he usually confines himself to astronomy, mathematics, mythology and religious and social conditions. He makes a few observations about law, judicial procedure and punishments, but his information seems to be merely a summary of some of the Smṛitis, he had studied. There is nothing original about it.

Among the literary works, we have naturally to attach great importance to the books on *Nīti-śāstra*. The important works in this category are *Kāmandakanītisāra* of *Kāmandaka*, *Śukranīti* of Śukra, *Nītivākyāmṛita* of Somadeva, *Bārhaspatya-Arthaśāstra* of Bṛihaspati and *Rājadharmakāṇḍa* of *Kṛityakalpataru* of Lakshmīdhara. We have two other minor works, the *Yuktikalpataru* of Bhoja and the *Mānasollāsa* of Someśvara; but they are not of much importance to our enquiry. The Smṛiti writers of our age also make some stray observations about the political thought of the period, but these are of a minor nature. These works are mostly concerned with ritualistic matters. Some of the Purāṇas have chapters on topics connected with the administration, but originality is not their strong point. Commentators like Medhātithi, Aparārka and Vijñāneśvara also have a few observations to make about the political thought and administration, but they have hardly any new light to throw upon the subject.

DATES OF SOURCE BOOKS

There is some difficulty, however, in utilising the above literary data. The precise time of the majority of the above writers is not known. The dates of some of them are subjects of great controversy. It is not possible here to enter into a discussion of the rival views; that would fall in the province of the historian of Sanskrit literature. For the purpose of this study we have generally accepted the dates proposed by scholars like Mahāmahopādhyāya P.V.Kane, Dr. A.B. Keith and Dr. R.C. Majumdar. The case of the date of the *Śukranīti* has, however, been discussed in detail in this chapter, as doubts have been expressed as to whether it can be legitimately utilised for reconstructing a picture of the administration of this period.

The question whether all the *Nīti* writers belonged to Northern India is also difficult to answer. The *Rājadharma-kāṇḍa* of *Kṛityakalpataru* was written in Madhyadeśa, as its author Lakshmīdhara is definitely known to have served the Gāhaḍavāla king Govindachandra as his minister of peace and war in the second quarter of the 12th century. Similarly the *Nītivākyāmṛita* of Somadeva was written in the Deccan; the author, who was a Jain, is definitely known to have flourished during the reign of the Rāshṭrakūṭa king Kṛishṇa III (*c.* 940-968). But as the Jain monks were usually travelling throughout India, it is very likely that Somadeva's book would have been based upon his observations in India as a whole. The internal evidence shows that the book is mostly based on the *Arthaśāstra* of Kauṭilya, which was certainly written in Northern India. Bhoja, the author of the *Yuktikalpataru* flourished in Mālwā in the first half of the 11th century and Someśvara, the author of the *Mānasollāsa* in the Deccan in the second quarter of the 12th century.

DATE OF KĀMANDAKA

As regards the remaining *Nīti* works, their dates and provenance are both unknown. K.P. Jayaswal had placed Kāmandaka in the 5th century; P.V. Kane in the period between 400 and 600 A.D., R.C. Majumdar in the 7th century (*Ancient India*, p. 471) and A.B. Keith in *c.* 700 A.D.

Out of these writers, P.V. Kane and R.C. Majumdar give no reasons for the dates they have accepted. Jayaswal's theory depends upon the identification of Kāmandaka with Śikharasvāmin of the Karmadaṇḍā inscription, for which there is no convincing evidence. A.B. Keith gives the following arguments :—

"It (*Kāmandakanītisāra*) is not known to the *Pañchatantra* in its oldest form nor to Kālidāsa, who both rather use the Arthaśāstra; even Daṇḍin seems to be unaware of it, but Bhavabhūti's mention of the nun Kāmandakī may have significance, though that dramatist, like Viśākhadatta in his *Mudrārākshasa*, used the Arthaśāstra. Vāmana knows it (*c.* 800), so that the date may be *c.* 700, though others have put it contemporaneous with Varāhamihira. Its presence on the island of Bali in the Kawi literature is of no importance, as it was not till the tenth century that that literature flourished to the greatest extent."[1]

The above arguments may not be weighty and conclusive, but it is not unlikely that the picture, which the book gives about the political thought, institutions and administration, may be true of the beginning of our period.

THE DATE OF THE ŚUKRANĪTI

It is necessary to fully discuss the problem of the date of *Śukranīti* as a wide divergence exists among scholars on the point. We therefore propose to discuss the question thoroughly, as we have utilised that work extensively in this study.

The date of the *Śukranīti* is still a question of great controversy among different scholars. G. Oppert, who edited the work first, thought that the book belonged to the same period which produced early Smṛiti and epic literature.[2] His view was, however, based on the assumption that the use of fire-arms was not unknown to ancient India. Pradhan while writing on the kingship in the *Śukranīti*, placed the work in the 4th century A.D. (*Modern Review*, February, 1916); K.P. Jayaswal, while reviewing *Criminal Justice in Ancient*

1. A.B. Keith : *History of Sanskrit Literature*, pp. 462-3.
2. As quoted in B.K. Sarkar's *Positive Background of Hindu Sociology*, p. 64.

India, expressed the opinion that the book is a product of the 8th century of the Christian era (*Modern Review*, February, 1916).

In his *Ancient India* (2nd edition), R.C. Majumdar has stated at one place (p. 471) that the *Śukranīti* is of quite a late date, as it refers to fire-arms; but in the same work, elsewhere on p. 442, he has pronounced the book as one of the latest political treatises written in ancient times and has utilised its contents to describe the political theory and administration between *c.* 300 to 1200 A.D. Beni Prasad holds that the book cannot be earlier than the 12th or the 13th century, and represents the last summing of Hindu political thought (*Theory of Government*, p. 245). B.K. Sircar points out that like the *Mahābhārata* and the *Manusmṛiti*, the book is a composite one and that it went on being expanded through several centuries (*The Positive Background of Hindu Sociology*, pp. 63-71). He, however, holds that the passages referring to the nine gems (IV, 2 41ff.) and to the doctrine of seven metals, would have been added to the book in the 10th and 14th centuries respectively.

U.N. Ghoshal places the book at the beginning of the period, 1200 to 1625 A.D. and considers it to be the last notable achievement of the Hindu genius on political speculation (*Political Theories*, p. 249).

Rajendralal Mitter, P.C. Ray and Panchanan Niyogi placed the work in the 16th century (*Positive Background*, p. 64).

It appears that, as observed by B.K. Sircar, the work is a composite one containing several early passages along with later ones. We also agree with U.N. Ghoshal and R.C. Majumdar in holding the work as one of the latest political treatises of the ancient Indian period. There are, however, some curious passages in the book, which contain a combination of the terminology of the late Vedic period with the coinage of the Muslim age, as where the incomes of *svarāṭs* and *virāṭs* are given as 50 lakhs and 10 crores of silver *karshas*, each weighing 100 *rattis* (I, 183ff.). Passages like those, which prohibit the killing of the enemy, when he is asleep or without arms (IV, 7, 355-7) are mere copies of the earlier rules in Manu (VII, 90) and are generally not true of our age; the same is the case of the statements, which deny any property to the wife and the son.

Let us first try to fix the approximate date of the passages referring to small and large guns and the composition of the gun-powder, which are probably the latest additions to the book. It is no doubt true that the most detailed information on these topics is supplied at IV. 7. 195-213; but this does not mean that the rest of the book was not at all touched by the latest redactor. In Chapter I, he refers to the soldiers with guns protecting the king (I. 231). In Chapter II also he insists that the commander-in-chief of the forces should be an expert in the use of the gun and the gun-powder (II, 95); he does not forget to garrison the forts with guns and the artillery corps (II, 195).

When did the latest redactor introduce these innovations? It is usually believed that as the gun-powder was used in India by the Mughal conquerors, the date of the latest additions to the book should be the 16th century. This view, however, need not be necessarily accepted, because we have now definite evidence to show that in the 14th century, Vijayanagar was not unaware of the use of the fire-arms. Firishtah, while describing the loot secured by the Muslim conquerors in the campaign of 1368 against Vijayanagar, includes three hundred gun-carriages in it (Saletore, *Social and Political life in Vijayanagar*, p. 430). Even if we reject this passage as of doubtful authenticity, we have the definite evidence of two Karnatak inscriptions, showing that guns were used by the Vijayanagar troops in the 14th century; one of them refers to the death of the matchlockman (*Koyi-kara*) Devayya Nayak in 1388 (*E.C.*, VIII, Sh. 433, p. 8 and part II, p. 218), while the other refers to an attendant, whose duty it was to supply gun-powder to the fighters riding on an elephant (*E.C.*, VIII, Sa., 68, p. 104, part II, p. 282). The epigraphical evidence thus clearly shows that in the 14th century, India was not unacquainted with the use of fire-arms and gun-powder and hence the date of even the latest additions in the *Śukranīti* need not be placed later than *c.* 1400 A.D.

In I. 385 ff., Śukra refers to a silver coin weighing 100 *rattis* and gives the revenues of villages and the incomes of the different grades of rulers in that currency. It is to be noted that a silver coin weighing 100 *rattis* or about 170 grains was not current in the first millennium of the Christian era; it was first popularised in India by the Pathan kings, who issued silver currency of the standard of 165 to 175 grains from the 13th century. Hence the passages in the *Śukranīti* referring to the silver coin of 170 grains should also be taken to be added to it in the 13th or the 14th century.

The pattern of the book is however fundamentally different from that of the books on the Dharmaśāstra and Nītiśāstra, which were composed after 1150 A.D. These later works are of the nature of Nibandhas or digests, discuss each topic, give the views of earlier writers upon it, but do not necessarily conclude it with their own views. The digest writers usually choose prose for making such comments as they want to offer. We give below some specimen pages of the *Rājadharmakāṇḍa* of the *Kalpataru*, pp. 22 to 26.

Athāmātyaḥ

Tatra narādhipa iti anuvrittau Yājñavalkyaḥ :—

(One and half verse quoted)

Manuḥ :—

One verse quoted with the remark, *labdhalakshyān paridṛishṭakarmaṇaḥ*.

(Four more verses of Manu quoted).

Matsyapurāṇe :—

(Three verses quoted).

Rājaguṇānuvṛittau Kātyāyanaḥ :—

(Three verses quoted).

Commentary on them :—*Mantriṇaḥ rājakṛityeshu. Sabhyāḥ prāyaśchittādau. Vaidyāḥ chikitsāyām.*

Mahābhārat :—

(One verse quoted).

Tathā (Three anonymous verses quoted).

Matsyapurāṇe :—

(Three verses quoted).

Commentary. *Vyūhatantravidhānajñaḥ, Chakradaṇḍādyākārasainyasanniveśaḥ. Tasya tantraṁ śāstraṁ, tena vyūhaprakāraṁ yo jānāti.*

(Five more verses from the *Matsyapurāṇa* quoted).

Commentary. *Anāhāryaḥ parairabhedyaḥ.*

(One more verse from the same Purāṇa quoted).
Commentary, *Aksharakshitā akshaparipālakaḥ*.

(22 more verses from the *Matsyapurāṇa* quoted).
Commentary, *Svāsano dṛiḍhāsanaḥ*.

The above will give an idea of the style and pattern of the *Rājadharmakāṇḍa* of Lakshmīdhara and it is generally followed by the *Rājanītikāṇḍa* of Devaṇabhaṭṭa (*c*. 1300 A.D.) the *Rājanītiratnākara* of Chaṇḍeśvara (*c*. 1325), the *Nītimayūkha* of Nīlakaṇṭha (*c*. 1625) and the *Rājanītiprakāśa* of Mitramiśra (*c*. 1650). The latest redactor of the *Śukranīti* does not follow this new pattern; on the other hand he copies the pattern followed by Kāmandaka, Bṛihaspati and Somadeva. The author discusses each topic, and gives his own independent view upon it in great detail; he, however, rarely refers to the views of earlier writers. The main body of the book therefore can hardly be later than *c*. 1200 A.D.

We have so far tried to show how the main portions of the book cannot be placed later than *c*. 1200 A.D.; we shall now see how far its polity reflects the condition of our period. It may be pointed out at the outset that though some portions were added to the book by *c*. 1400 A.D., the administrative structure and the designations of officers as given in the work do not show any points of contact with those of Vijayanagar, which was the most prominent Hindu kingdom in the 14th century. In Vijayanagar,[1] the provincial viceroys had their own ministers, but Śukra does not refer to them. The term Nāyaka, used to denote both the provincial viceroys and petty officers, is unknown to Śukra in that sense. In Vijayanagar, the secretary was called Rāyasa; Śukra calls him a Lekhaka; officers in Vijayanagar like Nirvāhaka, Kāryakartā, Śāsanāchārya are conspicuous by their absence in Śukra. Territorial divisions in Vijayanagar were known as Kheḍa, Kharvaṭa, Droṇamukha, Siṁhāsana, Nāḍu, Koṭṭam, etc., Śukra, however, does not at all refer to them.

All this evidence clearly shows that the latest redactor has not borrowed anything from the Vijayanagar polity. There was hardly any well-settled Hindu Government in the north during the period 1200 to 1400 A.D., whose polity could have

1. Saletore, *Social and Political life in Vijayanagar*, 265-268.

materially influenced the account of Śukra. We may therefore well conclude that the *Śukranīti* does not give much information about the polity of the period later than *c.* 1200 A.D., though it probably received its present final form in *c.* 1400. It may be further noted that words like the Diwān, the Kotwāl, the Peshvā and the Vakil, which became common in the Muslim period, are conspicuous by their absence in the *Śukranīti*.

It is felt in certain quarters that the designations of the different ministers have a modern air about them and may have been borrowed from the medieval Rajput polity. However, this is not corroborated by evidence from medieval Rajput History.[1] Out of the names of the ten ministers in Śukra, only Purohita and Pradhāna were current in Rajputana; Sachiva, Mantrin, Paṇḍita, Sumantra, Amātya and Prāḍvivāka were not at all known to Rajput polity.

We need not, however, suspect that the designations of the ten ministers may be modern merely because they are not referred to by any earlier writer on polity. It is interesting to note that Śukra alternatively speaks of a ministry of eight also (II, 71-72) and this is very nearly the position of Someśvara and Manu, who advise a ministry of seven or eight. In the Hindu period, we thus find a ministry of eight not unknown. When Shivaji performed his coronation, he formally constituted a ministry of eight, members of which were known as Ashṭapradhānas at that time. The Rājanīti of Chitnis and a contemporary paper known as *Jābatā*, both refer to eight ministers and their functions, while describing Shivaji's coronation.[2] It is from these two sources that we learn that the designations of Shivaji's ministers were similar to those of Śukra, though the functions of some of them were not identical. Out of the eight ministers of Shivaji's ministry, Pradhāna, Paṇḍitarāo, Senāpati and Mantrī were discharging functions similar to those in the *Śukranīti*. Prāḍvivāka of Śukra becomes Nyāyādhīśa of Shivaji. Sachiva is the war minister according to Śukra and the contemporary *Jābatā*, but

1. I am thankful to Dr. M.L. Sharma for information on this point.
2. B.V. Bhat, *Shivasichī Rājanīti*, pp. 107-16.

Chief Secretary according to Chitnis. Sumantra, who is a treasurer according to Śukra, becomes a foreign minister according to Chitnis and the *Jābatā*. Purohita is included in the ministry by the *Jābatā* but not by Chitnis. Pratinidhi of Śukra has been excluded from Shivaji's ministry, but when Rajaram had to leave Mahārāshṭra and take refuge in Jinji, this post was created and given to Ramachandra Panta Amātya. We may well conclude that in the ancient period also, it was only when the king was unable to function that this post was created and filled.

It is well known that Shivaji was a revivalist and tried to base his polity on the ancient tradition. The original kernal of the *Śukranīti* must have been a boo k of established reputation, at least about 300 or 400 years old since Shivaji chose to name his ministers more or less on the pattern suggested by Śukra. These names given by Śukra my well have been in vogue even before his time; only Manu and others somehow did not mention them.

We have so far tried to show that the *Śukranīti* in its present form cannot be placed later than the 14th century, we shall now try to settle the earliest possible date for the book as a whole. It appears from a number of passages that the work cannot be earlier than *c.* 800 A.D. The inclusion of Dharmaśāstra and Purāṇa in Trayī (I, 390), the numbering of Vidyās as 32 and not 14 (IV, 3, 24), the references to the Tantras and Tāntrikas (II, 184; II, 122), the mention of the *bhasmas* of metals (IV, 3, 33), all point out that the book cannot be earlier than *c.* 700 A.D. Then we have the references to Mlechchhas as residing in the north-west, and following their own scriptures (IV, 4, 35-36) and having their own Yāvana-mata, which maintained that God was invisible (IV, 3,30). These would obviously show that the book cannot be much earlier than *c.* 800 A.D.

The book seems to be belonging to the age of the *Yuktikalpataru* of Bhoja (*c.* 1050 A.D.) and the *Mānasollāsa* of Someśvara (*c.* 1125 A.D.). Its long sections on the *Khaḍgalakshaṇa*, (IV, 7, 215) *aśvaparīkshā* (IV, 7, 142-148). and *gajalakshaṇa* (IV, 7, 32-42) are unknown to earlier works on polity, but recall similar sections in the *Yuktikalpataru* (pp. 140-147; 181-193; 193-205) and the *Mānasollāsa* (BR II, Chap. VI, pp. 79-90). It may be therefore contemporaneous with them.

Besides these points, there are a number of facts to show that the general outlook of the book is that of the period 800-1200 A.D.; they are the following :—

(1) The book refers to the use of the term Sāmanta both for a feudatory and a high official (I, 189); this was common in the Deccan of our period.[1]

(2) The price of gold is stated to be sixteen times the price of silver (IV, 2, 92); this ratio is accepted by Bhāskarāchārya (J.N.S.I., II. p. 2-12). In the Pathan period, the ratio was 10 to 1.

(3) The author does not like women to become officers (III, 44). It will be shown in Chapter II how women officers were practically non-existent in northern India of our period.

(4) In IV, 2, 13, the author lays down the principle that the treasury should have a reserve equal to 20 years revenue; this principle seems to have been followed by the Hindu states during our period, for otherwise Mahmud of Ghazni and Mahmud of Ghor would not have been successful in carrying huge plunders from the defeated kings.

(5) The inclusion of the *deśabhāshā* (regional language) and *Yāvanamatam* in 32 *kalās* (IV, 3, 30) would also indicate *c.* 1200 A.D. as the time of the work.

(6) In IV, 3, 50, Śukra describes Vedānta as a doctrine, which advocates that Brahma alone is the reality without a second, that multiplicity has no real existence and that it is due to *Māyā* and *Ajñāna*; this is the view of the Advaita Vedānta of Śaṅkara; apparently the Visishṭādvaita of Rāmānuja (*c.* 1200 A.D.) had not yet become popular.

(7) The injunction that princes should not be made governors or allowed pensions (I, 345-347) was also followed in our period (*J.A.S.B.* XII. 104; X. 209; XIV. 104).

(8) The tax on houses and shops, referred to by Śukra

1. Datta, the foreign minister of Dhruva, was also a Sāmanta; *E.I.*, X, p. 89.

in IV, 2, 129, also existed during our period (see Chap. VII. *E.I.*, XIV. 309).

(9) In IV, 4, 63, Śukra refers to the building of the temples of Vishṇu, Śaṅkara, Gaṇeśa, the Sun and Devī; this Panchāyatana worship is believed to have been made popular by the great Śaṅkarāchārya.

(10) Śukra's section on the building of a capital (1, 214) recalls a similar section in the *Rājadharmakāṇḍa* of *Kṛityakalpataru* of Lakshmīdhara written in *c.* 1150 A D.

(11) The principle that the cavalry should be one-fourth the strength of the infantry (IV, 7, 19) was followed in our period at least by some states. In the Chandella army, that opposed Mahmud of Ghazni, there was the same proportion (Chap. V.).

(12) In I, 382, Śukra advocates resort to a strong fort in times of difficulty; many of the Hindu opponents of the Muslims were following this policy during *c.* 1000 to 1300 A.D.

(13) The injunction that peace should be concluded even with an Anārya, because otherwise he might uproot the kingdom (IV, 7, 243) recalls the conduct of many of the Hindu kings of the 11th to 13th century, who decided to make terms with the Muslim conquerors with the hope that they might thereby survive.

(14) In IV, 2, 95 ff, Śukra refers to the prices of a number of articles in silver *pala,* which was a coin weighing 320 *rattis*, equal to ten silver Kārshāpaṇas. Several Orissa inscriptions belonging to the early medieval period (*c.* 800 to 1000 A.D.) mention the annual revenues of villages in silver *palas* (*J.N.S.I.* XV, 139). So the time of *Śukranīti* would not be very much later than 1000 A.D.

Each of the above fourteen points by itself may not carry any definite conviction about the date of the work. But when they are taken together, they tend to show that the main kernal of the work, apart from the passages borrowed bodily from earlier works and later additions referring to silver *karshas*, and gun-powder etc., belongs to the period, c. 800 to 1200 A.D.

I think that we are therefore well justified in utilising the work as a source book for our period.

We have utilised the political thought contained in the Nīti works of our period in the body of the book. Nevertheless some remarks are necessary about the contents and important features of these books as works on polity. The account given in these books is sometimes traditional; sometimes it is merely a summary of the theories of earlier works like the *Arthaśāstra* and the *Manusmṛiti*. But there are several sections in some of them, which give us a glimpse into the new features of the polity as developed in our age.

Let us now discuss the important features of the above-mentioned *Nīti* works. We shall give a brief and running commentary upon their contents, which will be useful in judging them as source-books.

KĀMANDAKANĪTISĀRA

The *Kāmandakanītisāra* need not detain us long, as it is merely a metrical version of certain portions of the *Arthaśāstra* of Kauṭilya. Kāmandaka himself has admitted that he is merely summarising the work of Kauṭilya; however, occasionally he gives his own views also. He recognises the importance of *daṇḍa* and holds before us the traditional social and moral ideals. He discusses the ends and aims of the state and maintains that the interests of the ruler and the ruled are identical. He extols moral discipline in the king and describes his duties, functions and responsibilities. He refers to a number of rulers, who perished due to their wickedness and immoral character. Considerable space is also devoted to the education of the prince and the personal safety of the king. The duties of the *anujīvi* (courtier) towards the king are also discussed in great detail. Valuable information is also supplied about the criminal (*Kaṇṭakaśodhana*) court. The seven constituents of the state are also discussed in detail. Importance is given to the proper control of the army. Considerable attention is paid towards the problem of the *Maṇḍala*.

There are certain important omissions in the *Kāmandakanītisāra* as compared to the original work. Kauṭilya devotes one chapter to republics (or oligarchies), but Kāmandaka does not do so, probably because they did not exist during his period. Similarly chapters dealing with the personal, civil and criminal law, which are among the important contributions of the *Arthaśāstra*, are not at all touched and discussed by Kāmandaka. The probable reason for this was that during our period, some writers like Bṛihaspati and Nārada had specialised in this branch and Kāmandaka did not feel it necessary to cover the same ground again.

We may in vain look into the book for information either about the ministry or about the departmental heads, either about the provincial or about the district administration. Taxation is also passed over. The king and the courtiers dominate the picture indicating thereby that the royal court with its numerous courtiers had now become the most important feature of the state.

ŚUKRANĪTI

The Śukranīti is a more comprehensive and important book on the Political Science than any other book dealing with the subject with the exception of the *Arthaśāstra* of Kauṭilya. According to Śukra, it is the *nīti*, which is the main cause of the stability of society, so necessary to secure livelihood of the citizens. Nīti is the source of *dharma*, *artha* and *kāma*. It enables us to follow the correct path of duty, so that we may get salvation.[1] It secures livelihood to all and promotes social peace and order, rendering family life and pleasures possible. Non-conformity to *Nīti* is usually dangerous to a king; he should therefore always act according to *Nīti* for the welfare and prosperity of his kingdom and his subjects. The kingdom will become weak, the army will be inefficient, the civil service will be disorganised and the state will get topsyturvy, if the king will not follow the rules of *Nīti*.[2]

1. Sarvopajīvakaṁ lokasthitikṛinnītiśāstrakam,
Dharmārtha-kāmamūlaṁ hi-smṛitaṁ mokshapradaṁ yataḥ, *Śukra*, I, 5.
2. Bhinnaṁ rāshṭraṁ balaṁ bhinnaṁ bhinno'mātyādiko gaṇaḥ,
Akauśalyaṁ nṛipasyaitadanīteryasya sarvaād. *Śukra*, I, 19.

Śukra deals only with the monarchical type of Government and divides his book into four chapters. The first chapter deals with the king and discusses in great detail his qualities, duties, functions and responsibilities. Valuable information is given about king's education. The problem of the divinity of the king has also been tackled in this chapter in an interesting manner. Unlike any other work, it supplies information about the different grades of feudatories and their incomes. The rules of inheritance are also discussed in great detail. While describing the lay-out of the capital, it informs us at what place the capital should be built, where the king's palace should be situated, how many courtyards it should have, where the court and the museums should be situated, what should be the length and width of the *rāja-mārgas*, *mārgas*, *vīthis* and foot-paths. Considerable light is also thrown upon the construction of the council chamber. Town-planning is also discussed in detail. Interesting and minute instructions are given about the seating arrangement in the court. Where, how, and in what direction, the princes, their sons, the king's brothers, uncles, elder members of the royal family, the preceptor, the ministers, etc., should sit in the court, is described in an interesting way.

Incidentally there is a discussion in this chapter about the weights and coins, which is not relevant to its main theme. There are however many such *obiter dicta* in the book.

The second chapter mainly deals with the high officers of the state, their duties and functions and their relations with the king. The members of the ministry naturally come first in this connection, and their functions are fully described. We are also given a clear insight into the day-to-day working and functions of the ministry. The state expenditure is also discussed in this chapter, probably because the officers were mainly connected with it. It may be pointed out here that no other writer on polity has discussed the different items of state expenditure and the percentages to be spent on them. Valuable and detailed information is also given about the different kinds of state documents like *jayapatra* or the document of judgment, *ājñāpatra* or the document of order, *prajñāpatra* or the document of notification, *śāsanapatra* or the document of public notice, *prasādapatra* or the document of royal favour, *bhogapatra* or the document of possession; these are not mentioned in the earlier works. It may be noted here that duiing our period, numerous royal grants were issued for different purposes and hence they were given different technical titles. The attitude of the king towards the courtiers and followers is also discussed in this chapter. How the courtiers are to be treated, how they should behave towards the king, what are their duties towards the ruler, all these questions are fully discussed.

The third chapter does not deal with the political thought or the administration. It describes certain customs and traditions and deals with some problems connected with social organisation. Problems connected with the family life like the attitude of the father towards his son, the attitude of men towards women, are also tackled here. There is also some discussion about the extent of the educational courses. Greater concern is shown towards the branches of learning like Mīmāṁsā, Tarka, Itihāsa, Arthaśāstra, Kāmaśāstra, Śilpaśāstra, Alaṅkāra, Kāvya, etc., and prejudice is expressed against the Vedic scholarship. Emphasis has been laid upon the importance of Āchāra and Dharma. The relative importance of Āchāra and Śṛuti is also discussed. The advantages of travel are also referred to.

The fourth chapter deals with a number of topics like the forts, allies, judicial and military administration, and the problem of taxation. There is also a section dealing with the different arts and sciences, and the social customs and institutions.

The section devoted to the 'forts' describes their eight kinds of varieties and discusses their importance. It may, however, be noted here that Kauṭilya refers to only four varieties of forts and is silent about the *parikhā*, *parighā*, *sahāya* and *sainya* forts mentioned by Śukra.

The section dealing with 'Allies' does not reveal any thing new. Like other political writers, Śukra also describes the nature of different kinds of policies, namely *sāma*, *dāna*, *daṇḍa* and *bheda*, and the circumstances under which they are to be followed. The use of *daṇḍa* is recommended to be avoided as far as possible. The king is advised to ascertain his own limitations as well as those of his subjects.

As regards the judicial administration a number of principles are laid down, but there is nothing new about the information given.

The section devoted to the army administration is very important. Nowhere else we get so detailed and interesting an account about the army, its constituents and administration. How the soldiers were recruited from all the castes, how they were trained, how they had to go through daily exercises, how they were paid and rewarded—all these topics are discussed in great detail. There is also interesting information about the different varieties of horses, camels and elephants, which formed part of the army. How to judge the age of these animals, how to select the best among them and how to train them—all these are dealt with in great detail. Different kinds of weapons are also described. The description of gun and gun-powder is a special feature of this chapter; it is not referred to by earlier writers. This section is perhaps the latest addition to the original work as already stated above.

As regards taxation, a number of interesting principles are enunciated. Valuable information is supplied about the different kinds of taxes that were imposed upon merchants, cultivators, shop-keepers, traders, etc. We are also given a clear insight into the nature and varieties of different kinds of gems and precious stones. The prices of a number of articles are referred to; this enables us to have an idea of the economic life during our period.

It is worth noting that there are several striking points of resemblance and difference between the *Arthaśāstra* of Kauṭilya and the *Śukranīti* of Śukra. Both discuss the duties and daily time-table of the king and hold similar views on the topic. Proper education of the prince is emphasised by both; Śukra, however, includes new sciences like astrology and useful arts in the king's curriculum, which are not mentioned by Kauṭilya. Both deal with the topic 'restraints of organs', the discussion is, however, more systematic in the *Arthaśāstra* than in the *Śukranīti*. Necessity and importance of the ministry is recognised by both; Śukra, however, gives a better glimpse into the working of the ministry and into the functions of different ministers than Kauṭilya. Both attach importance to the careful selection of the ministers. Testing of ministers is, however. more detailed systematic in the *Arthaśāstra* than in the *Śukranīti*. Distinction between *amātya* and *mantrin* is made by Kauṭilya, while Śukra does not do so. Both deal with the topic *rājaputrarakshaṇa*; Śukra, however, deals with it in greater detail than Kauṭilya. Both discuss the topic *anujīvi-vṛittam*; Śukra however gives more detailed information about it than Kauṭilya. The sixfold policy and the nature of alliance are discussed by both. In this connection, Kauṭilya gives a more comprehensive account about the nature of different kinds of expedients than Śukra, who only enumerates them. About the replenishment of treasury, Kauṭilya suggests a larger number of expedients than Śukra. Principles of taxation are discussed by both, but the treatment of Śukra is more vivid. Spies do not occupy a prominent place in the *Śukranīti*, while in the *Arthaśāstra*, there is a detailed description about the spy organisation.

Topics of civil and criminal law are not dealt with by Śukra as by Kauṭilya. Problems connected with the law of marriage, divorce, remarriage, maintenance of women, rules regarding the sale of buildings, boundary and field disputes, recovery of debts, taking of oaths, resumption of gifts, ownership, sale without ownership, robbery, gambling, protection of artisans and merchants etc. are not discussed by Śukra. The reason was probably that in this period Nārada and Bṛihaspati had separately dealt with the civil and criminal law, and hence Śukra had merely touched some of the topics concerning them in order to make the book more comprehensive.

According to Śukra an ideal state is one where the use of force is non-existent and where every thing goes on right lines without any external compulsion;[1] society has become law-abiding by instinct and so there is no necessity for the use of force. The king and the subjects both should act according to law, for it is only by following Dharma that one gets happiness in this world.[2] The king is not above the law but subject to its jurisdiction.

1. Apreritahitakaraṁ sarvarāshṭraṁ bhaved yathā,
Tathā nītistu sandhāryā nṛipeṇātmahitāya vai. *Śukra*. I, 18.
2. *Śukra*, I, 24.

The state, as described by Śukra, is an organism composed of seven elements, namely the king, the minister, the treasure, the territory, the fort, the army and the ally. It may be noted that earlier writers had also recognised these seven constituents of the state and regarded them as the limbs of the body politic. Śukra, however, goes a step further in comparing them to the different limbs of the body, which hardly any writer before him had done. The king is compared to the head, the minister to the eye, the ally to the ear, the treasure to the mouth, the army to the mind, the fort to the arms and the country to the legs.[1] The state has been thus regarded as a living organism; it may, however, be pointed out that the cells and limbs of the living organism have no separate existence of their own and cannot function independently, while the seven constituents of the state have their own separate existence. New states can also be established with the help of only some of the constituents like territory, treasure, forts and king.

The king, as the head of the body politic, is the main cause of social progress and prosperity. He is to identify his interest and welfare with those of his subjects and look upon them with equality. He has to promote *dharma*, *artha*, *kāma* and learning. He has to work hard for the material prosperity of the subjects and has to make arrangements for their amusement and recreation. He has to impose only just taxes and has to protect the properties of infants, minors, widows and of all persons, who are unable to manage their estates. He is further called upon to support the helpless, the aged, the blind, the cripple, the lunatics, the widows, the orphans and those suffering from diseases and calamities by giving them medicines, shelter, food, and clothing according to their requirements.

The king is to be virtuous and self-disciplined, for otherwise, he cannot rule successfully and cannot enjoy prosperity. He is also himself expected to be well-versed in the arts and sciences and to be skilled in the use of arms and weapons (I, 47-48).

1. Dṛigamātyāḥ suhrit śrotroṁ mukhaṁ kośo balaṁ manaḥ,
Hastau pādau durga-rāshṭrau rājyaṅgāni Smritāni hi. *Śukra*, I, 62.

As regards the theory of the divinity of the king, Śukra has merely conceded a certain functional resemblance between the king and the divine guardians. He only admits a good and virtuous king to be divine and boldly declares unlike any of his predecessors that a bad and vicious king is *rākshasa* (demon) incarnate; he does not hesitate to add that the subjects do not owe the duty of obedience to such a ruler. He further states that the king, who forsakes his duty, oppresses his subjects and falls from the high ideal, is a dacoit in the form of a ruler (II, 257) and unhesitatingly allows the subjects to oust such a king and to put an end to his maladministration (II, 275).

Unlike any other political writer, Śukra has made a further advance in declaring the king to be a trustee, while describing his duties. He has asked him not to spend the royal treasury for his own private use. The king was of course to tax the people; but he must promise that in return of taxation he will protect them. The king is thus regarded as the servant of the people (IV, Sect. 2, 130).

The king is further not regarded as infallible. Śukra points out that it is the king, who sets the fashions, people follow them more or less due to helplessness. If, therefore, he leads a vicious life and the subjects follow his example, he is accountable to God for not only his own sins but for those of his subjects as well, and is thus liable to be condemned to hell (I, 87).

As regards the problem of the succession to the throne, the eldest son is to succeed the king. Other princes should be given an allowance equal to one-fourth of the privy purse of the king. They should also be appointed as governors of the provinces. In the absence of a son, the daughter's son is allowed to succeed. There is, however, no reference to an adopted son as a possible successor (II, 15, 32).

No other writer on polity except Śukra gives us the names of different departments held by various ministers, Śukra's ministry consisted of the following 10 ministers, namely the Purohita, the Pratinidhi, the Pradhāna, the Sachiva, the Mantrī, the Prāḍvivāka, the Paṇḍita, the Sumantra, the Amātya and the Dūta. The functions of these ministers are described in detail in chapter III.

Officers, says Śukra, should be appointed not on caste consideration, but according to their capability, merit and character (II, 54). They should be promoted to the post of the minister in due course (II, 115), if they have proved their capacity by their merit and achievements. Śukra further recommends the occasional transfer of ministers from one department to another, so that an able minister may get the chance of working in a department, more important than the one to which he had been originally appointed. It is worth noting that the transfer of a minister from one department to another is not referred to by any earlier writer on politics.

Śukra also lays down that in disputes and complaints, the king should take the side not of his officers but of his subjects and should dismiss a government servant, who is accused by one hundred men.[1] He should also dismiss those members of the public service, who go astray more thna once.

The state, as envisaged by Śukra, was an organisation for the welfare of the subjects. It was not only to preserve law and order by suppressing crime and disorder and supervising and controlling gambling and drinking, but it was also to maintain hospitals and to establish rest houses, where new-comers should be allowed to take rest after proper examination of their bonafides. The State was to increase the resources of the country by developing forests and working mines. Agriculture was to be promoted by constructing and repairing tanks, dams, and canals and by bringing waste land under cultivation; Important economic transactions were to be under the supervision of the state. The state was not to tolerate counterfeit currency and false measures and weights (II, 358). It was to promote commerce by securing the safety of roads.

The state was not merely to be content with promoting the material prosperity of its citizens, it was to promote their

1. Prajāśatena saṅdviṣṭaṁ saṁtyajedadhikāriṇam, Amātyamapi saṁvīkshya sakṛidanyāyagāminam, Ekānte daṇḍayet spashṭamabhyāsāt-pakritaṁ tyajet, Anyāyavartinām rājyaṁ sarvasvaṁ cha harennṛipaḥ. *Śukra*, I, 376-77.

moral and spiritual welfare also by appointing special religious inspectors. It was also to improve the social order and to encourage learning, education and art by subsidising learned academies and extending patronage to scholars

Famine was to be provided against by keeping large stock of grains sufficient for the needs of three years.[1] There were no war loans; in case of need, the state had to rely on the hoarded wealth of the rich people by promising them to return it, when prosperity returned.[2]

Unlike any other book, the *Śukranīti* deals with the leave rules and holidays of the royal servants. In cases of illness, the servants were to get leave on 1′2 or 3′4 of the pay drawn by them.[3] Men with forty years of service were to get pensions equal to half of the salary enjoyed by them;[4] in cases of premature death, their wives and children were to receive pensions.[5]

NĪTIVĀKYĀMṚITA

The *Nītivākyāmṛita* of Somadeva is a book mainly devoted to the political institutions and administration. Its value, however, is relatively not so great as that of the *Kāmandakanīti*. Somadeva, like Kāmandaka, also follows Kauṭilya, while discussing the political topics. He has got a happy way of expressing ideas in a concise form, as he had a nice command over Sanskrit. His work is characterised by pun, humour and short pithy sentences. He emphasises the harmony between the different *Purushārthas* and recommends a balanced synthesis, when he states that everything has got its own value except when it is carried to an excess.

Somadeva recognises the supreme importance of political discipline and regards the state as an end in itself. He lays great emphasis upon the proper education of the king, who was expected to be well-versed in the four branches of learn-

1. *Śukra*, IV, Sect II, 40.
2. *Śukra*, IV, Sect II, 26.
3. *Śukra*, I, 406.
4. *Śukra*, II, 410.
5. *Śukra*, II, 413.

ing, namely, *ānvikṣhikī trayī, vārtā*, and *daṇḍanīti*. He also discusses the qualities necessary for a good king, and gives us a clear insight into royal functions and duties. He recognises the importance and necessity of the ministry and insists upon the careful selection of the ministers and discusses their qualifications. He considers the problem of the strength of the ministry and gives a careful analysis of all the possibilities regarding its number. He describes in detail, how deliberations should be held in the council and how they were to be kept confidential. He warns the king against the dangers of overtaxation; taxes should not be unjust and excessive. He insists that the state expenditure must not exceed the income. He supplies interesting information regarding the oaths taken by the members of the four castes in the law courts.

While dealing with the army, Somadeva lays down that it should be kept under control and should be in readiness to ward off attacks. The forces should be regularly paid. He also recognises the importance of diplomacy and deprecates severity and treachery in war. He refers to a number of historical instances of bad kings perishing through misconduct. Some of these are known to us from earlier works, while some others like Śūdraka, Śaktikumāra, etc. have not yet been identified. He has obviously utilised some later events in history and does not rely merely upon old and traditional instances.

Along with the Rājanīti, Somadeva also deals with some social topics and problems. He recognises the social importance of castes and disapproves intercaste marriages. He, however, had no inherent prejudice against lower castes; he believes that even a Śūdra can be a pious and useful citizen, if he has sincerity and good conduct. He is harsh against those who take or offer bribes.

The *Nītivākyāmṛita* on the whole is not of much importance as a source of information on polity and administration, as it is mostly conventional in its information.

BĀRHASPATYA ARTHAŚĀSTRA

The *Arthaśāstra* of Bṛihaspati is a small book on polity, hardly of any important value. The book is written in the

Sūtra style, but its contents show that it does not belong to the Dharmasūtra period (*c.* 500 to 100 B.C.), it obviously belongs to a much later age. It professes to deal with the administration as a whole, but all the topics are not dealt with. Bṛihaspati exalts *daṇḍanīti* to the rank of the supreme and only science. He lays down the qualities that are necessary both for the king and the ministers. He insists upon the proper selection of ministers; he is not in favour of young men being appointed to the office of the counsellor. He recognises the importance of ministerial advice and recommends the king to act according to it. While dealing with the working of ministry, he states that a policy is to be executed only after it has been carefully examined by councillors. The king is further advised to follow the policy of conciliation, diplomacy, and if necessary, that of gifts to ensure success.

The state, as envisaged by Bṛihaspati, has to preserve law and order. It was to promote religion by maintaining temples and encouraging festivals. Agriculture was to be promoted by constructing and repairing tanks. The state was to establish rest-houses for the convenience of travellers. It was to encourage education and to extend protection to all. Bṛihaspati, however, gives special privileges to Brāhmaṇas, for he exempts them from the capital punishment.

RĀJADHARMAKĀNDA OF KṚITYAKALPATARU OF LAKSHMĪDHARA

The *Rājadharmakāṇḍa of Kṛityakalpataru* is an important source for the polity of our period. It was composed by Lakshmīdhara, who was himself the foreign minister of the Gāhaḍavāla king Govindachandra. One may expect from the title of the book that it should be dealing with all the topics connected with the administration. But such is not the case. Lakshmīdhara gives unequal treatment to different topics. It is further to be noted that the book being a digest (*nibandha*) merely quotes the views of earlier writers like Manu, Yājñavalkya, Vishṇu, Kātyāyana, Śaṅkha, Gautama, Nārada and Bṛihaspati; the Purāṇas are also requisitioned. It however occasionally gives the views of Lakshmīdhara himself in short explanatory notes.

The author divides his book mainly in three parts. The first part deals with the seven elements of the state. It begins with the *rājapraśaṁsā* and devotes about one hundred pages in describing the king's qualities and duties, the qualifications of the ministers and other royal officers, the different varieties of forts and the importance of treasury, kinds of allies, princes' training, judicial administration and the development of the kingdom's resources. The fundamental principles are hardly discussed by the author while dealing with these topics; he merely quotes the views of his predecessors. We are therefore not enabled to draw from the work any realistic picture of the actual administration during the 12th century.

The second part of the book deals with the six-fold policy and military march. In the discussion of these topics, nothing new is revealed.

Religion was in ascendancy during this period; Lakshmīdhara therefore devotes one-fifth the portion of the book in describing the different rituals connected with coronation. Even while doing this, the author nowhere refers to the political importance of the ceremony; he only describes the different rites that are to be performed and the different *mantras* that are to be recited. The coronation oath, which once formed one of the most important features of the ceremony, is nowhere referred to. It may be noted that while describing the rituals, Lakshmīdhara attaches great importance to superhuman factors in ensuring worldly success. According to him, rituals should be correctly performed and certain deities should be worshipped for the welfare of the state. He further holds that every one should act according to Dharma; even the king cannot go against it. He has to maintain the norm in order that the society may progress and the individuals, who compose it, may succeed in the aims of life.

The main importance of the work lies in its giving us a glimpse into the new attitude of our age, where religion dominated. To Lakshmīdhara, rituals were of great consequence than the principles of administration and *mantras* were more important than the administrative details. The impression left on our mind is that the ideal king of the author is more concerned in following the requirements of rituals than the rules of administration.

MĀNASOLLĀSA OF SOMEŚVARA

The *Mānasollāsa*, composed by or attributed to the Chālukya king Someśvara, who flourished in the first half of the eleventh century, professes to be a work on polity. It is divided into five *viṁśatis*, namely, *Rājyaprāptikāraṇa*, *Rājyasthairyakāraṇa*, *Bharturupabhogakāraṇa*, *Pramodakāraṇa* and the *Krīḍāviṁśati*; out of these, the second *viṁśati* alone deals with some aspects of polity.

The first *viṁśati* deals with the requisite qualifications of an ambitious king, who desires to extend his dominion. The king is advised to be truthful, to avoid excessive anger, to follow the correct path, etc. He is asked to offer oblations to his forefathers (*pitṛtarpaṇa*) and to respect and to take proper care of his guests (*ātithipūjana*).

The second *viṁśati*, as has been already pointed out deals with polity. The qualities of the king are enumerated first, but there is nothing noteworthy in the treatment of the subject. The author merely gives the summary of the views of the earlier writers in this connection. He then discusses the strength of the ministry and holds that it should consist of seven or eight ministers and that the king should consult them separately on important matters (II, 39-59). As regards the duties and qualifications of the different ministers and officers like the Koshādhyaksha, Pratīhāra, Sārathī, Sūda, Vaidya and Antaḥpurādhyaksha, there is nothing particular about them, their functions are the same as those described by the earlier writers. The author, however, gives interesting information about the duties and qualifications of the Dharmādhikārin, Sāndhivigrahika, and Senāpati. The Dharmādhikārin was to be well-versed in Smṛitiśāstra (II, 22). The Sāndhivigrahika was to summon the different feudatories at proper time, to have discussions with them and then to send them back with proper instructions (II, 138). The Senāpati, apart from possessing the military qualities, was required to have the knowledge of omens and medicine; the former was probably for ensuring victory in the battlefield and the latter for the proper arrangement and care of the wounded soldiers. The treasury should always be full of gold, silver, jewels, costly clothes, ornaments and *nishkas* in order to meet any national calamity (II 394-7). The king should keep one-fourth of the state revenue in the treasury, as a kind of national insurance and should spend the two-thirds for *dharma*, *artha* and *kāma* (II, 540). Land tax should be 16 per cent. The king should impose 6% tax upon honey, butter, meat, flowers, fruits, medicinal plants, etc. 10% duty should be levied upon the goods brought to the harbour by the sailors (II, 374-76). Brāhmaṇas should be exempted from taxation.

Forts should be constructed as protection against the enemies and they should be stored with plenty of cash, arms, drugs, horses, tigers, lions and serpents. The inclusion of lions, tigers and serpents in this list is rather unexpected. They were not intended for any zoo in the fort, but were to be let loose on the besieging army to create panic and confusion. Besides the six traditional types of forts, Someśvara refers to three more, those built with stones, bricks and mud (II, 5). It would appear that these new types of forts were getting popular in our period. He speaks of the traditional four-fold army and mentions a number of weapons like clubs, battle-axes, knives, tridents and machines to throw missiles. He also refers to a weapon called *sella-chakra*, whose nature is not clear (II, 683). According to him, warfare permits all kinds of acts, like the burning of houses, destruction of crops (II, 1076-78), breaking of dams (*jalāśaya*), amputation of the limbs of the civil population in enemy's country, etc. He refers to the different kinds of expedients, but interprets *Āsana* and *Dvaidhībhāva* in a different sense. According to him *Āsana* is encampment of the army and not a policy of neutrality and *Dvaidhībhāva* is duplicity and treachery and not the policy of war on one front and that of peace on another.[1] The king should always protect his subjects from wicked persons, thieves, army officers and revenue officers (Kāyasthas). While

1. This latter is the view of Kauṭilya, *A.S.* VII. 1.

emphasising upon the duty of protection, the author puts before us a beautiful simile; just as a man loses his strength due to diseases, so also the king, due to rebellions (II, 158). As regards the internal administration, the author advises the king to appoint officers over one, ten and hundred villages, who are to report to the king about what is wrong within their jurisdiction.

The second *viṁśati* on the whole does not give any new and valuable information about the polity of our age. The author is more concerned in displaying his knowledge of other subjects than that of politics. Thus while enumerating the king's qualities, he devotes much space to the description of chemical science (Rasāyana) necessary for king's health, and of the fevers and other deseases, from which he may suffer. Similarly, while describing the duties of Purohita, he deals with Pañchāṅga-nirṇaya in great detail. We also get detailed information about mathematics, multiplication, division, *trairāśika* and *bṛihadrāśika* in the section dealing with the Koshādhyaksha. Different kinds of *nidhis* are mentioned in the section dealing with treasure troves and various popular beliefs are given as to how to discover them. We have also a discussion about the different *ratnas*, namely, *mauktika*, *padma*, *indranīla*, *marakata*, etc.; long sections are devoted to describe how to examine them. One whole chapter is devoted to Aśvavaidyaka (II, 570-619) and another to Gajachikitsā (II, 630-674) in connection with the section dealing with the army. The author also refers to a number of astrological beliefs like *Nakshatraśūla Śvaśakuna*, *Kākaśakuna*, *Piṅgalā-śakuna*, etc. (II, 753-948), while dealing with an enemy's invasion.

We thus see that there are many topics discussed in this book, which have no connection with its subject-matter. The author hardly refers to the administrative machinery of his age. We do not get sufficient and adequate information about the functions and duties of ministers and the departmental heads, the provincial and the district administration are hardly touched. The book, on the whole, discloses no originality of thought or treatment.

While the second *viṁśati* deals at least with some aspects of polity, the third, fourth and fifth *viṁśatis* deal with only the personal and private life of the king. the administrative structure of the period, is altogether passed over in them.

The third *viṁśati* deals with the twenty kinds of *upabhogas* or enjoyments. Long sections are devoted to describe the building of new houses (*mandira-nirmāṇa*), worship of Vāstu or the site of the palace, painting, iconometry, varieties of pictures, etc.

The fourth *viṁśati* treats of the twenty kinds of Vinodas or royal sports among which the *Gaja-vāhyālivinoda* (the sport with elephants in the arena) and the *turagavāhyāli-vinoda* (Modern Polo) are quite interesting. There is also a long section on Music, which equals in length the whole of first two *viṁśatiṣ*. The fifth *viṁśati* deals with different *krīḍāṣ* or sports of the king and is not even remotely connected with government and administration.

YUKTIKALPATARU OF BHOJA

The *Yuktikalpataru* is traditionally attributed to the king Bhoja of the Paramāra dynasty, who flourished in the first half of the 11th century. It is a small and unimportant book on *Nīti* containing hardly any new political thought or theory. The author's interest in polity seems to be limited, he devotes only 20 pages out of 230 to the topic. The remaining portion of the book deals with diverse topics like the precious stones and their varieties and values, weapons, vehicles, ships, ship-building, animals like the elephant and the horse and their varieties etc. It also discusses at length town planning and its administrative machinery.

As observed above, the book devotes only twenty pages to polity and discusses a few topics without giving any new information. The first chapter deals with the importance of *Nīti* and informs us, how the prosperity of a king, who does not follow Nīti, fades away (p. 2, V. 10-11). Among the principal officers mentioned by it are the royal preceptor, the priest, the minister, the secretary, and officer of the harem, etc., who are to be appointed after a careful examination (p. 2, V. 13) The second chapter deals with the qualifications for the different officers; they are, however, traditional and do not reveal anything new. The third chapter, besides discussing the qualifications, functions and duties of different superintendents like those of horses, elephants, forests, etc., emphasises upon the importance of the prosperous treasury It may be pointed out here that like Śukra and Somadeva, Bhoja also states that the treasury is more valuable to the king than the breath itself (p. 5, Vs. 30-31). In order to meet the national calamities, the king is advised to keep an overflowing treasury (p. 5, V. 32). Agriculture is to be promoted by protecting and helping farmers, as it is the main source of prosperity (p. 6, V. 40). The fourth chapter deals with the four-fold divisions of the army, namely, the infantry, the cavalry, the elephants and the chariot corps, and informs us how the particular arm is useful for a particular place of warfare (p. 7, V. 45). The navy is also referred to. The Chapters V to XIII dilate at length on the problems of the foreign policy and warfare, but there is nothing new in the treatment as the author usually gives the views of his predecessors bearing upon these and similar topics. The 14th chapter deals with justice, law and punishment. *Daṇḍa* alone is the cause of the stability of the society. It promotes *dharma*, *artha* and *kāma* and establishes law and order in the society (p. 15, V. 103). The king is asked to inflict upon the offenders just punishment otherwise people will be distressed and will lose faith in him (p. 15, V. 106). A policy is to be settled in a secret meeting; women and foreigners should not be present at that time (p. 17, 116). The chapters XV to XVII deal with forts and their different varieties. It may be here noted that Bhoja gives a new term called *dvandva* to denote the fort; this is not used by any other writer.

The book, on the whole, possesses no intrinsic value to the student of political science, as it merely gives the summary of the views of the earlier writers. It hardly describes the administrative machinery of the state, nor does it inform us how the central secretariat used to function. Taxation is passed over. The provincial, the district and the village administrations are not touched at all.

PURĀṆAS

The *Purāṇas* also help us to some extent in understanding the political ideals of the period. They are no doubt religious in character, but some of them like the *Agni-Purāṇa* and the *Matsya-Purāṇa* deal in great detail with the state and the administrative structure. They describe the origin of the state and inform us, how there was an ideal state of nature in the *Kṛita Yuga*, how later on people became greedy, how they began to fall foul with one another, how the law of the jungle began to prevail in society, how then Brahmadeva, the chief of gods, composed a code of law and created and appointed Virājas as a king. The *Purāṇas* also lay down elaborate rituals for coronation, which will be discussed in the second chapter. They also give us a clear insight into the different duties of the king. The king is advised to rule righteously, for otherwise he will be condemned to hell. The Purāṇas discuss the problem of the divinity of the king and while doing so, they usually accept only the functional resemblance between the king and some of the deities. They advocate the *saptāṅga* theory and regard the seven elements of the state as interdependent upon one another. They regard the ministry as essential for the good government and refer to a number of officers in charge of various departments. The conduct of courtiers is also discussed in great detail. Problems connected with taxation are also dealt with. The dishonesty in commercial dealings, the use of false weights, etc., are to be severely punished. Great space is also devoted to an exhaustive discussion on the problems connected with the foreign policy, peace and war. Considerable light is also thrown upon the *maṇḍala* of kings, and the policy to be followed in connection with its different members and the ways and means by which to establish one's ascendancy among them. They also comment upon the manner in which the warfare is to be carried on. They emphasise the importance of maintaining a powerful and efficient army. They also insist upon the proper administration of justice and deal with civil and criminal law

It may, however, be noted that while dealing with these topics, the *Purāṇas* usually summarise the views of Smṛitis and Nīti-writers and rarely enunciate their own theories. They therefore hardly throw any new light upon the subject under discussion.

The above account will give an idea of the light, which books on polity throw upon the political institutions and administration of our age. Their account is more than 75% traditional and based upon the views of earlier writers. To rely upon them for reconstructing the picture of the state and administration during our period would not be very sound. We shall have to check their views from purely historical evidence supplied by contemporary inscriptions. We shall therefore now make some observations about the inscriptions as a source material for our purpose.

B

EPIGRAPHICAL SOURCES

The stone and copper plate inscriptions are, as already observed, the most important source of information for reconstructing a picture of contemporary administration. They are no doubt usually donative in character, but they throw considerable light upon some of the aspects of the administrative system that prevailed during our period. It is true that all the statements made in these records may not be trustworthy, as they are mostly written by the court poets. But the eulogists would make exaggerative statements usually regarding the merits and achievements of kings and the nature of their victories in war, and not about the administrative structure and political ideals of the age. Inscriptions often discuss the duties and functions of the king. They sometimes enunciate interesting maxims about the aims and ideals of the Government. They also inform us how provision used to be often made for the maintenance of queens and princes by giving them land or revenue assignments. Now and then they reveal the important part played by the crown-prince and other princes in the administration.

Several inscriptions supply considerable information about the ministry. They refer to a number of ministers, describe their duties and dilate upon their relations with the king. They also inform us, how very often, the hereditary principle was followed in making ministerial appointments. How the ministers were honoured by the feudatory titles is revealed to us by some records.

Some inscriptions also give us a good insight into the working of the secretariat. How the secretariat used to control and inspect the provincial, district, town and village administrations, how it used to take steps to counteract fraudulent grants, how the documents concerning the land grants were kept carefully in the office, how they were renewed, is discussed by some of our epigraphs in an interesting way.

The inscriptions also give us valuable information regarding the different nomenclature used for the different territorial divisions that prevailed during our period.

Considerable information is also supplied by the epigraphs about the district, town and village administrations. They inform us how the popular elements played an important part in the local administration. They describe how the members of the village and town councils were elected or selected. They refer to the executive committees of these councils and inform us how they were constituted. They give us a clear insight into the different works of public utility carried out under the auspices of village and town councils.

The records also supply valuable information about the taxation, when they enumerate the dues from which the donees were exempted. Taxes collected from farmers and merchants often figure in our records. We see how the customs duties were levied upon ordinary articles of consumptions like leaves, barley, coconuts, fruits, grains and cattle-fodder, how the excise duties were levied upon oil, butter, sugar, and jaggery, how taxes were imposed upon the houses, wells and water wheels,—all these facts are disclosed by our records. The inscriptions also refer to a number of taxes imposed upon the shopkeepers, dancing girls, gamblers and distillers. Besides, these taxes, some epigraphs also refer to a number of other sources of state income. They will be discussed in detail in the chapter VII.

Our records often throw light on interstate relations and give us an idea about the relations between the suzerain and the feudatories. They often describe the causes of the war and the punishment that was inflicted upon the rebels They sometimes refer to a number of indignities inflicted upon the feudatories, when the former had rebelled and were deposed from the throne,—how they were forced to surrender their forces, treasures, horses and elephants for their disloyalty and how they had to do the menial work in the camp of the emperor. The records sometimes give us a clear insight into the measure of the internal autonomy enjoyed by the feudatories of different grades. They also inform us how the activities and the affairs of the kingdoms of the feudatories were often controlled and supervised by some imperial officers. The inscriptions are thus a very important source of information about the political ideals, institutions and administration of our period, if they are used with proper circumspection.

Chapter II

KINGSHIP

Section A : The King

King-in-ministry was the normal form of government throughout India during our period of survey. The feudatory states were also governed by the same machinery. So far we have not yet come across any literary or epigraphic evidence, which can prove the existence of the non-monarchical form of government during our period. The foreign travellers also do not speak of any republic existing during our period, they refer to the existence of monarchy only.

(1) *Kingship hereditary, not elective*

Kingship at this time was hereditary. References to a king's election occur extremely rarely, and they are more figurative than real. Gopāla, the founder of the Pāla dynasty, is no doubt described in one record as being elected by the *prakṛiti*.[1] Since this statement is made in the course of an eulogy, we should carefully examine it to find out whether it is true. The record clearly declares that Gopāla had put an end to anarchy and restored law and order in Bengal, people therefore must have welcomed his rule enthusiastically. This circumstance would have led the court poet to state that Gopālā was elected by the *prakṛitis*.[2] Even if such was the case, numerous Pāla records show that none of his successors owed his crown to any election, the principle; of heredity, and not the method of election, governed the succession in the Pāla dynasty.

In the Deccan also we come across a similar case. In

1. Mātsyanyāyamapohituṁ prakritibhirlakshmyāḥ karaṁ grāhitaḥ Śrī Gopāla iti Kshitiśaśirasāṁ chūḍāmaṇistatsutaḥ. *E.I.*, *IV*, 248.
2. *Prakṛiti* can denote the people, ministers or high officials. If Gopāla was at all elected king, it was probably by his ministers rather than by the people. Harsha was offered the crown of Kanauj by its ministers, and not by its 'people.'

one of the Rāshṭrakūṭa records, we are told that Amoghavarsha III was requested by the feudatories to accept the throne for supporting the glory of the Rāṣhṭrakūṭa empire; but as pointed out by Dr. Altekar, such a statement appears to be rather figurative than real;[1] from other Rāshṭrakūṭa records we learn how Amoghavarṣha III owed the throne more to the exertions of his crown prince Kṛishṇa than to the votes of his feudatories.

These two instances of Gopāla and Amoghavarsha III will thus show that when owing to unusual circumstances, there was a change in dynasty or a claimant other than the heir-presumptive came to the throne, the latter's supporters often described his accession as due to the election. If there was at all any election, only ministers and feudatories took part in it.

Normally we see that kingship was hereditary in our period both in the North and in the South. There is of course no doubt that something like a real election did occur once in Kashmir during our period; for the *Rājataraṅgiṇī* clearly informs us that at the end of the Utpala dynasty in 939 A.D., when general Kamalavardhana had got an effective control of the situation and was in possession of the palace, he asked the Brāhmaṇas to elect some one as king[2] instead of ascending the throne himself. This he did, says Kalhaṇa, 'because he was deluded by Karman or guided by bad advisers......Encountering alone a young woman, who has been difficult to meet, in private and flushed with drink, he who being inexperienced does not have the joy of love with her and prays for favours the next day through a procuress, and he who having by his dash gained glory, gives it up at the moment and wooes through diplomacy the next day, who else is to be pitied more than these two ?" The above remaks of Kalhaṇa make it quite clear that the election of king was regarded in our period as quite a foolish procedure

1. Sāmantairatha Raṭṭarājyamahimālambārathamabhyarthitaḥ, *E.I.*, XI. Chitaldrug, No. 76.
2. *Rāj.*, V.454-60. In this particular case the Brāhmaṇas did not elect Kamalavardhana to the throne, but Yaśaskara, who had got the control of the capital in the meanwhile.

and must therefore have gone out of vogue long ago. The tradition of an elective king was however remembered in some quarters.

We have a large number of inscriptions of different dynasties, and they generally show the crown passing from the father to the son or to some other member of the royal family.

The books on polity of our period like the *Śukranīti*, the *Kāmandakanītisāra*, etc. also do not refer to the election of the king. Nor have we any evidence to show that in our period there existed any institution like the Parliament or the Paura-jānapada with power to elect the king.

(2) *Order of Succession*

Let us now consider some problems connected with the hereditary monarchy. As far as succession to the throne is concerned, the law of the primogeniture normally prevailed in all the dynasties of Northern India. The crown therefore usually passed from the father to the eldest son, who was installed to the office of the heir-apparent, when he had come of age and finished his education and training. That the heir-apparent was selected during the life-time of the ruling king is evident not only from the epigraphical evidence but also from the accounts of foreign travellers. The Arab writer Sulaiman, who flourished during our period, observes that 'the princes in India used to select their own successors.'[1] This clearly indicates that the practice of the nomination of the Yuvarāja by the king during his life-time was widely prevalent. There are a number of epigraphical cases to show that the heir-apparent was selected during the life-time of the king.[2] Thus under the Gāhaḍavālas, Madanapāla was selected as Yuvarāja by his father.[3] The Basahi grant,

1. Elliot and Dowson, I, 6.
2. This practice was followed in the Deccan also; for instance, the Rāshṭrakūṭa King Kṛshṇa I had installed his son Govinda as Yuvarāja before the latter was sent to lead the expedition against Vengi (*E. I.* VI, pp. 210-3).
3. *I. A.*, XVIII. 9-14.

dated 1104 A.D.,[1] and the Kamauli grant, dated 1105 A.D.,[2] inform us that Govindachandra was acting as Yuvarāja during his father's rule. The same was the case with Āsphoṭachandra, who was the son of Govindachandra.[3] Jayachandra was selected as the heir-apparent by his father Vijayachandra.[4] Some records of the Chāhmānas of Nadol also mention *Yuvarāja* along with the reigning king. Thus when Aśvarāja was ruling as a king, his son Kaṭukarāja was discharging the duties of the heir-apparent.[5] Similarly when Kaṭukarāja and Sāmantasiṁha were the kings, they selected Jayantasiṅha and Kānhaṇadeva respectively as their heirs-apparent [6] Under the Pālas also the same practice generally prevailed. Tribhuvanapāla and Rājyapāla were selected as *Yuvarāja* by their fathers Dharmapāla and Devapāla respectively in their old age.[7] Probably the same was the case with Nārāyaṇapāla; v. 15 of the Bhagalpur plate of this ruler states, 'Let asceticism be mine and kingdom thine' thus two men have spoken to two others, Vigrahapāla to him and Sāgara to Bhagīratha' (*I.A.*, XV, 305). If Vigrahapāla had abdicated the throne for his son, it is not unlikely that he might have earlier invested him with the powers of Yuvarāja. The coronation of the Chedi king Yaśaskarṇa, in which his father Karṇa participated, marked most probably his selection as heir-apparent.[8]

We thus see that the advice of the Nīti writers that an heir-apparent should be selected in the life-time of the ruling king was generally followed. The prince usually selected was the eldest son and his selection was often formalised by a regular *Yuvarājābhisheka*, which is expressly referred to in several Gāhaḍavāla records.[9] The formality of this *abhisheka*

1. *I.A.*, XIV, 101-4.
2. *I.A.*, XIX, 101-104.
3. *E.I.*, VIII; 155-6.
4. *E.I.* IV, 118.
5. *E.I.*, XI, 20-30.
6. *E.I.*, XI, 29-30; 60-61.
7. *E.I.*, IV, 248.
8. *E.I.*, 1, part I, p. 294.
9. Asmatsammatyā samastarāja-prakṛiyopeta-yauvarājābhishikta-mahārājaputra-Śrī-Jayachandradevena. *E.I.*, IV, 118; *E.I.*, VIII, 155-6.

would suggest that the prince was usually not recognised as Yuvarāja before the actual ceremony was performed.

Yuvarāja is often seen issuing land grants and actively participating in the military and administrative duties but he was not a co-ruler or a joint ruler. Theoretically he was always subordinate to the ruling monarch. The idea of dual or joint rulership was unknown in our period.

It is, however, important to note that our writers on polity have not allowed the crown to pass on to the eldest son, if he suffered from any physical or mental defect. Śukra has clearly stated that if the eldest prince suffers from deafness, dumbness, blindness, leprosy or importance, he is unfit to rule and that in such a case, his brother or son should succeed.[1] There is sufficient evidence to show that when the eldest son happened to be less competent and a younger brother more promising, the latter was selected for the throne. This would of course sometimes lead to the internecine war, as happened at the accession of the Rāṣṭrakūṭa king Govinda III, which had resulted in the supersession of his elder brother, Stambha in 793 A.D.[2] Such wars, however, are so far not known in the case of Northern dynasties; they were also rather an exception than the rule in the Deccan. The younger princes as we shall see later on, were usually given land grants or revenue assignments to maintain their high status; they were also appointed to high administrative posts.

There is hardly any evidence to show that an actual division of the kingdom took place either in the south or in the north during our period to satisfy the claims of rival princes, as probably happened under the Vākāṭaka dynasty, where Pravarasena I seems to have entrusted the different parts of his empire under the charge of his sons, who established practically independent houses, after their father's death and thus weakened the empire.[3] Śukra also is not in favour of the

1. Jyeśṭhopi badhiraḥ kushṭhī mūkā'ndhaḥ shaṇḍa eva hi,
Sa rājyārho bhavennaiva bhrātā tatputra eva hi.

Śukra, i, 343.

2. A.S. Altekar, *Rāshṭrakūṭas*, pp. 61-62.
3. R.C. Majumdar and A.S. Altekar, *The Age of the Vākāṭakas*, p. 101.

partition of the kingdom, for he says 'the kingdom divided into parts is exposed to the enemies'.[1]

If the king had no son, the crown usually passed to his younger brother. Thus under the Chandellas, Devavarmā had no son; he therefore appointed his younger brother Kīrtivarmā, as an heir to the throne.[2] Under the Chedis, Lakshmaṇarāja was succeeded by his younger brother Yuvarāja II, as he left no issue.[3] When the Chedi king Narasiṁha died in c. A.D. 1155, his younger brother Jayasiṁha became the king, because his elder brother had no issue. Under the Paramāras when the kings Lakshmadeva and Jaitugi left no issue, they were succeeded by their younger brothers, Naravarman and Jayavarman II respectively.[4] Under the Chāhamānas Vigraharāja was succeeded by his younger brother Durlabharāja[5] (c 999 A D.) and Jājalla by his younger brother Āśarāja or Aśvarāja[6] (c 1110 A D.), because the elder brothers had left no sons to succeed them.

In the absence of a son or a brother, a nephew was sometimes succeeded by his uncle. Thus when the Chandella king Jayavarmadeva died without leaving any issue, his uncle Pṛithvīvarmadeva, who was the younger brother of his father Sallakshaṇa, ascended the throne.[7] Rāshṭrakūṭa king Dantidurga was also succeeded by his uncle Kṛishṇa I, probably because the former had left no son.

Sometimes a war of succession used to take place between the uncle and nephew. The Sevadi Inscription of Ratnapāla informs us how he ousted his uncle Āśarāja from Nadol by carrying out a rebellion against him.[8] There are many such cases in the course of Indian history of ancient, medieval and modern periods. The uncle being the most experienced

1. Rājyavibhajanāt śreyo na bhūpānāṁ bhavet khalu,
Alpīkritaṁ vibhāgena rājyaṁ śatrurjighṛikshati. *Śukra*, I, 346.
2. *E.I.*, I, 195.
3. *E.I.* XI, 142, II. 3.
4. H.C. Ray; *Dynastic History of Northern India*, p. 795.
5. *E.I.*, V, 180-95, H. C. Ray ; *Dynastic History of Northern India.*
6. H.C. Ray, *Dynastic History of Northern India*, II, p. 1067.
7. *Ibid*, II, p. 1109.
E.I., I, 198.
8. *E.I.*, XI, 304-13.

claimant was usually allowed to succeed. Thus under the Yādavas, Mahādeva worked as a crown prince during the reign of his elder brother Kṛishṇa and also succeeded him on the throne; as Kṛishṇa's son Rāmchandra was too young to rule, it is however important to note that his efforts to secure the crown for his own son Ammaṇa in supersession of his nephew Rāmchandra did not meet with ultimate success. Under the Chālukyas also Maṅgaleśa tried to secure the throne for his own son, superseding the claim of his elder brother's son Pulakeśin, but failed in the effort.

It is interesting to note that Śukra also suggests that if a king has no male issue, then his uncle or younger brother or his elder brother's son, or his daughter's son or his sisters's son should be selected as a crown prince.[1] The *Nītivākyāmṛita* of Somadeva also lays down a more or less similar order of succession.[2] It states that if the king has no son, the crown should then pass to the full brother, failing him to half-brother failing him to uncle, failing him to the male of the same family, failing him to daughter's son, failing him to a stranger.

It is interesting to note that this order of succession given by Śukra and Somadeva postpones the succession of the daughter's son to a stage much later than that contemplated by Yājñavalkya. It appears that the patriarchal conception was more powerful in the case of the royal succession than in the case of the succession to private or individual property.

Whether the throne passed to a member of a collateral branch on the failure of heirs in the main line is not known from northern Indian inscriptions. Such was sometimes the case in South India; when Parameśvaravarman died leaving behind no son, the crown passed on to Nandivarman, who belonged to a collateral Pallava branch.

The succession was usually limited to males during our period. There is hardly any epigraphical or literary evidence

1. Svakanishṭhaṁ pitṛivyaṁ vānujaṁ vāgrasambhavaṁ.
Putraṁ putrīkṛitaṁ dattaṁ yauvarājc'bhishechayet.
Śukra, II, 15.

2. Suta-sodara-sapatna-pitṛivya-kulyadauhitrāgantukeshu pūrvapurvābhāve bhavatyuttarasya rājapadāvāptiḥ.
(Rājarakshāsamuddeśaḥ), *Nvk*, p. 247.

to show a female becoming a sovereign as the first choice after the death of the last king. In the history of Kashmir and Orissa, we come across some cases of women rulers or regents, but it is clear that they were usually exceptions due to dire difficulties. It is no doubt true that Sugandhā, the widow of Śaṅkaravarman (*c.* 883—900 A.D.) became a queen for the short period of two years, 902—04 A.D., but it was merely a stop gap arrangement. It was upon the prayer of her subjects that she ascended the throne, when two sons of her husband had died after short reigns and there was the prospect of anarchy. (*Rājataraṅgiṇī*, V. 243). She was waiting for the birth of a grandson to succeed her and when this hope came to an end, she had to summon a conference of ministers and grandees, Tantrins and Ekāṅgas, to select a successor. Their choice fell upon Pārtha and Sugandhā had to vacate the throne for him. The Kashmir historian says, 'Shorn of royal power Sugandhā went out of royal residence and the failing tear-drops served her as her necklace" (V. 257). The case of Diddā is of a different nature; she ruled Kashmir effectively for about 22 years, (981 to 1003 A.D.). But even this woman of extraordinary energy and ability had to wait for 22 years after the death of her husband Kshemagupta and work for the removal of three kings Abhimanyu, Nandigupta and Tribhuvanagupta before she could get the coveted throne. In the Kara dynasty of Orissa, the accession of Tribhuvanamahādevī must be regarded as an unusual event. Her husband Śāntikaradeva I had been succeeded by her son Śubhakaradeva III, but he also died soon. Tribhuvanamahādevī was unwilling to ascend the throne, but was persuaded to do so by the assembly of great feudatories; she however abdicated when her grandson Śāntikaradeva II came of age. Towards the end of the Kara dynasty, we have the phenomenon of four queens Gaurī, Daṇḍamahādevī, Bakulamahādevī and Dharmamahādevī ruling one after the other. But this was not a regular instance of normal succession, it indicates, as observed by Dr. R.C. Majumdar, troublesome times on the eve of the downfall of the dynasty.[1] Śubhakara V, the

1. R.C. Majumdar, *The Age of Imperial Kanaul*, p. 67.

husband of the first of the above queens Gaurī, had probably no son, so his widow succeeded him and was followed by his daughter, Daṇḍīmahādevī. But how she should have been succeeded by her step-mother Bakulamahādevī and the latter by a widowed queen of the predecessor of her husband Śubhakara V passes one's comprehension. Obviously there was something wrong in the Kara kingdom and most of these queens were probably mere puppets in the hands of interested parties seeking power. To conclude, in normal times in the northern India of our period, society did not welcome women as ruling monarchs. They did not succeed as first choice to the last ruler.

A number of queens do appear in the records of our dynasties under consideration, but as a general rule they do not seem to be entrusted with any administrative duties. Somaladevī, queen of the Chāhamāna king Ajayarāja (c. 1125) was apparently authorised by her husband to issue coins in her own name with the legend *Śrī-Somaladevī*, but whether she was entrusted with any administrative duties, we do not know.

(3) *Minority Administration*

How the administration was carried on, when a king died leaving a minor heir behind, is not disclosed by our epigraphs. Under the Vākāṭakas, dowager queens used to supervise and direct the administration, if the heir-apparent to the throne happened to be a minor. Thus Prabhāvatīguptā, the widow of Rudrasena II, is known to have successfully steered the ship of the state through troubled waters for a long time.[1] Queen Tribhuvanamahādevī, the widow of king Śāntikaradeva I of the Kara dynasty, is stated to have been persuaded by the feudatories to ascend the throne afer her son's death, but she was really acting as a regent, for she abdicated the throne on her grandson attaining majority. We, however, do not get any instance of women as regents in the dynasties included in this work. Even Śukra is silent on the point; he does not give any suggestion as to who should look after the

1. *I.A.*, XVII-37.

administration during the king's minority. Very likely a male relative was usually appointed to act as the regent, as was the case under the Rāshṭrakūṭas.[1] The case of Tribhuvanamahādevī acting as regent in the Kara dynasty is unusual for the northern India of our period.

(4) *Training of the princes*

Our writers on polity have laid considerable emphasis on the proper training of the princes, but unfortunately our epigraphs give us no glimpse of the actual arrangement made during our age. In the earlier period, we find that sometimes the princes were sent to the famous university centres like Takshaśilā for training. In the 7th century A.D., an arrangement of a special school with expert teachers was made for the training of princes, as shown by the *Kādambarī* of Bāṇa; in our period also most probably the same method might have been followed.

As regards the course of instruction for the prince, our writers on polity devote a good deal of space to it and maintain that the would-be king should master the four Vidyās namely Ānvīkshikī, (the study of Logic and Philosophy), Trayī[2] (the study of three Vedas), Vārtā (the science of agriculture and commerce) and Daṇḍanītī (the science of administration). Besides this theoretical study, our writers on polity have also prescribed practical education, which included training in the administration and proficiency in the military art and tactics. The *Agni-Purāṇa* maintains that the king should be a good bowman, a skilful horseman and an expert controller of elephants. It also prescribes the study of various arts and crafts.[3]

How far in actual practice the king's curriculum

1. A.S. Altekar, *Rāshṭrakūṭās*, p. 153. During the minority of Amoghavarsha I his cousin Karkka was appointed to carry on the administration on behalf of the emperor.
2. In the earlier period the study of Trayī included the study of three Vedas. Its meaning however changed during our period. It included a number of sciences, namely *Mīmāṁsā*, *Dharmaśāstras* and *Purāṇas*, which had no connection with *Tray*ī at all.
3. *Agni-Purāṇa*; 227, 2-3.

included all these subjects it is difficult to state. Naturally, the study of Dharmāśastras, Mīmāṁsā and Purāṇas, which Śukra includes in *Trayī*, must have been not very deep. Emphasis must obviously have been laid on Daṇḍanītī, Vārtā and practical training in the military art.

Such evidence as we get from contemporary records shows that not *Trayī* and *Ānvīkshikī* but law and classical Sanskrit literature were king's favourite subjects in humanities. Thus the Charakhāri plate of the Chandella king Devavarmā informs us, how king Devavarmā had mastered the Kāvya, Alaṅkāra and Chhandas.[1] The Paramāra king Vākpati was a great orator, poet, logician and had mastered all the Śastras.[2] The Gāhaḍavāla king Chandradeva is described as an abode of all the Vidyās and arts.[3] The Chandella king Sallakshaṇa-Varman is described as a leader of those versed in sacred lore, a kinsman of the virtuous, a store of arts and abode of good conduct.[4] The Chedi king Yuvarāja was the lover of classical literature.[5] The Gāhaḍavāla king Chandradeva is described as solely devoted to the logic.[6] The Paramāra king Jayasiṁha was also expert in law.[7] All this evidence shows that the views of our political writers, who emphasise the necessity of training the princes in Dharmaśāstra, law and political science were generally followed in practice.

After the training was over, the prince was made a Yuvarāja. A major crown-prince became king immediately after the death of his father. Al Masudi's statement that no one could become a king before he was forty does not appear to be correct (Elliot I p. 20).

1. Kāvyālaṁkāra-chhandopalakshaṇa-guṇa-gaṇādhishṭhānaḥ *E.I.*, XX. 127.
2. Vaktritvochcha-kavitva-tarka-kalana-prajñāta śā (strā) gamaḥ. *E.I.*, I. 257.
3. Ākaraḥ sarvavidyānāṁ ālayaḥ kalānāṁ...*E. I.* XV, 193.
4. Dhaureyaḥ śrutaśālināṅguṇavatāṁ bandhuḥ kalānāṁ nidhiḥ, Sadvrittasya cha sadma kalpa-viṭapī niḥśesha-pushṭyarthinām. *E.I.* I, 198.
5. Sāhitya-vidyā-lalanā-bhujaṅgaḥ... *E.I.* XXIV, 111
6. *Nayaika-rasikah*... *I.A.* XV, 6.
7. Prādurbhāva-viśārado nayapathaprasthāna-sārthādhipaḥ, *E.I.*, I, 301.

(5) *King's Qualities and Qualifications*

Let us now discuss the necessary qualities required for the king. The theoretical qualifications laid down by Śukra and Kāmandaka are numerous but we need not devote much space to them, as they are the same as those described by the earlier political writers. Inscriptions and works on polity of our age emphasise that a king can become a successful ruler only if he waits upon the elders, studies the art of government, cultivates righteousness and protects his subjects as efficiently as the divine guardians. He was expected to be always in constant association with virtuous and learned men in order to derive the benefit of their experience and advice. He was to be kind-hearted and was not to oppress his subjects for his own selfish interest. A king, says Śukra, who is virtuous is divine in nature, one who is otherwise is devilish, he is destined for hell.[1] The king had to observe discipline, for it brings prosperity to him. He was to be well-versed in Śāstras and in different branches of learning. A king, who is well-grounded in all the Vidyās, is respected by the good; he can never be inclined to a wrong course even if impelled by evil advisers.[2] Prowess, strength, intelligence and valour were other necessary qualities required for the king, a king devoid of these qualities, says the *Matsya Purāṇa*, though wealthy, can never administer even a small kingdom."[3] The king is also advised to keep an even balance between *dharma*, *artha* and *kāma*.

On the negative side the king is advised to give up excessive gambling and hunting. He was not expected to sleep by day, nor was he to be too much talkative. Over-indulgence in music and dancing was to be avoided. Six enemies namely excessive indulgence, anger, intoxication, envy, convetousness, and self-delusion were to be carefully guarded against. All the *vyasanas* were to be avoided. According to Somadeva, 'A

1. Guṇijuṣṭastu yo rājā sa jñeyo devatāṁśakaḥ,
Viparītastu raksho'ṁśaḥ sa vai narakabhājanaḥ.
Śukra, I, 86-87.
2. Śāstrāya gurusaṁyogaḥ Śastraṁ vinaya-vṛiddhaye,
Vidyāvinīto nṛipatiḥ satāṁ bhavati sammataḥ.
Preryamāṇo'pyasadvṛittairnākāryeshu pravartate:
Śukra, I, 148-9.
3. *Agnī-Purāṇa*, 239, 2-5 enumerates similar qualities.

single *vyasana* is enough to destroy a powerful king, even possessing four kinds of armies, what to say if there are all of them combined.[1] A good king should exert to eradicate these evils, keeping himself in the association of the learned men and away from the evil-doers.[2]

The records of our period usually describe the kings as possessing the above qualities prescribed by the Nīti works. The Ratnapur inscription of the Chedi king Jājalladeva, dated 1114 A.D., informs us how king Pṛithvīdeva possessed nobility, bravery and depth.[3] The Khajuraho inscription dated *c.* 954 A.D. states that the king Harsha combined in himself eloquence, statesmanship, heroism, vigour, ambition, modesty and self-confidence.[4] The Chandella king Sallakshaṇavarman is described as a master of the sacred lore, a kinsman of the virtuous, a store of arts and an abode of good conduct.[5] The Pratīhāra records usually describe the kings as endowed with bravery, valour and modesty. The Chedi king Jājalladeva (*c.* 1160 A.D.) is described as the sun of prowess, who secured success and prosperity by his heroism.[6] Pṛithvīdeva (*c.* 1141 A.D.) is described as the sun, endowed with the most intense brilliancy.[7] Generosity, truth, statesmanship and heroism were the qualities of the Chandella king Jayavarmadeva.[8] (*c.* 1117 A.D.). The king Vairisiṁha is described as endowed with might, generosity, bravery, resoluteness and good fortune.[9] Intelligence, bravery, religiousness, truthfulness and gratitude were the qualities possessed by the Chandella king Devavarman (*c.* 1051 A.D.), who had full control over all his senses.[10] The Chedi king Kokkalla (*c.* 875 A.D.) possessed generosity and was a man of active habits.[11] King Kakka of the Pratihāra dynasty was

1. *Nvk.* p. 62.
2. *Ibid,* ,,
3. *E.I.*, I, 35.
4. *E.I.*, I, 131.
5. *E.I.*, I, 195.
6. *E.I.*, I, 41.
7. *E.I.*, I, 33.
8. *E.I.*, I, 205.
9. *E.I.*, II, 183.
10. *I.A.*, XVI, 205.
11. *E.I.*, I, 152.

the master of prosody, grammar, logic and astronomy. He was also a store of arts and could compose poetry in many languages.[1] The Paramāra king Bhoja (*c.* 1025 A.D.) was also a great poet. The Udayapur record describes him as a king among poets (*Kavirāja*).[2] The Pāla king Vigrahapāla III (*c.* 1055 A.D.) was acquainted with fine arts.[3]

(6) *Divinity of the King*

The precise attitude of our period towards the doctrine of the divinity of the king is not easy to determine. The political writers of our age have, as a rule, postulated the functional resemblance between the king and some of the deities, as is generally done by earlier works like the *Manu-Smṛiti* and the *Mahābhārata*. Thus Śukra states 'Like Indra, the king protects the wealth; like Vāyu, he is the cause of good and evil actions; like Yama, he is the punisher of offences; like Agni, he is the purifier and enjoyer of all the gifts; like Varuṇa, he nourishes his subjects and like Chandra, he delights everybody by virtuous activities.[4] The *Agnipurāṇa* does the same, when it states that the king assumes the forms of nine deities, namely, the Sun, the Moon, Vāyu, Yama, Agni, Kubera, Varuṇa and *Pṛithvī*, when he discharges the different[5] regal functions, e.g., like *Chandra*; the king gives delight to his subjects; like *Vāyu*, he surveys the whole kingdom by means of spies etc. Several other Purāṇas like the *Matsya*[6], the *Padma*[7] and the *Mārkaṇḍeya*[8] also accept the functional resemblance between the king and some of the deities. All this evidence shows that the king was not regarded by our political writers as divine, though they regarded the king's office as such. They generally state that the king resembles the deities only in the performance of his regal functions. It is further to be noted

1. *E.I.*, XVIII, 95.
2. *E.I.*, I, 235; V.18.
3. *E.I.*, XV, 296.
4. *Śukra*, I, 73-77.
5. *Agni-Purāṇa*, 225, 16.
6. *Matsya-Purāṇa*; Ch. 22.
7. *Padma-Purāṇa*, I, 30.45 ff.
8. *Mārkaṇḍya-Purāṇa*, 27, 21, ff.

that if they compare the king to some deities, they also compare him to the father, the mother and the preceptor because of a similar resemblance of functions.[1]

Śukra, the principal writer for our period, further emphatically points out at one place that kingship is due to previous merit (*Prāk-karma*)[2] and at another place attributes it to mere valour and bravery.[3] But at no place does he state that the kingship arises because particles of different gods enter into the body of a king, as has been crudely done by Manu. He neither invests him with infallibility, nor enjoins absolute obedience to him, even if he was a wicked or worthless ruler, as was done by Nārada in the earlier period.[4] On the other hand, he regards the bad, vicious and reprobate king as a demon incarnate, and advises the subjects not to obey him.[5] He further calls that king a dacoit, if he forsakes his duty, disobeys the high ideal of kingship and oppresses the subjects.[6] According to Śukra the question does not arise at all as to whether the subjects are to obey such a king; he openly encourages them to intrigue and conspire against him,

1. Pitā-mātā-gururbhrātā bandhur Vaiśravaṇo Yamaḥ,
Nityaṁ saptagunaireshāṁ yukto rājā na chānyathā.
Guṇa-sādhana-sañdakshaḥ svaprajāyāḥ pitā yatahā.
Kshamayitryaparādhānāṁ mātā pushṭi-vidhāyinī.
Hitopadeshṭa Śishyasya suvidyādhyāpako guruḥ,
Svabhāgoddhārakṛid bhrātā yathā-śāstraṁ piturdhanāt.
Śukra, I, 78-80.

2. Tapasā teja ādatte śāstā pātā cha rañjakaḥ,
Nṛipaḥ svaprāktanāddhatte tapasā cha mahīmimām.
Śukra, I 20.

3. Nṛipaḥ svadharmanirato bhūtvā tejaḥkshyo'nyathā,
Abhishikto'nabhishikto nṛipatvantu yadāpnuyāt.
Buddhyā balena śauryeṇa tato nītyānupālayan,
prajāḥ sarvāḥ pratidinamachchhidro daṇḍadhṛik sadā.
Śukra, I, 26-27.

4. Rājani praharedyastu kṛitāgasyāpi durmatiḥ,
Śūle tamagnau vipached Brahmahatyāśatādhikam.
Nārada, XVIII, 31.

5. Guṇijushṭastu yo rājā sa jñeyo devatāmśakaḥ,
Viparītastu raksho'ṁśaḥ sa vai narakabhājanaḥ.
Śukra, I, 87.
Yāvat tu dharmaśīlaḥ syāt sa nṛipastāvadeva hi,
Śukra, IV, Sect. I, 114.

6. Hitāhitaṁ na śṛiṇoti rājā mantrimukhāchcha yaḥ,
Sa dasyū rājarūpeṇa prajānāṁ dhanahārakaḥ.
Śukra, II, 257.

and even to attempt to dethrone him[1] with the help of neighbouring or feudatory kings, and to offer the crown to a virtuous prince or to any other capable member of the royal family.[2] This advice was not so difficult to follow in the past, when there were several feudatory rulers aspiring to the imperial position and when the ruler possessed an army not much more efficient than the forces that could be raised by the oppressed subjects in co-operation with the feudatory, whom they wanted to enthrone.

There was however another school, probably of courtiers, which was inclined to accept the divinity of the king more or less in a literal sense. According to this school, the king was regarded as a divine incarnation. Some of the epigraphs of our age were written by authors, who subscribed to this view. Thus the Chaulukya king Kumārapāla is described as an incarnation of God Hari, who had descended from heaven.[3] The Chedi king Pṛithvīdeva is stated to be an incarnation of God and the guardian of the world.[4] Gāhaḍawāla rulers Chandradeva, Govinda Chandra and Jayachandra are described as incarnations of Brahmā,[5] Hari[6] and Rāma[7] in contemporary records. Pirṭhvīrāja II was regarded as an incarnation of Rāma,[8] as also Rāmpāla of the Pāla dynasty. The Dāwara followers of Bhikshachara proclaimed him as a divine incarnation in order to secure popular support for his cause (Raj. VIII. 305).

The climax of this tendency is to be seen in the practice of building temples not only in honour of dead kings, as was the case under the Kushāṇas, but even of living kings. In

1. Adharmaśīlo nṛipatiryadā taṁ bhīshayejjanaḥ,
Dharmaśīlātibalavadriporāśrayataḥ sadā.
Śukra, IV, Sect. I, 113.
2. Tatpade tasya kulajaṁ guṇayuktaṁ purohitaḥ,
Prakṛityanumatiṁ kṛitvā sthāpayedrājyaguptaye.
3. *E.I.*, I, 302.
Devaḥ (sotha) kumārapālanṛipatiḥ Śrī-rājyachūḍāmaṇi
......gādavatīrṇavān Haririti jñātaḥ prabhāvājjanaiḥ.
4. *E.I.*, I, 35, V. 15.
5. *I.A.*, XVIII.15.
6. *E.I.*, IX.319.
7. *Rambhāmañjarī*, p. 6.
8. *Prithvirājavijaya*, VII. 620.

one of the Chāhamāna records, king Luntigadeva is said to have set up images of himself and his queen; this obviously must have been done for being enshrined in the temple.[1] It is quite possible that the prevailing tendency of ascribing divinity to the royal personages and of regarding them as divine incarnations may be responsible for the erection of temples to living kings.

Whether the advocates of this school, which regarded the king as a divine incarnation, were prepared to hold him as infallible and above public scrutiny, we do not know. Probably they did so, as would appear from a passage in the *Kādambarī*.[2] It is very likely that the political writers of our period like Śukra may have propounded their theories as a reply to the extreme views advocated by the courtiers and expressed in some of our epigraphs.

(7) *King's functions*

The king was the supreme head of the executive, judicial and military administration. His paramount duty as the head of the Government was to protect the people and work for their welfare. Śukra clearly states at one place that the highest Dharma of the king is to protect the subjects and to put down the wicked.[3] Kāmandaka says that the protection of the subjects is possible only if law and order are preserved in society; the king should take proper steps to achieve this goal.[4]

Being the head of the judicial administration, the king was to administer law impartially and to ascertain carefully whether proper justice was administered by lower courts. The monarch, states Śukra, who proceeds according to the dictates

1. *E. I.*, IX, 79-81, We have got only a summary of this record here; the original text has not been given. Statues of secular for decorative purposes were not common in temples.
2. Śukanāsa's address, *Kadambarī*, p. 206.
3. Nṛipasya paramo dharmaḥ prajānāṁ paripālanam,
Dushtanigrahaṇaṁ nityaṁ na nītyā te vinā hyubhe.
Śukra, I, 14.
The text appears to be corrupt in the last quarter.
4. Tasmāddharmaṁ puraskṛitya yatetārthāya pārthivaḥ.
Dharmeṇa vardhate rājyaṁ tasya svādu phalaṁ śriyaḥ.
Kāmandaka, I, 15.

of law, is blessed with virtue, wealth and enjoyment.[1] Kāmandaka advises the king to impose just punishment upon the culprits according to the offences committed by them.[2]

Being the head of the military administration, the king look after the proper maintenance of the army and had to take steps to increase its efficiency. He was to make proper arrangements for the training and discipline of the fighting forces. The king, who does not increase the strength of his army, who does not protect his subjects and who does not make other princes to pay him tributes is compared to barren sesame.[3]

Besides these functions, the king had to promote *Dharma*, *Artha* and *Kāma* for the religious, socio-economic and aesthetic progress of the society. He was to encourage virtue and morality. He was to help all the religious sects. He was to maintain or support hospitals, rest houses and educational institutions, and had to encourage trade, industry, agriculture and fine arts.

(8) *Coronation*

In our period, the coronation ceremony was usually performed soon after the death of the last ruler. There is no evidence to show that it was postponed to the time when the king attained majority. Of course if a king was minor at the time of the ceremony, a regent carried on the administration for him.[4]

The coronation ceremony of our period differed consderable from that in the Vedic and post-Vedic times; it will be therefore necessary to survey its earlier history in

1. Nyāyapravṛitto nṛipatirātmānamatha cha prajāḥ,
Trivargeṇopasaṁdhatte nihanti dhruvamanyathā.
Śukra, I. 67.
2. Udvejayati tīkshṇena mṛidunā paribhūyate,
Tasmād yathārhato daṇḍaṁ nayet pakshamaṇāśritaḥ.
Kāmandaka, VI, 15.
3. Na vardhitaṁ balaṁ yaistu na bhūpāḥ karadīkṛitāḥ,
Na prajāḥ pālitāḥ samyak te vai shandḥatilānṛipāḥ.
Śukra, I, 126.
4. Amoghavarsha I was a minor of 12 at the time of his formal coronation and king Karikala of the Sangam age a boy of 5 only.

some details in order to understand the new developments in our age.

The history of coronation goes back to hoary antiquity. Even in the Vedic period we find it being solemnly performed with sacred *mantras*. It consisted of several rituals among which the Rājasūya was the most important one; next to it were the Vājapeya and the Sarvamedha. According to the *Aitareya-Brāhmaṇa*, the king would secure *Sāmrājya*, *bhaujya*, *svarājya*. *Vairajya*, etc., by performing the Rājasūya sacrifice.[1] According to the *Śatapatha-Brāhmaṇa*, however, the ceremony was not to be undertaken to achieve a particular distinction, but to inaugurate the reign of the king, however small.[2] In this sacrifice the king used to take an oath[3] undertaking not to work against the interest of the priestly order.[4]

The Vājapeya sacrifice lays down some rituals, which are followed by the chariot race, which was its main feature. The king was of course expected to win in this race and was then proclaimed and installed to the high office. It is however important to note that in the Vedic period the Vājapeya was of lesser political importance than the *Rājasūya*. In the later Vedic period the Vājapeya however obtained the higher rank than the Rājasūya because it was believed that by performing the former, one secures the imperial position, while by performing the latter, one attains to mere royalty.

Another important feature of the *Vājapeya* sacrifice was the Ratnin oblations, which were offered by the king to the Ratnins, (important courtiers and officials) by repairing to their houses.

In the epic period, the royal oath formed an important part in the coronation ceremony. The *Mahābhārata* admonishes

1. *A.Br.* p. VII, 2.6 . VIII, 3, 13.
2. Rājāsvarājyakāmo rājasūyena yajeta. *Śa. Br.*, V.2-3.
3. *A. Br.*, VIII, 15.
4. The oath is wrongly taken by some scholars as coresponding to the coronation oath of the modern times. It only means that the royal power should be in harmony with the priestly power, for it is the priest who invokes the divine powers at the time of coronation for the safety and prosperity of the king. The context of the passage contains no undertaking given by the king to the people to rule according to Dharma for their welfare. Neither does it indicate that the officiating priest was the representative of the society.

the king 'Take the oath in mind, word and deed, nemely I shall always look after the welfare of the people, regarding it as supreme; whatever is prescribed by the rules of ethics, I shall always abide by, I shall never be self-willed."[1]

In the coronation ceremony of our period, however, the Vedic rituals like the Vājapeya and the Rājasūya do not figure at all. The Vedic *mantras* had become unintelligible; due to the complicated and complex nature of the sacrificial rituals and greater repugnance for sacrificial slaughter, Vedic religion had gone out of vogue. The Ratnins, who played an important part in the Vājapeya sacrifice of the Vedic period also disappear in our age. There is no doubt that the ministers had taken their place, but it was no longer customary for the king to go to their houses to offer any oblations at the time of the coronation.

During our age king's power was regarded as supreme and the tendency to deify him was getting stronger. That the king should take an oath to rule without oppressing the people was probably regarded as incompatible with his power and dignity. Chariot race and the dice play also ceased to be important elements of the ceremony.

We thus see that the Vedic form of coronation had gone out of vogue. Some Vedic rituals like Vasodhārā were performed and a number of Vedic *mantras* were recited, but they do not appear to be connected with coronation. A number of Paurāṇic rituals like Graha and Nakshatra-śānti were introduced, attesting to the faith in astrology of the age. These rites are described by Lakshmidhara in the *Rājadharmakāṇḍa of Kṛitya-Kalpataru*, relying upon the authority of epics and Purāṇas.

Let us now survey the important features of the coronation ceremony of our period.[2] The proper date and auspicious time for the coronation were first settled by the court astrologer. It may be noted here that the Vedic rituals do not refer to any astrological considerations; in our period,

1. *Mbh.*, XII, 58, 115-6.
2. Epigraphs refer only to the holy bath in connection with this ceremony; other religious details are not mentioned.

however, astrology became a popular science and people began to have more faith in it, so the advice of the astrologer was usually taken on every important occasion. A chief priest was then chosen, who was to direct the rites. It was essential that he should not be the chief priest of any other ruler; only in that case he can pray to God for the paramount sovereignty and prosperity of only one ruler and none else. The preceptor of the king and the ministers were then to be presented to the king.

A number of preliminary arrangements were made for the coronation. The palace and the capital were beautifully decorated. The main roads were washed by clean and fresh water.[1] Gold, precious stones, jewels white garlands, fried rice, honey, ghee, weapons, new raiments, a white umbrella, a complete tiger skin and many other similar things required for the occasion were collected. An elephant with auspicious marks was also brought for the state procession after the coronation. Similarly a chariot was also made ready, so that the king might mount on it before going to make a circuit of the capital.

The ceremony[2] started with a ceremonial bath, given to the king by the water procured from the confluence of the Gaṅgā and the Yamunā at Prayāga and from other holy streams as well.[3] The king then performed a number of propitiatory rites, among which the Vināyaka-śānti, the Grahaśanti, the Aindrī-śānti and the Abhyudaya-śrāddha were the most important.[4] The Vināyaka-śānti, was performed to overcome obstacles, the Graha- or Nakshatra-śānti was intended to ward off evil influences of the planets and stars. Then followed the Abhyudaya- or Nāndī-śrāddha, which was

1. *Kkt.* R., Chap. II, p. 9.
2. If the coronation pandal was away from the palace, the king must have been taken there in a procession, at the end of which he must have been received by the officials assembled there.
3. Ābhishechanikaṁ dravyaṁ sarvamevopakalpitam.
Gaṅgā-Yamunayośchaiva saṅgamādāhṛitaṁ jalam.
Yās'chānyāḥ saritaḥ puṇyāstābhyaścha jalamāhṛitam.
Sarva-bījāni gandhāścha ratnāni vividhāni cha.
Kkt. R. Chap. II, p. 16.
4. Ādau kṛitvā mahāśāntiṁ puṇyāṁ vaināyikiṁ śubhām,
Grahaśāntim tathā śreshṭhāṁ tṛitīyāmāhutiṁ tathā.
Kkt.R., Chap. II, p. 10.

an inevitable ritual to be observed on every auspicious occasion. After the Abhyudaya-śrāddha, the king used to worship Vishṇu and Divine Mothers. The Vasordhārā sacrifice, which followed this worship consisted of 401 ghee offerings made continuously to fire in order to fulfil all varieties of desires. For a long time, it was connected with the royal coronation and was performed at the time of the consecration ceremony, as is shown by the Nāndsā inscription. It was regarded as a kind of superior consecration ceremony for the royal sacrificer himself, more potent than the Rājasūya or the Vājapeya.

The *Aindrī-śānti*, the most important rite, which was performed before the actual coronation, followed the Vasordhārā sacrifice. Its aim was to overcome internal and external enemies of the king. It was thus an important element in the coronation ceremony.

On the day of the actual Abhisheka, the priest decorated with turban and earrings, used to start the ceremony by propitiating the sacred fire with offerings. A few Vedic Mantras were then recited, but they are really not connected with the royal coronation. Some of them like Ritāshāḍi[2] and Yata-Indra[3] are calculated to make the king powerful and to promote the prosperity of the nation. Majority of Mantras, however, like Indrigaṇya, which is not yet traced, *Āshuḥ-śishāṇa*[4] which, describes the power of Indra, Āgatsatya[5], which refers to the oblation to truth, *Yaste-agne*[6] which refers to the sanctification of fire on an altar and *Svastidā*[7], in which, Indra is asked to drink *Soma* juice, have no connection at all with the coronation ceremony, and thus are not of any political significance.

After the recitation of the Vedic Mantras, the king was

1. *E.I.*, XXVII, 263.
2. *V.S.*, 18.38.
3. *A.V*, 19.15.1; *R.V.*, 8.61, 13.
4. *R.V.*, 10, 103, 1; *A.V.*, 19.13.2.
5. *T.Br.*, 3.12.32.
6. *T.Br.*, I, I.7.3.
7. *R.V.*, 10, 116, 2.

again given a bath[1] with Pañchagavya,[2] consisting of Milk, curds, ghee, sugar and honey. It is interesting to note that the bath with Pañchagavya is not referred to by the Vedic texts; it is therefore an innovation of the Paurāṇic age. Further, in the Vedic period, it was the priest only, who used to give this bath to the king; none others enjoyed this privilege. In our period, such was not however the case. Representatives of all the four castes, including the Śūdra, were permitted to besprinkle the king. The Śūdras, the Vaiśayas, the Kshatriyas, and the Brāhmaṇas standing respectively to tho west, south, east and north used to besprinkle the king by the water, milk, curd and ghee (also described as nectar) using earthen, copper, silver and gold pots[3] respectively. This perhaps indicates that the king was anxious to have the good-will of all the classes of his subjects on the occasion of his coronation.

After the bath, the limbs of the king were rubbed by the earth collected from twelve different localities.[4] The selection of the spots from which the earth was collected is not quite at random; some of them have symbolic importance. For instance, the mountain is the highest place on the earth, and the rubbing of the king's head with the earth obtained from the summits of mountains was naturally believed to make the king as prominent as a mountain peak. The right hand of the king was rubbed with the dust dug with the tusk of an elephant and the left hand with that found adhering to the horns of a bull. Now we know that the elephant and the bull are both the symbols of strength and power and the earth dug by them was thought to make the king most powerful. The temple was regarded as the most holy place, and

1. The coronation baths were believed to make the person of the king holy, as is expressly mentioned in Rāshṭrakūṭa record describing the coronation of Amoghavarsha III, Altekar, Rāshṭrakūṭas, p. 109.
2. Rājasnātaḥ punaḥ snāpya pañchagavyena devavat,
Mṛittāmra-raupya-hemotthairjalapūrṇaistatc ghaṭaiḥ.
Kkt. R., Chap. II, p. 11.
3. Toyena Sūdraiḥ snāpyaścha paśchimāṁ diśamās'ṛitaiḥ,
Tataḥ kshīreṇa vaiśyais'cha dakshiṇasyāṁ diśi sthitaiḥ.
Kshatriyaiścha tato dadhnā pūrvasyāṁ diśyavasthitaiḥ,
Amṛitena tato vipraiḥ ghṛitenottarataḥ sthitaiḥ.
Kkt. R. Chap. II, p. 11.
4. *Kkt. R.* Chap. II, 11-12.

the earth obtained from it was used to rub the king's face. The face is the most significant limb of a person, and its rubbing with this holy earth was obviously to sanctify the entire person of the king. The rubbing of the remaining of the king's limbs with the earth obtained from other diverse localities like an ant-hill, a house of a prostitute, a confluence of streams, a horse-stable, a cowshed and a river bed had probably similar significance, though it cannot be now fully understood.

After this symbolic rubbing, the king was asked by the priest to sit on a *bhadrāsana*; he was then besprinkled with water falling through a golden sieve (having hundred and eight holes) by the members of four castes, by chaste women and by women with living husband and children. The king then used to see hundred auspicious objects and hundred and eight holy articles.[1] The remaining rites were then performed and lastly the *pūrṇāhuti* or the final oblation was offered to the fire.[2] All these are new details in the coronation ritual introduced in our age reflecting to changed outlook.

Later on the king used to worship Gaṇesha, Brahmā, Vishṇu and Śiva and also other deities popular in contemporary times. For the satisfaction of the planets, the gods and the manes, he used to bestow gifts on worthy recipients; an assurance of safety was also given to all living beings.[3] The prisoners were then released.[4] It is interesting to note that the custom of releasing the prisoners was prevalent in India since very early times; we find the great emperor Aśoka releasing the prisoners on every anniversary of his coronation.

1. Maṅgalānāṁ śataṁ paśyetpuṇyamashṭottaraṁ śatəm,
Śāntyai prādhānike sthāne sarvametadythākramam.
Kkt. R. Chap. II, p. 12.

2. Kṛitvā śeshaṁ tato hutvā dadyātpūrṇāhutiṁ tataḥ,
Abhishiktastato rājā saṁpūjyādau Vināyakam.
Kkt. R., Chap. II, p. 12.

3. *Paṭṭabandha*, the tying of the fillet round the forehead and *mukuṭa dhāraṇa*, wearing the crown, are curiously enough not described by Lakshmīdhara. Probably these were secular elements in the coronation ceremony for which there were no *mantras* prescribed and hence Lakshmīdhara omits them. They are not refered in this Vedic coronation ceremony also.

4. Athātaśsthānagān sarvān paśūnapi vimochayet.
Bandhana-sthāna-saṁsthāṁścha pramochayati śāstravat.
Kkt. R. Chap. II, p. 12.

The release of cattle, advocated by Lakshmīdhara, is perhaps a grotesque extension of the principle of the release of all under confinement at the coronation time. Probably only a few cattle were let loose as a matter of formality.

When this was done, the king was seated on a lion throne covered with a tiger skin and the chief priest used to present him the customary *madhuparka* offering. Having worshipped his weapons and royal umbrella (Chhatra), he used to give audience to his subjects. Then started the coronation procession. For a time the king used to ride a charger, but after a short while, he used to exchange the horse for an elephant. The royal procession went through the principal thorough-fares of the metropolis. The city gods in temples were visited and worshipped at that time and largesses were scattered all the way. After returning to the palace, royal servants and guests were offered a feast, which marked the end of the coronation.

Comparison with the modern English coronation

Before concluding this topic, we may passingly compare the Indian coronation with its English counterpart. It is interesting to note that the principle features of the modern English coronation show a striking resemblance to that of India. In both we find the ceremony essentially religious in character, the difference lies only in degree. In English coronation, prayers and offerings are given to God, his Son and the Holy Ghost, so that they may bless the sovereign and secure the welfare of his kingdom, while in Indian coronation, the divinities together with various natural and supernatural forces credited with power for good and evil were propitiated through prayers, offerings and other religious rites. In both the systems there occur, crowning, blessing for universal dominion, presentation of nobles and officials, jail delivery, and the state procession through the metropolis. The coronation oath, which is the principal feature of modern English coronation, was of course not taken by kings during our period, though it was not unknown earlier.

(9) *King's titles*

We will now discuss the different royal titles in use in

our period. During the last half of the 1st millennium before the Christian era, Indian kings were content with the simple title Rājā. In all his records, the great Mauryan emperor Aśoka calls himself merely a Rājā; he does not bear any high sounding epithet. When the Scythians and the Kushāṇas established themselves in northern India, they popularised the imperial title Rājātirāja, 'king of kings'. Later on when the Guptas became imperial rulers, they transformed the title Rājātirāja into Mahārājādhirāja, which soon became popular with the great conquerors and imperial rulers of India.

During our period the title Mahārājādhirāja was usually used by emperors. In Rajasthan, Bihar and Bengal kings used to have variations of this title like *samastarājāvalivirājita*, *parameśvara* and *paramabhaṭṭāraka*.

Many Gāhaḍavāla kings assumed the title Vividhavidyā-vichāra-vāchaspati, 'deep scholar engaged in pondering over the different branches of learning'. This shows that some kings were anxious to assume titles testifying to their scholarship or patronage of learning. In one of his inscriptions, the king Hammīravarmadeva calls himself Paramabhaṭṭāraka Shāhīrāja (c. I. XX, 135). The title Shāhīrāja was undoubtedly adopted by him from the Muslims, who had established themselves in the northwest by his time. In earlier times, of course, this title was used by the Kushāṇas.

It is somewhat surprising to note, that the title Mahārājādhirāja was sometimes used by the feudatories also. Thus for instance, Mathanadeva, who was a feudatory of the king Vijayapāladeva calls himself Mahārājādhirāja Parameśvara in the Rājor inscription.[1] Dhārāvarsha, the feudatory of the king Yaśovarman, is described as Mahārājādhirāja Mahāmaṇḍaleśvara in the Kalavan plates.[2] This tendency probably indicates the growing aspirations of feudatories and the waving power of their overlords.

There were also some titles in use, indicating the king's faith in a particular religion or sect. Thus Dharmapāla and Devapāla, the two great Pāla rulers, called themselves as

1. *E.I.*, III, 266-67.
2. *I.A.*, LVI, 50.

Paramasaugata in their records, clearly showing that they were the followers of Buddhism. The title Paramamāheśvara which was assumed by a number of kings of the dynasties in Northern India, indicates that the rulers were the worshippers of Śiva. Similarly some of the Pratīhāra kings assumed the title Paramaśaktibhaktas, which indicates their faith in the worship of Śakti.

The records of our period refer to some additional epithets assumed by the rulers of the Gāhaḍavāla, Pratīhāra, Chedi, Pāla and Sena dynasties. These epithets were Aśvapati, Gajapati and Narapati. Of these titles Narapati was a general one and could hardly have had any special significance. But there is some evidence to show that originally the titles Aśvapati and Gajapati might have been used by the Gurjara-Pratīhāras and the Pālas respectively. A verse in a Śilāhāra record of Aparājitarājadeva, dated 993 A.D. refers to the Gajapati taking refuge in a cave on the bank of the Gaṅgā and to the Vājīśa being constantly tormented as a consequence of the military exploits of the Rāshṭrakūṭa emperor Kṛishṇa III.[1] Gajapati's taking refuge in a cave on the bank of the Gaṅgā can well be applicable to a Pāla ruler of Bengal; the Vājīśa of the record was probably the Pratīhāra ruler; the Rāshṭrakūṭas were at constant wars with the Pālas and the Pratīhāras. Sulaiman also informs us that the Pratīhāras were strong in cavalry and the Pālas in the elephant force. It is therefore not improbable that for sometime the kings of the Pāla and the Pratīhara dynasties were known as Gajapatis and Aśvapatis. Very soon, however, these titles ceased to have any dynastic significance; for instance, we find the Gāhaḍavālas describing themselves as both Aśvapatis and Gajapatis;[2] the same was the case with the Chedis and Senas.

(10) *Was monarchy limited ?*

It is important to note that though the king was the centre of all military, political, administrative and judicial

1. Cholo Lolo bhiyābhūdgajapatirrviśadjāhnavī gavharāntaḥ Vājīśastrāsaśeshaḥ samabhavadabhavat śailarandhre tathāndhraḥ. C. V. Vaidya, *History of Medieval Hindu India*, Appendix VI, p. 349.

powers, he was expected not to behave arbitrarily. Hindu political writers have imposed a number of checks upon the king to prevent him from becoming an autocrat.

In ancient India, sovereignty was executive rather than legislative. In other words, the king had no legislative power. He was expected to act according to the rules and laws framed not by himself but by the wise sages and immemorial custom. He had to respect *deśadharma* (local customs), *jātidharma* (caste rules), *kuladharma* (family traditions), and *śreṇidharma* (guild regulations), which together constituted the law of the land. Śukra clearly says that it is only by following the Dharma or law that the king can earn fame in the world.[1] He could not however make the law, nor could he act against it, because the law was regarded as more divine, than the king himself. He was made to realise that there was nothing higher than *Dharma* and that he must and he should act according to it. Kāmandaka says that it is only by following the law that the king can enjoy the kingdom for a long time. One, who acts against the rules of *Dharma*, goes to hell.[2] *Dharma* alone brings prosperity to the kingdom and fame to the king. The king should therefore act according to its dictates.

The political writers of our period like those of the earlier ages[3] regard the king as a servant of the people appointed to protect them. Nārada says that taxation is nothing but king's pay for the protection of his subjects.[4] According to Aparārka, who flourished in our period, no one ever makes a payment without expecting a return; the taxes are therefore paid in return for protection expected from the king.[5] Śukra goes a step further and says that since the people pay him

1. Deśadharmā jātidharmāḥ kuladharmāḥ sanātanāḥ,
Muniproktāścha ye dharmāḥ prāchīnā nūtanāścha ye.
Te rāshṭraguptyai saṁdhāryyā jñātvā yatnena sannṛipaiḥ,
Dharmasaṁsthāpanādrājā śriyaṁ kīrttiṁ pravindati.
Śukra, IV, Sect. III, 10-11
2. *Kāmandaka*, I, 14-15.
3. *B.D.S.*, I, 10, 6; *A.S.* X, 3.
4. *Nārada*, XVIII, 48.
Anyaprakārāduchitādbhūmeḥ shaḍbhāga-saṁjnitam,
Baliḥ sa tasya vihitaḥ prajāpālana-vetanam.
5. On *Yaj*, I, 366.

taxes, the king should serve them as a *dāsa* or a servant.[1] The above statements are not to be taken literally; but they are obviously intended to convey to the king that if the people paid the taxes, it was his duty to protect them as their servant, specially appointed for this work.

The political writers of our period have gone a step further and declared the king to be a trustee for the people. They have advised him not to spend the state revenues for his own personal enjoyment. They have clearly maintained that the taxes, which the king collects, are held by him only as a trust for the subjects, and are to be used only for their welfare. The king is repeatedly informed that the treasury is not his own personal or private property. Śukra maintains that the king, who spends the revenues for the maintenance of the army, for the welfare of the subjects and for the performance of sacrifices, gets the happiness in this as well as in the next life, but the king, who spends it otherwise, goes down to hell.[2]

The *Agni-Purāṇa*, however, goes a step still further and declares that the king's responsibilities are greater than those of a trustee; the latter is not called upon to sacrifice his own interests in favour of the object of trust; the king has to do so. This authority compares the king to an expectant mother and states that just as the latter sacrifices her own pleasures and conveniences for promoting the growth and welfare of the baby in her womb, in the same way the king must sacrifice his own ease, convenience and happiness, so that the subjects committed to his care may prosper both materially and spiritually.[3] The *Mārkaṇḍeya-Purāṇa* also advocates the same view, when it states that the body of the king is not meant for pleasures and enjoyment; it has to put up with great troubles

1. Sarvataḥ phalabhugbhūtvā dāsavat syāttu rakshaṇe.
Śukra, IV, Sect. II, 130.

2. Bala-prajā-rakshaṇārthaṁ yajñārthaṁ kośasaṁgraḥ,
Paratreha cha sukhado nṛipasyānyaścha duḥkhadaḥ.
Strī-putrārthaṁ kṛito yaścha svopabhogāya kevalam,
Narakāyaiva sa jñeyo na paratra sukhapradaḥ.
Śukra, IV, Sect. II, 3-4.

3. Nityaṁ rājñā tathā bhāvyaṁ garbhiṇī sahadharmiṇī,
Yathā svaṁ sukhamutsṛijya garbhasya sukhamāvahet.
Agni-Purāṇa, 222, 8.

and worries, while carrying out the royal duty of protecting the subjects and fulfilling the Dharma.[1]

To sum up, a passage in *Śukra*, I, 78-81 gives us perhaps a very good glimpse into the views of the age about the king. Like a father, the king was to promote the building up of good character in his subjects; like a mother, he was to forgive them; like a teacher, he was to offer them good advice; like a brother, he was to ensure them a proper share in the revenues of the states; like a friend, he was to guard their secrets; like Kubera, he was to grant them wealth and like Yama, he was to mete out just punishments. In IV, 2, 131 Śukra sums up the whole position, when he maintains that the king was a servant of the people as he received his wages from them, but he was also their lord as he offered them protection.

A functionary, who was to discharge so many diverse duties, could of course not afford to act capriciously. He is at every step asked to act after consulting his ministers, preceptors and Brāhmaṇas. Śukra advises the king to act normally according to the advice of his ministers and preceptors. He clearly states that the king, who does not listen to his ministers and acts according to his own whims, will be soon destroyed. Even the wisest king cannot know everything, for different persons have different aptitudes.[2] Even Manu, who has put forth the rather crude theory that the king's body is fashioned out of the particles from the bodies of Dikpālas, reminds him that he can never hope to govern the kingdom well, except with the genuine co-operation of his ministers and advisers. We thus see that the ministers are expected to play an important part in preventing the king from becoming an autocrat.

Kings usually become arbitrary when they are not given good education and training. Our political writers have therefore insisted that proper steps should be taken in this direction. The training of the king taught him to be

1. Rājñāṁ śarīra-grahaṇaṁ na bhogāya mahīpate.
Kleśāya mahate pṛithvī-svadharmaparipālane.
Mārkaṇḍeya-Purāṇa, 130, 33.

2. *Śukra*, II, 2-7.

pious and religious to cultivate good manners and to respect the public opinion.

Our political writers have also imposed a number of religious and moral checks upon the king in order to prevent him from becoming an arbitrary ruler. They assert that a king, who does not rule according to the law and oppresses the subjects, will go to hell. This threat of hell had a great terror in ancient times and it served as a great deterrent.

Public opinion was also expected to play an important part in checking the arbitrary powers of the king. Through his spies, he was to ascertain what his subjects thought of him and his administration and was to mend matters, if necessary.[1]

We thus see that the political writers of our period have devised a number of administrative, moral and religious checks in order to prevent the king from becoming an autocrat. The records of our period, however, further reveal how a great decentralization of the functions of the Government was brought about, and how it served to protect the interests of the people. Large powers were vested in district, town and village administrations, which could be effectively supervised and controlled by local non-official councils, in which the voice of the people had the upper hand. The village and town councils of our period discharged almost all the functions of Government, except that of organising a regular army, determining foreign policy and declaring and conducting a war. This extensive decentralization was an effective check upon the powers of the king in ancient India.

1. Svadurguṇa-śravaṇato lokānāṁ paripīḍakaḥ
Nṛipo yadā tadā lokaḥ kshubhyate bhidyate yataḥ
Gūḍhācharaiḥ śrāvayitvā svavṛittaṁ dūshayanti ke
Bhūshayanti cha kairbhāvairamātyāśyāścha tadvidaḥ
Mayi kīdṛik cha saṁprītiḥ keshāmaprītireva vā

Śukra, I, 13-12.

Prāyopaveśana (fast into death) resorted to by Brāhmaṇas in Kashmir can hardly be described as a form of public opinion. It was usually undertaken for the class privileges e.g. exemption from forced labour (*Rāj*, VII 1888); very often it was at the instigation of interested political parties, as in the case of *prāyopaveśana* against minister Tunga (Raj, VII, 13).

How far the above checks and devises were successful in serving as breaks on royal power and in preventing it from becoming arbitrary is however difficult to determine. During our period there were some virtuous and able kings, who worked hard for the welfare of the people and for the all round progress of their kingdoms. But there were also some tyrants, who oppressed the subjects and ruled arbitrarily. The *Rājataraṅgiṇī* supplies many instances of such cruel and unprincipled rulers, who were helped by the Damara, Ekaṅgas and Kayastha in their oppressive activities Very probably some of the monarchs of the dynasties surveyed in this work might have belonged to the same category. An account of their maladministration does not occur in our inscriptions probably because they were composed by their court poets Or it may be that normally a successful rival to the throne did not care to describe the administration of the ruler, he had ousted. The Rāshṭrakūṭa king Amoghavarsha III describes the maladministration of his predecessor Govinda IV, but such cases are few. What was the percentage of tyrants to good rulers cannot be unfortunately ascertained at present.

The kings, who ruled in an arbitrary way in our period, could do so, because moral checks like those described above, were not always effective and constitutional checks like those in modern times did not exist in our age. In the Vedic period, the Samiti apparently functioned as a constitutional check and controlled the king more or less like a modern Parliament. But during our period, there was no such body, which could control a wicked ruler or bring his administration to a standstill. It may be noted that the same was the case in Europe also in contemporary times. The ministry could sometimes control a king, but normally this was difficult for it because ministers were appointed by king and held office during his pleasure.

The philosophy of the resistence to misrule was not properly developed by our age. We have already shown how our political writers regarded the king to be a servant and the kingdom to be a trust. What action was to be taken by people, if the august servant and trustee did not discharge the duties properly is not discussed by our writers. Rights of the people have not received that attention, which the modern age would have liked to be paid to them. The result was that there were no constitutional checks developed in our period, as was the case everywhere else.

(11) *King's Privy Purse*

The question of what may be conveniently described as king's privy purse has been discussed by the writers of the age; some epigraphical records also throw light upon it. Proceeds of taxes and revenues were regarded as the state income and a portion of it was given to the king as his privy purse. Śukra states that one-sixth of the state revenue should be allotted to the king for his own expenditure. He, however, does not inform us how this amount was made up. Most probably the king would have received a part of it as a cash allowance and a part as income from the crown lands. The inscriptions of our period do not mention the cash allowance, probably because there was no occasion to do so in land grants. They usually refer to royal fields and villages allotted to kings.

The extent of the crown lands naturally differed from time to time and place to place. The Chaulukya king Bhīmadeva II enjoyed a number af Pathakas, namely Gaṁbhūta pathaka,[1] Chālīsā-pathaka,[2] Daṇḍahī-pathaka,[3] Dhāṇḍābāra-pathaka[4] and Vālauya-pathaka. Pathakas were normally equal to a Tehsil or Taluka of the modern period.

Sometimes kings received as part of their privy purse, revenues of an entire Maṇḍala, or a Vishaya or a town. Thus under the Chaulukyas, Bhīmadeva II was enjoing the revenues of the entire Kaccha Maṇḍala[5] in 1030 A.D.; under the Paramāras, Devarāja was receiving the revenues of an entire Vishaya[6] or district. Under the Chedis, the king Karṇa

1. *E. I.*, XXI, 172.
2. *I. A.*, VI, 194-5.
3. *I. A.*, VI, 199-200.
4. *I. A.*, XI, 71-2.
5. *E. I.*, XXI, 172.
6. *I. A.*, VI, 203.

enjoyed the revenues of the town of Ānandapur.[1] Unfortunately we do not know what was the exact amount of the income derived from these different Maṇḍalas or Vishayas or Pathakas, as the records are silent on this point.

(12) *Abdication and Suicide*

The kings during our period are sometimes seen abdicating the throne in favour of their sons, usually under the influence of the theory of *Vānaprastha* and *Sannyāsa*. Thus under the Pālas, Vigrahapāla is stated to have entrusted the reins of the government to his son Nārāyaṇapāla and become an ascetic. 'Let asceticism be mine and kingdom thine', says he, in his Bhagalapur grant.[2] Under the Chandellas, the king Jayavarman is also stated to have abdicated the throne. The Kālañjara inscription clearly declares that being wearied of administration, this monarch handed over the government to Pṛithvīvarman and went to the Gaṅgā to wash his sins.[3] The Jodhapur inscription of Bauka informs us that Bhillāditya, after entrusting the reins of the Government to his son, went to the Gaṅgā and lived there for eighteen years, he then observed a fast unto death and then went to heaven.[4] Jhoṭa, the father of Bhillāditya, is also said to have proceeded to the Bhāgīrathī after enjoying the pleasures of the kingdom.[5] It is very likely that he also renounced the worldly life sometime during his old age. Jāṭa, a member of the family of Pratīhāra Bauka, also retired to the pious hermitage of Māṇḍavya, adorned with streams and rivers, after entrusting the administration to his younger brother Bhoja, and practised there the rites of pure religion.[6] In the Sena dynasty, Sāmantasena is said to have frequented the sacred hermitages in the woods by the sandy banks of the Gaṅgā where he

1. *E. I.*, I, 317.
2. *I. A.*, XV, 306.
3. *J. A. S. B.*, 1848, Vol. I, 318-19; H. C. Ray, *Dynastic History of Northern India*, Vol. II, p. 704.
4. *E. I.*, XVIII, 95.
5. *Ibid.*
6. *Ibid.*

spent a long time.[1] The Chedi king Lakshmīkarṇa probably abdicated the throne in favour of his son, though it is difficult to say whether he did it due to the desire of renunciation.[2] The inscription merely states that Lakshmīkarṇa took part in his son's coronation; it does not, however, inform us whether he accepted *Sannyāsa* in his old age.

Besides the epigraphical evidence, the Jain sources record a number of cases of such abdications. Thus the *Prabhāvaka-carita* informs us that the king Āma, a son of Yaśovarman of Kanauj, abdicated the throne in favour of his son Duṇḍuha and spent his life in religious devotions.[3] The *Dvyāśraya-Kāvya* also informs us that Durlabharāja of Chaulukya dynasty abdicated the throne in favour of his nephew Bhīma and devoted his remaining life to religious pursuits.[4] Bhīma I is also stated to have abdicated the throne in favour of his son Karṇa.[5] The *Hammīramahākāvya* also states that Jaitrasiṁha handed over the administration to his son Hammīra and himself went to the forest.[6] The contemporary South Indian records also refer to a number of instances of kings' abdications.[7] Both Amoghavarsha I of the Rāshṭrakūṭa dynasty and Mārasiṁha of the Gaṅgā family[8] are stated to have abdicated the throne in favour of their sons in order to pursue spiritual ideals.

All this evidence clearly indicates that some of the pious rulers of our period actually followed the teachings of Hinduism and Jainism which lay down that a person should retire from life at the advent of old age in order to realise the spiritual ideal of human life. In the earlier periods, such instances are relatively few. This may perhaps indicate that the ideal of renunciation was becoming more popular in Hinduism in our period.

1. *E. I.*, I, 305-15.
2. *E. I.*, XII, 205; *E. I.*, II, 1-17.
3. *S. I. G. M.*, XIII, 108, V. 709.
4. *D. V.*, VIII, V.20.
5. *Ibid.* IX, V.74.
6. *H. M. K.*, VIII, 54-57; 106-108.
7. A. S. Altekar, *Rāshṭrakūṭas*, p. 89.
8. *Ibid*, p. 132. The Sanjan plates state that Amoghavarsha I gave away his kingdom more than once saying 'Of what account are external objects to me ?'

There are only two instances in northern India of kings committing suicide under religious motif, that of the Chandella King Dhaṅga and the Chedi King Gāṅgeyadeva. The Mau inscription of Madanavarmā states that Dhaṅga after living for more than hundred years 'at last abondoned the body in the waters of the Gaṇgā and the Yamunā and entered into beatitude, closing the eyes, fixing his thought on Rudra and muttering holy prayers'.[1] The Chedi king Gāṅgeyadeva is also stated to have thrown himself into the Gāṅgā.[2] In the Deccan also during our period, the Rāshṭrakūṭa king Indra IV[3] and the Gāṅga king Mārasiṁha are stated to have committed suicide[4] by fasting unto death, as recommended by the Jain religion.

Jainism permits an old man to commit suicide by fasting. *Manusmṛiti*[5] allows a Vānaprastha to walk straight in north eastern direction, till he meets his death, by falling into water or fire. It is these teachings which were responsible for the above religious suicides. Examples of Hindu rulers followings the advice of Manu in the earlier periods are not known. Probably the growing influence of Jainism was responsible for their decisions.

SECTION B : MEMBERS OF THE ROYAL FAMILY

(1) *Yuvarāja*

We now turn to a discussion of the role of the various members of the royal family in the administration of our period. The first person to consider is the Yuvarāja or the crown prince. It may be observed at the outset that the Yuvarāja was regarded as an important member of the administration by our political writers. Śukra compares him to the right eye and the right ear of the king; he was to be consulted on important administrative problems.[6]

1. *E. I.*, I, 195.
2. *J. A. S. B.*, VIII, part I, p. 489, V. 11.
3. A. S. Altekar, *Rāshṭrakūṭas*, p. 89.
4. *Ibid*, p. 132.
5. *Manu*, VI 31.
6. Yuvarājo'mātyagaṇo bhujāvetau mahībhujaḥ,
Tāveva nayane karṇau dakshasavyau kramāt smṛitau.
Śukra, II, 12.

Naturally great care was bestowed upon the proper training of the crown prince; we have already referred to this topic (pp. 43-44). The crown prince is particularly warned that he should not become insolent on account of his privileged position. He was to be respectful to the king and considerate to his brothers. He was to help his father in carrying on the administration on proper lines and to the satisfaction of the subjects.[1]

Though the Yuvarāja was an important member of the administration, our political writers do not include him in the ministry, probably because an heir-apparent, old enough to participate in administration, was not always available. We may presume that when a Yuvarāja, old enough to bear the burden of administration, was available, he was included in the ministry. Possibly he may have occupied the status of the Pratinidhi in Śukra's cabinet.

We often find the Yuvarāja exercising the royal prerogative of granting villages, of course with the permission of the reigning king. Thus under the Gāhaḍavālas, Yuvarāja Govindchandra is seen granting a village in 1104 A.D., after taking his father's permission.[2] Similarly Yuvarāja Jayachandradeva donated the village of Haripur to Praharājaśarman with the consent of his father.[3] Yuvarāja Āsphoṭachandra issued a copper-plate in 1134 A.D., bearing his father Govindachandra's seal.[4] All this evidence shows that under the Gāhaḍavālas, the crown prince enjoyed the right of making land grants after taking the emperor's permission. Probably such was also the case with other dynasties, though it is not revealed by their records.

Some records of the Chāhamānas of Nadol refer to the rule of both the king and the crown prince at the beginning. Thus the Sevadi inscription refers both to Mahārājādhirāja Aśvarāja and the Yuvarāja Kaṭukarāja.[5] Another inscription

1. *Śukra*, II, 35-50.
2. *I. A.*, XIV, 101-4.
3. *E. I.*, IV, 118.
4. *E. I.*, VIII, 155-56.
5. Mahārājādhirāja-śrī-Aśvarāja-rājye śrī-kaṭukarāja-yauvarājye. *E. I.*, XI, 29-30.

from the same place refers to the king Kaṭukarāja along with the heir-apparent Jayantasiṁha.[1]

These cases would show that when the ruling kings were old, or incapacitated, the heir-apparent naturally exercised almost all the powers of the ruling king. The seal of the Yuvarāja was often regarded as necessary even when the seal of the king was there. Thus Madanapāla as Yuvarāja put his own seal on his father's grant.[2]

(2) *Queens*

Let us now see what was the position of the queens during our period. It is important to note that a number of queens figure in the records of the different dynasties of our period, but we hardly find any one of them being entrusted with any administrative duties in Northern India. There is no doubt that in two of the records of the Gāhaḍavāla king Madanapāla, the crown prince Govindachandra is stated to have taken consent not only of his ministers and Purohita but also of the queen Rālhāṇadevī at the time of the land grant;[3] whether her permission was a mere formal affair or whether it was due to her being a member of the government is difficult to say. It appears very probable that the queen-mother being the most important member of the royal family, the crown prince would have thought to honour her by taking her formal consent at the time of making the grant, and that she did not occupy any important post in the administration. The consent was thus probably a formal affair in her case, and more certainly in the case of other persons like Pratīhāra and Mahattama mentioned in the record.

The queens during our period hardly played an important part in the administration. In the copper-plate records they are sometimes seen making land grants, but we should remember that they could do this only after taking the

1. *E. I.*, XI, 34.
2. *I. A.*, XVIII, 9-14.
3. Pratīhāro Gautamaścha Jāgukaścha purohitaḥ,
Jananī Rahladevī cha Vālhaṇaścha mahattakaḥ.
Eteshāṁ saṁmatiṁ prāpya samyaglikhitavānidam.
Nāmnā Vijayadāsākhyaḥ śāsanaṁ rājaśāsanam.
I. A., XIV, 103-4; *E. I.*, II, 359-61.

permission of the king. Thus, when under the Gāhaḍavālas, the crowned queen Prithvīśṛīkā wanted to grant the village of Bahuvarā to Purohita Devavarmā and other Brāhmaṇas, she had to take the consent of the emperor Govindachandra.[1] Nayanakelidevī, another queen of Govindachandra, had to supplicate for the king's permission, while granting the village of Daravali to Mahāpurohita Jāguśarman.[2] Ghosalādevī, another queen of Govindachandra, took her husband's permission while granting the village of Ghaṭiārā to Thakkura Kulhe.[3] Under the Chedis also the same practice prevailed. The Karatalai inscription informs us that the queen Rahaḍā granted the village of Chakrahaḍi to the temple of Vishṇu with the permission of the king Lakshamaṇarāja[4]. Similarly queen Ghosalādevī took the consent of king Vijayasiṁha when in 1180 A.D, she donated the village of Coralaya in the Semvala-pattala to a Brāhmaṇa named Sitha-Śarmā[5]. All this evidence clearly indicates that the queens during our period were not given the right to make land grants with their independent authority.

There is of course one rare instance, where we find the queen making a grant without taking the permission of the king. Thus the Chedi queen Ālhaṇadevī, widow of the king Gayakarṇadeva and the mother of the reigning king Narasiṁha, is seen assigning the income from the villages of Nāmmauṇḍi in the Jāutipattala; but the document is silent about any permission taken for the transaction.[6] The non-reference to the permission may however be accidental. Or it may be that the reigning king, out of his regard for his mother, did not like the permission to be formally rocorded in the copper-plate.

The queens are also sometimes seen making land grants along with their sons. Thus under the Gāhaḍavālas, in 1124 A.D., the queen Rālhaṇadevī granted the village of

1. *E. I.*, II, 187-88.
2. *E. I.*, IV, 108.
3. *E. I.*, V, 117-8.
4. *E. I.*, II, 177.
5. *I. A.*, XVIII, 219.
6. *E. I.*, II.13.

Tribhāṇḍa to Brāhmaṇa Paṇḍita Bhūpatiśarman along with her son Govindachandra.[1] Another inscription of the same dynasty informs us that the same queen along with her son Govindachandra granted 10 *Nālukas* of land to Thakkura Jayaśarman[2] in 1133 A.D. The association of the dowager queen with the son in the land grant seems to be due more to religious feeling than to any administrative necessity. Even now the mother is associated with the son, when she visits sacred places like Banaras and offers *Śrāddha* to her departed husband.[3]

For their private expenditure, the queens during our period were often given land allotments known as *Rājakīya-bhoga*[4] under the Gāhaḍavālas and *Grāsabhūmi*[5] under the Chāhamānas. They perhaps correspond to modern pin-money or *Strīdhana*. Due to want of evidence it is difficult to say with certainty whether the queens of all the dynasties enjoyed such grants.[6] Nor can we say definitely whether they enjoyed full proprietory rights over their *Rājakīyabhoga*. In one case, we find the Gāhaḍavāla queen Āṇaladevī granting one plough of land from her own *Rājakīyabhoga* to Tirthaṅkara Mahāvīra without taking the king's permission.[7] It is very likely that under the Gāhaḍavālas, queens could if they liked, make land grants from their own *Rājakīyabhoga*, if the land to be given was a small piece. It is, however, not unlikely that the omission of the king's permission in the above grant may be accidental.

Sometimes taxes were assigned to the queens as part of their income, probably in addition to the *Rājakīyabhoga* lands. In one of the Chāhamāna records, three queens are stated

1. *J. A. S. B.*, LVI, 114-16.
2. *E. I.*, V, 114.
3. One of the Nasik inscriptions (*E. I.*, VIII, Nasik No. 5) refers to an order of Gautamiputra Sātakarṇi and his mother Balaśrī to an officer at Govardhana in connection with a religious grant. Here also mother's association may be due to the religious desire to associate her with charity.
4. *E.I.*, IX, 47.
5. *E.I.*, XX, 33.
6. It is worth noting that the inscriptions of the earlier periods do not refer to such grants to queens; they were probably becoming common in our period.
7. *E. I.*, IX, 47.

to have made a grant of two *ghāṇakas* of oil from their own royal share.[1] This of course, they could have done, only if the tax had been assigned to them for their own personal use.

The question of dowager queens functioning as regents has been discussed already (*ante*, pp. 42-43).

The contemporary South Indian records show that queens and princesses in the royal family were appointed frequently to important administrative posts; for instance Revakanimdi, a daughter of Amoghavarsha I and the wife of Erragaṅga, was the governor of the important district of Edatore in *c.* 850 A.D[2]. Similarly under the Western Chālukyas, Vijayabhaṭṭārikā, the senior wife of Chandrāditya, the elder brother of Vikramāditya I, also acted as a governor.[3] Under the later Chālukyas of Kalyāṇī also, we have several examples of queens being appointed to important government offices. Thus Mailādevī, one of the wives of Someśvara, was the governor of Banavāsi in 1053 A.D.;[4] Ketaladevī, another wife of the same monarch, was the governor of the Agrahāra of Poonavada;[5] Akkādevī, an elder sister of Jayasiṁha III, was ruling over the district of Kirsukad in 1022 A.D.[6] Kuṁkumadevī, an elder sister of Vijayāditya, was administering Purigere 300 in 1077 A.D.[7] Lakshmīdevī, who was the chief queen of Vikramāditya VI, was in charge of 18 Agrahāras in 1095 A.D.[8] Under the Yādavas also, queens and princesses are seen taking part in the administration. Lakshmī, who was a sister of Kholeśvara, the Khandesh feudatory of Siṅghaṇa, is seen governing her brother's principality during her nephew's minority. Bhāgubāi, who was probably a relation of Siṅghaṇa, was in charge of Tarewadi. Under the Gaṅgas also, the queens exercised considerable political power. Their inscriptions

1. *E. I.*, XI, 35.
2. A. S. Altekar, *State and Government in Ancient India*, 2nd edition, p. 57.
3. *I. A.*, VII, 163.
4. *I. A.*, XIX, 274.
5. *I. A.*, XIV, 271.
6. A. S. Altekar, *State and Government in Ancient India*, p. 57.
7. *I. A.*, XVII, 37.
8. A. S. Altekar, *Rāshṭrakūṭas*, p. 154.

clearly inform us how the queens of Śrīpurusha, Būtuga and Paramadi were taking active part in administration, acting as governors, making land grants, etc.[1] It is difficult to say why such cases are altogether unknown to Northern India. Is it likely that due to the influence of the matriarchal notions, the queens in the Deccan and Southern India might have been allowed to take an active part in the administration ?

(3) *Younger Princes*

The younger princes during our period enjoyed suitable titles; thus Rājyapāla, a younger son of Gāhaḍavāla king Govindachandra, is described as '*Samastarājaprakṛiyopeta*'.[2] They were often appointed to some important posts in the administration. Sometimes they were in the ministry also. Thus under the Chāhamānas, prince Sallakshaṇapāla was appointed as the prime minister by his own father, king Vīsaladeva.[3] This practice does not seem to be very common, for there was the danger in such cases that the junior prince may conspire to secure the succession for himself.

Princes are often seen taking keen interest in tihe administration. One of the Chāhamāna inscriptions descrebes prince Jājalla as *Rājyachintaka*,[4] i.e. supervising or pondring over the problems of the administration. Another inscription of the same dynasty informs us, how even the king sometimes used to take help from the princes in the important administrative matters. Thus in the *Amaridakshiṇā* proclamation of the king Ālhaṇadeva, his two sons, Gajasiṁha and Kelhaṇadeva, are both stated to be concurring with him.[5] This clearly shows that grown-up princes under the Chāhamānas exercised considerable influence in the administration. It is also possible that Ālhaṇadeva had become old by this time and was being assisted in administration by his two sons.

1. M.V. Krishna Rao, *The Gaṅgas of Talkad*, p. 129.
2. Śrīmad-Govindachandradeva-pāda-padma-saṁmatyā samastarāja-prakriyopeta-mahārājaputra-śrī-Rājapāladevaḥ, *E. I.*, XIII, 217.
3. *I. A.*, XIX, 218.
4. *E. I.*, XI, 53-54.
5. *E. I.*, XI, 45.

Princes more frequently appear as the governors of towns in our records. Thus under the Chāhamānas, king Gajasiṁha appointed his son Chāmuṇḍarāja as the governor of Māṇḍavyapura in 1170 A.D.[1] Similarly the king Kelhaṇa appointed his son Vikramasiṁha to the same post in 1180 A.D.[2] In 1185 A.D. Māṇḍavyapura had another royal governor Soṭala, who was also a son of king Kelhaṇa[3] We thus see that different princes were appointed as governors of Māṇḍavyapura at different times. Even if they would have enjoyed it as a fief, they could do so only for a short period, for it was regranted in succession. The above cases hail from Rajasthan only, but it is not unlikely that the same was the case with other provinces also.

To carry on the town administration properly, the prince governors were aided by military officers. Thus when Gajasiṁha was acting as a governor of Māṇḍavyapura, Sauliki Jasadhana assisted him as his Balādhipa; this officer had been allotted the revenues of village Jhamara, probably as part of his pay.[4] He, however, could not make any alienations from his income, for we are told that when he was assigning a *dramma* from his income, he had to take the consent of the royal governor Gajasiṁha.

Sometimes princes also enjoyed considerable prestige. Thus when Mahārājaputra Rājyapāla, younger son of the Gāhaḍavāla king Govindachandra, granted the village of Camawāmi together with some *pattalas* to Paṇḍita Dāmodaraśarman, he was allowed to put his own seal on the charter, though he had to take the permission of his father for the grant of the village.[5]

For their personal enjoyment and expenses, princes were usually given fiefs known as *Sejā* under the Chāhamānas. It is, however, important to note that usually the princes had no full rights over their fiefs, i.e. they were not regarded as their personal property. For sometimes we find the central

1. *J. A. S. B.*, XII, 104.
2. *J. A. S. B.*, X, 209.
3. *J. A. S. B.*, XIV, 104.
4. *J. A. S. B.*, XII, 102-3.
5. *E. I.*, VIII, 157-8.

government exercising the power of assigning revenues out of these fiefs. Thus Kelhaṇadeva granted a well in 1165 A.D., which was situated within the fief of Ajayapāladeva.[1] We may well presume that similar practice prevailed in other dynasties also.

Princes usually could not alienate land out of their fiefs. But they seem to have often enjoyed the right of assigning small portion of the income as a gift for a charitable purpose without taking the king's permission. Thus the Chāhamāna prince Kīrtipāla, who was given a fief of twelve villages, granted a yearly sum of two *drammas* from each of the twelve villages to the Jina Mahāvīra at Naddulai.[2]

Prabably the extent of a prince's fief differed according to circumstances. Sometimes we find that a number of villages were given as a fief, as was the case with the Chāhamāna prince Kīrtipāla, who was enjoying twelve villages as his fief.[3] On the other hand, sometimes, only one village was given as a fief to two princes, as was the case with the Rājaputras Lākhaṇapāla and Abhayapāla, who were both enjoying one village as a fief in 1177 A.D.[4] It appears that the extent of the fief depended upon the extent and resources of the kingdom and the importance of the grantee.

1. *E. I.*, XIII, 210.
2. *E. I.*, IX, 68.
3. *E. I.*, IX, 68.
4. *E. I.*, XI, 50.

Chapter III

MINISTRY

(1) *Nīti Writers on Ministry*

The writers on the Hindu political science, as a rule regarded the ministry as an indispensable wheel of the administrative machinery, next in importance only to the king. Śukra, the most important writer for our period, attaches great importance to the ministry. He observes, 'it is difficult for a person single-handed to accomplish even an easy task; how then can a kingdom, which entails heavy responsibility, be managed by an individual without the aid of assistants'?[1] The king should therefore never act without the advice of his ministers, though he may be well grounded in all the sciences and a past-master in state-craft.[2] The king, who relies only on himself, will generally be in calamities. He will create hatred for himself among his subjects and will be soon deposed from the throne.[3] It is therefore necessary for a king to act according to the advice of his ministers, so that there may be neither any disorder in the kingdom, nor any danger to the head of the state. There are diversities in human aptitudes and they should be utilised to meet the different situations. It is, however, difficult for a single individual to be well-grounded in all spheres; the king should therefore enlist the help of competent ministers; otherwise he will bring about the destruc-

1. Yadyapyalpataraṁ karma tadapyekena dushkaram.
Purushenāsahāyena kimu rājyaṁ mahodayam.
Śukra, II, 1

2. Sarvavidyāsu kuśalo nṛipo hyapi sumantravit.
Mantṛibhistu vinā mantraṁ naiko'rthaṁ chintayet kvachit.
Śukra, II, 2

3. Prabhuḥ svātantryamāpanno hyanarthāyaiva kalpate.
Bhinnarāshṭro bhavet sadyo bhinna-prakṛitireva cha.
Śukra, II, 4

tion of himself, as also that of his kingdom.[1] Śukra further compares an autocratic king, who does not listen to the counsel of his ministers to a thief in the form of a ruler, and calls him an exploiter of the people's wealth.[2] It was the delicate duty of the minister to bring him round to the correct path.[3] 'A king' says Somadeva, 'who is assisted by his ministers, Purohita and Senāpati, is generally victorious and successful.'[4] He further states that even an unintelligent king can get success in his adminisration, if he acts in consonance with the advice of his ministers. He may himself have no sterling merit, yet he will be honoured.[5] Kāmandak also regards the ministry as one of the limbs of the body politic and advises the king to appoint good ministers and regard them as his best friends, because they can check him from following a wrong course.[6] He says that the king will never be able to rule successfully and will himself soon perish, if his council will consist of wicked ministers.[7] The *Matsya-Purāṇā* observes. 'The king, while his head is still wet with the waters of coronation, should act according to the advice of his ministers, and thereby secure stability for his kingdom'[8].

1. Purushe purushe bhinnaṁ dṛiśyate buddhivaibhavam.
   Āptavākyairanubhavairāgamairanumānataḥ.
   Na hi tat sakalaṁ jñātaṁ nareṇaikena śakyate
   Ataḥ sahāyān varayedrājā rājyavivṛiddhaye.
   Śukra, II, 57,
   Vinā prakṛitisanmantrādrājyanāśo bhaved dhruvam
   Rodhanaṁ na bhavet tasmād rājñaste syuḥ sumantṛiṇaḥ.
   Śukra, II, 81
2. Hitāhitaṁ na śṛiṇoti rājā mantrimukhāchcha yaḥ
   Sa dasyū rājarūpeṇa prajānāṁ dhanahārakaḥ.
   Śukra, II, 257
3. Kumārgagamapi nṛipaṁ buddhyodhartuṁ kshamān śuchīn.
   Śukra, II, 9
4. Mantrī-purohita-senāpatināṃ yo yuktamuktaṁ karoti sa ahāryabuddhiḥ. *Nvk*. Chap. 10
5. Asugandhamapi sūtraṁ kusumasaṅsargātkiṁ nārohati devaśirāṁsi ?
   Nvk., Chap. 10.
6. Nṛipasya ta eva suhṛidasta eva guravo matāḥ,
   ya enamutpathagataṁ vārayantyanivāritam.
   Kāmandaka, IV, 51
7. Nirundhānāh satāṁ mārgaṁ bhakshayanti mahīpatim,
   Dushṭātmānastu sachivastasmātsusachivo bhavet.
   Kāmandaka, IV, 12
8. *Matsya-Purāṇa*, 215-2.

'The *Agni-Purāṇa* also asks the king to consult ministers on weighty problems.[1] Writers of the earlier age also hold similar views about the importance and the necessity of the ministry.[2]

(2) *Epigraphs on Ministry*

Ministry was a regular feature of administration since early times[3] and the same was the case in our age. Ministers are invariably mentioned in the records of Gāhaḍavāla rulers.[4] The records of the Chandella kings of Mahoba refer to several ministerial families.[5] The Badal pillar inscription of Nārāyaṇapāla states that several generations of the Brāhmaṇa family of Garga served as ministers under successive Pāla rulers.[6] The Parmāra inscriptions refer to Mahāpradhānas and Amātyas.[7] Mahāmantrins and Mahāmātyas are both mentioned in the Chedi records.[8] Śaṅkaradhara appears as the chief of hundred councillors in the India office plate of Lakshmaṇasena.[9] The Chaulukya and the Chāhmāna inscriptions also frequently refer to Mahāmātyas.[10] They should not, however, be taken as the chief ministers; for in one of the Chaulukya inscriptions, the finance minister is also called Mahāmātya. This shows that the title Mahāmātya was probably given to other important ministers also in the Chaulukya administration.

(3) *Ministry under Provincial Government*

In ancient India, not only the king used to have his own ministry, but the same was often the case with some provin-

1. *Agni Purāṇa*, 24. 16-18.
2. Cf. *Mbh.*, V. 37. 38; *Manu*, VII. 53; *A.Ś.*, I, Chap. 3.
3. For ministers in the earlier dynasties, see Aśoka's Rock Edicts, III and IV; *Mālavikāgnimitra*, Act V; Junagada Inscription of Rudradāman I, *E.I.*, VIII, 42; Walter, *On Yuan Chwang*, I, p. 343.
4. *E.I.*, XXIV, 291.
5. *E.I.*, I, 197.
6. *E.I.*, II, 161.
7. *E.I.*, XX, 79.
8. *E.I.*, II, 309.
9. *E.I.*, XXVI, 12.
10. *E.I.*, XI, 308; *I.A.*, XVIII, 112-14.

cial governors. We have ample evidence to show that the provincial governors were guided by the ministers in carrying out the administration successfully. This clearly indicates how ministry was regarded as indispensable for good government. Even as early as the time of the Mauryas, the province of Taxila was governed by a viceroy assisted by a ministry. There is evidence to show, how the subjects at Taxila revolted against the ministers and how Aśoka was sent there by Bindusāra to establish peace and to restore order. The *Mālavikāgnimitra* informs us that Agnimitra, the crown prince of Pushyamitra and the governor of Mālwā, had his own council of ministers.

It is difficult to say whether such a council of ministers existed under provincial viceroys during our period of survey. Our inscriptions supply very little information about provincial government. The officers called Kumārāmātyas do occur in the Pāla records, but they should not be taken as ministers to the prince of the blood royal, who was appointed as an heir-apparent or viceroy. It is very likely that the Kumārāmātyas were something like I.C.S. officers under the British administration, who sometimes worked in the district and sometimes in the provincial and sometimes in the Central secretariat. They were also sometimes appointed as the members of the government.

The contemporary south Indian records, however, point to the existence of ministries functioning under the crown-prince and governors. In one of the records of the Yādava dynasty, a minister of the crown prince Jaitugi is referred to in one place, while in another inscription there is a mention of the premier of Tikkamadevarāya, the Southern Viceroy of Rāmachandra.[1]

(4) *Influence of the Ministry*

The ministers exercised great power and influence in the administration of different dynasties. They were respected even by kings, as is suggested by the Badal pillar inscription, which informs us how Darbhapāṇi, the minister of Devapāla, kept

1. *S.I.I.*; IX, 367, 387; *E.I.* III, 219.

his king waiting at his door.[1] This is no doubt an exaggeration, but the inscription leaves no doubt that the king showed utmost reverence to this minister. The Baghari stone inscription graphically states how through the advice of the minister Sallakshaṇa, the king Paramadideva became as it were the lord of the earth (Śiva) with three eyes.[2] Obviously the minister was regarded as the third eye of the king.

Good and able ministers were highly honoured and respected; and others were urged to follow their example. The Mau inscription declares how Mahīpāla, the prime minister of the Chandella king Vijayapāla, became the standard of comparison among the good ministers due to his blameless policy.[3]

Success in foreign policy depended upon the efficiency of ministers. It is described how the minister Śivanāga secured for the king Vidyādhara a paramount position in the circle of kings by means of his clever policy.[4] It was due to the policy of Darbhapāṇi that the Pāla emperor Devapāla was able 'to make tributary the earth between Revā's parents (Vindhya Mountains) and Gauri's father (Himalayas)' and enjoyed it 'as far as Rama's bridge in the South'.[5] It was by following the advice of Kedāramiśra that Devapāla was successful in eradicating the race of the Utkalas. He also humbled the pride of the Hūṇas and scattered the conceit of the rulers of Draviḍa and Gurjara.[6] These statements, even though exaggerated, undoubtedly indicate that ministers did take a leading part in determining the foreign policy of the king.

Ministers were also regarded as the main cause of the prosperity of the kingdom and the happiness of the subjects. The Karitalai Inscription states how the kingdom of the Chedi king Yuvarāja went on prospering during the ministership of Brāhmaṇa Bhākamiśra.[7] It was the minister

1. *E.I.*, II, 161.
2. *E.I.*, I, 207-214.
3. *E.I.*, 195-207, V. 26.
4. *Ibid.*, 199, V. 24.
5. *E.I.*, II, 161 V. 5.
6. *Ibid.*, V. 13.
7. *E.I.*, II, 174.

Gaṅgādhara, who through his wonderful ability, made the kingdom of Ratnadeva III free from all foes and thus restored peace and prosperity.[1] The Paramāra king Jājalladeva was able to maintain the stability and prosperity of his kingdom only through his minister Lālārka, who is said to have crushed forcibly the powerful enemies.[2]

The ministers' advice was also expected to bring to the king the three objects of life, Dharma, Artha and Kāma. The Chandella kings Dhaṅga and Gaṇḍa are stated to have obtained them by following the advice of the minister, Prabhāsa.[3]

In the Deccan also during our period of survey, ministers were highly respected and honoured by their kings and were able to exercise considerable influence on the administration. In the Salotgi inscription of the Rāshṭrakūṭa king Kṛishṇa III, his foreign minister Nārāyaṇa is described to be as dear to him as his own right hand.[4] The Pathari pillar inscription of Parabala, who was a Rāshṭrakūṭa feudatory, informs us how he used to regard his premier as worthy of salutation.[5] The Yādava king Kṛishṇa compares his minister to his own tongue and right hand in one of his records.[6] Another inscription of the same ruler states, how his premier's feet were brightened by the crest jewels on the head of the feudatories.[7] All this evidence clearly indicates that ministers occupied a place of honour in the Deccan also.

We have thus seen that the status of ministers was very high. The contemporary Deccan records show how sometimes they were honoured with the feudatory titles and how they were entitled to the use of Pañchamahāśabdas. Thus Dalla, who was a foreign minister of the Rāshṭrakūṭa king Dhruva, was invested with the title Sāmanta and also authorised to use five great musical instruments.[8] Kālidāsa,

1. *E.I.*, XXI, 164.
2. *E.I.*, XXII, p. 159-62.
3. *E.I.*, I. 195.
4. *E.I.*, IV. 60.
5. *E.I.*, IX, 254.
6. *I.A.* XIV, 60.
7. *A.S.* Altekar, *Rāshṭrakūṭas*, 161.
8. *E.I.*, X, 89.

the war minister of the Chālukya king Jagadekamalla, is described as entitled to the Pañchamahāśabdas.[1]

It is difficult to say whether such a practice prevailed in the North also during our period of survey. Our inscriptions do not confer any such titles upon the ministers. There is no doubt that in one inscription Ajayadeva, who was the prime minister of the Paramāra king Jayavarman II, is designated as Rājā,[2] but it is difficult to say whether it was a feudatory title.

(5) *Ministers' Qualifications*

Let us now see what were regarded as the main qualifications for a minister. The views of the writers of our period are generally the same as those of their predecessors. According to Śukra, the minister should belong to a good and well-to-do family, should have studied the political science, should be a man of character and personality and should be pre-eminent for his modesty in behaviour, courage in action and sweetness in speech.[3] He further states that while selecting a minister, one should not attach an undue importance to the caste and family.[4] Somadeva says 'Ministers must be endowed with real character, for lack of principles vitiates all personal merits and qualities. They must be well-born, since an ill-bred person is proof against all shame and is capable of misdeeds. They must be free from passions, for to possess a sensual minister is like riding a mischievous elephant. They must be resourceful and courageous, for there is no use of a minister who is not of help in adversity.[5]' Bṛihaspati says 'Ministers must be men of high character, free from the vices of gambling, drinking, sensuality and recklessness. They must be acquainted with the Śāstras also.'[6] The *Agni-Purāṇa* pres-

1. *I.A.*, VI, 140.
2. *E.I.*, XX, 79.
3. *Śukra*; II, 52-64.
4. Naiva jātirna cha kulaṁ kevalaṁ lakshayedapi
   Karmaśīlaguṇāḥ pūjyāstathā jātikule na hi.
   Śukra, II, 54
5. *Nvk.* Chap. X, 111.
6. *Bārhaspatya*, II. 42.

cribes similar moral and intellectual qualifications for ministers.[1] All this evidence clearly indicates that while selecting the ministers great attention was paid towards loyalty, efficiency, character, merit and family extraction.[2]

Let us now see how far ministers conformed to this high standard in actual practice during our period of survey. A number of epigraphical passages give us a vivid idea of the qualities regarded as indispensable to the minister. Thus Prabhāsa, the minister of the Chandella kings Dhaṅga and Gaṇḍa, besides possessing excellent qualities, is described as expert in the science of politics.[3] Ananta, the minister of the Chandella kings Kīrtivarman and Sallakshaṇavarman, combined in himself 'spotless sacred knowledge, bravery and efficiency in the very high office of counsellers.' He is described as upright, intelligent, eloquent, versed in the sciences, resolute and yet compassionate and well grounded in practical administration. Rudrarāja, the minister of the Paramāra king Naravarman, was well grounded in the Śāstras.[4] Śivanāga, the minister of the Chandella king Vidyādhara, was a past-master of sacred knowledge and also an expert in military art.[5] Mahīpāla, the minister of the Chandella king Vijayapāla, is described as 'fulfilling the purport of his word by truth, that of his understanding by actions, which bore good fruits, and that of his wealth by pious and beneficial deeds.'[6] This shows that he was always truthful, active and pious. Gadādhara, the premier of the Chandella kings Pṛithvīvarman and Madanavarman, is stated to have surpas-

1. *Agni-Purāṇa*. 121, 16-17.
2. It may be noted in this connection that some of the writers on Hindu polity hold that only loyal persons should be selected as ministers, while others attach more importance to efficiency than to loyalty. Some writers also hold that the selection of ministers should be made from among king's school companions; others thought that the choice should be restricted to the members of certain loyal and tested families. Cf. *Manu Smṛiti* VII, 60-64; *A.S*, I Chap. 5. It is difficult to say which of the above views prevailed in actual practice. Most probably persons combining in themselves both efficiency and loyalty were appointed to the posts of ministers.
3. *E.I.*, I, 195-97.
4. *Tr. R.A.S.*, I, 266.
5. *E.I.*, I, 195-97, V, 23.
6. *E.I.* I, 195, V. 25.

sed the preceptor of gods in understanding.[1] Lāhaḍā, the premier of the Chandella king Madanavarman, was well-versed in sacred lore and different arts.[2] Gadādhara, the minister of peace and war of the king Paramarddi of the same dynasty, is expressly described as an excellent poet.[3] Vatsarāja, the premier of Kīrtivarman, was like Vāchaspati in both counsel and action.[4] The Badal Praśasti[5] of the time of Nārāyaṇapāla graphically describes the qualifications of the ministers, who served under the Pāla rulers. Thus Garga, the minister of Dharmapāla, is said to have excelled Bṛihaspati in knowledge. His son Darbhapāṇi was well versed in the four Vidyās. His son Someśvara, the minister of Devapāla, was very liberal and was like Dhanañjaya in point of prowess. His son Kedāramiśra, the minister of Śūrapāla, was a liberal donor and a great scholar. His son Gauravamiśra, the minister of Nārāyaṇapāla, was a great orator and was well-grounded in the Āgamas, Vedas and Astrology. Narapati, the minister of both Jaitrasiṁha and Hammīra of Raṇathambhor, is described as a master of the science of politics.[6] Gaṅgādhara, the minister of the Chedi king Ratnadeva III, besides being brave, courageous, kind and intelligent, was of upright behaviour and well-grounded in the science of polity and law.[7] Lālārka, the minister of the Paramāra king Jagaddeva, was brave, truthful and pure-hearted.[8] Bhākamiśra, the minster of the Chedi king Yuvarāja, was a great poet and was well-versed in the sacred lores.[9]

It is important to note that our writers on Hindu polity rarely refer to military proficiency as an essential qualification for the ministers. There is no doubt that Kāmandaka observes at one place that the ministers should be brave and Soma-

1. *E.I.*, I, 195, V. 36.
2. *E.I.*, I, 208, V. 19.
3. *E.I.*, 211, V. 30.
4. *E.I.*, I, 203.
5. *E.I.*, II, 161.
6. *E.I.*, XIX, 49.
7. *E.I.*, XXI, 164.
8. *E.I.*, XII, 174-76.
9. *E.I.*, II, 174-76.

deva adds that they should know the use of missiles,[1] but even such general statements are not made in this connection by any of the remaining writers of our period. A perusal of the epigraphical evidence, however, shows that ministers were usually military leaders or generals. Thus Ananta, the minister of Kīrtivarman, is said to have been expert in controlling the elephants, horses and chariots.[2] He was also skilled in archery. Jagapāla alias Jayasiṁha, the minister of Jājalla, assisted the latter in his victories.[3] Vatsarāja, the minister of Kīrtivarman, was also a general, who had wrested away from the enemy a whole district by his counsel and valour.[4]

The contemporary South Indian records also show that ministers were generally military leaders. Jaitrapāla, the prime minister of the first Yādava emperor Bhillama V, was as great a general as a statesman.[5] Nāgarasa, the premier of Yādava king Kṛishṇa, was also as great a general as a scholar.[6] Chāmuṇḍarāja, the minister of the Gaṅga king Mārasiṁha, was a great military leader, for he is said to have won the battle of Gonur for his king.[7] In 1024 A.D. the Minister of Records and the Director-General of Registration in the administration of the later Chālukyas, had the title Mahāprachaṇḍadaṇḍanāyaka, showing that he was a high military officer.[8] All this evidence clearly indicates that both in the north and south, military leadership and ability were considered to be necessary qualifications for ministers during our period. Shivaji's ministers were also good generals with the exception of the Purohita (royal priest).

Most of the works on Hindu polity prescribe that the ministers should be hereditary.[9] This hereditary character is

1. A.S. Altekar, *Rāshṭrakūṭas*, p. 163.
2. *E.I.*, I, 197.
3. *I.A.*, XVII, 35.
4. *E.I.*, I, 195.
5. *E.I.*, III, 219.
6. *I.A.*, XIV, 76.
7. *E.I.*, V, 173.
8. *I.A.*, XIV, 26.
9. *Manu*, VII, 54 and *Yājñavalkya*, I, 312 use the word *Maula* in connection with ministers, which is interpreted as hereditary by Kullūka and Vijñāneśvara.

also borne out by many inscriptions. The Mau inscription of the time of Madanavarman informs us that under the Chandellas, five generations of one family, Prabhāsa, his son and grandson Śivanāga and Mahīpāla, the latter's son and grandson Ananta and Gadādhara, served as ministers under nine generations of the dynasty represented by Dhaṅga, his son, grandson and great grandson Gaṇḍa, Vidyādhara and Vijayapāla, the latter's son Devavarman, his brother Kīrtivarman, the latter's sons Sallakshaṇavarman and Pṛithvīvarman, and the former's son Jayavarman.[1] A little later under the same dynasty, we find that Lāhaḍā was a minister under Madanavarman and his son Sallakshaṇa and grandson Purushottama under Paramarddideva, the grandson of Madanavarman.[2] Under the Pālas, the hereditary principle was followed in appointing the ministers. The Badal Praśasti of the time of Nārāyaṇapāla associates the members of the ministerial Brāhmaṇa family representing Garga, his son Darbhapāṇi, his son Someśwara, his son Kedāramiśra and his son Gauravamiśra, with four successive Pāla rulers, namely Dharmapāla, Devapāla, Śūrapāla and Nārāyaṇapāla.[3] Similarly, Brāhmaṇa Bhākamiśra and his son Someśvara acted as chief ministers in the reign of the Chedi kings Yuvarāja and Lakshmaṇarāja.[4] It is thus clear that the hereditary principle in appointing the ministers was often followed in actual practice. A later work, the *Rājanīti-Prakāśa*, expressly states that this hereditary principle is to be given up, if the son of a former minister has not the requisite qualifications; under such circumstances the descendant is to be employed only in such state work as is suited for his attainments.[5] Probably this practice was followed in our age also.

An analysis of the above evidence indicates that an ideal minister, besides being the citizen of the state and belonging if possible to a hereditary ministerial family, was expected to be an administrator of character and ability, well versed in

1. *E.I.*, I, 197.
2. *E.I.*, 208-11.
3. *E.I.*, II, 161.
4. *E.I.*, II, 174-76.
5. *Rājanītiprakāśa*, p. 176.

the political science and able to lead the army in case of necessity.

In actual practice not all ministers came up to the ideal standard. Just as there were oppressive kings, there were also greedy and unscrupulous ministers. It is interesting to note that Mānasollāsa[1] couples them with robbers and exhorts the king to protect his subjects from both.

Sometimes ministerial appointments were made from among the members of the royal family. Thus under the Chāhamāna king Vīsaladeva, his own son Sallakshaṇapāla was functioning as a minister.[2] The *Rājatarangiṇī* also informs us that in Kashmir, the king Harsha had appointed two sons of a former ruler as his ministers.[3] It appears that this practice of selecting ministers from the members of the royal family was not very common in Northern India, for we come across very few such cases during our period. The main reason for this appears to be that it was feared that the royal minister may revolt against the king and usurp the throne for himself.

Early Smṛitis have laid down the dictum that only Brāhmaṇas should be appointed to the post of ministers. We do not know how far this principle was followed in actual practice. Our inscriptions do not always refer to the caste of any minister; but it appears very probable that members of all the four castes were often represented in the ministry. Śukra expressly observes that the ministerial appointments should not be made on caste considerations.[4] It is only on the occasion of marriage and dinner that one should enquire about the caste; but while selecting ministers, consideration of caste should not be taken as important.[5] Somadeva recommends that the king should select ministers only from among the members of the three regenerate castes, namely Brāhmaṇa, Kshatriya and Vaiśya.[6] Śukra, however, allows even a Śūdra

1. Mānasollāsa, I, 155.
2. *I.A.*, XIX, 218.
3. *Rājatarangiṇi*, VIII, 874.
4. *Śukra*, II, 54.
5. *Śukra*, II, 55.
6. Brāhmaṇa-kshatṛiya-visāmanyatamaṁ svadeśa-janmā-chārābhijanaviśuddhaṁ avyasaninamavyabhichāriṇamadhītākhila-vyavahāratantramastrajñamaśeshopadhi-viśuddhaṁ mantriṇaṁ kurvīta.
Nvk., Chap. 25

to be in charge of the military department, if he is capable and loyal.[1] It is thus clear that in the ministry, the three twice born castes were usually represented, and also the Sūdra caste on some occasions. During our period, kings were usually non-Brāhmaṇas; it is therefore very likely that they might have often preferred to have at least a few ministers from their own caste.

(6) *Composition of the Ministry*

Let us first consider the strength of the ministry. Unfortunately due to divergence of views among the writers on Hindu polity, we are not able to make any definite statement on this point. The *Mahābhārata* is in favour of a ministry of eight.[2] According to Manu, this number may be reduced to seven also.[3] The *Arthaśāstra* quotes the different views on the topic from which we learn that the *Mānava*[4], *Bārhaspatya*[5] and the *Auśanasa*[6] schools were in favour of a council of 12, 16 and 20 members respectively. Kauṭilya himself, however, is in favour of a small ministry of three or four members.[7]

The writers of our period also do not insist upon any particular number of ministers. Kāmandaka mentions the different views of the three schools given by Kauṭilya.[8] Somadeva is of opinion that there should be three, seven or eight ministers.[9] He also suggests that if one minister possesses all the qualifications necessary for the proper administration of the kingdom, more need not be appointed.[10] Obviously Somadeva was in favour of a very small ministry. Śukra, however,

1. Svadharmaniratā nityaṁ svāmibhaktā ripudvishaḥ Śūdrā vā Kshatriyā Vaiśyā Mlechchhā saṅkarasambhavāḥ. Senādhipāḥ sainikāścha kāryā rājñā jayārthinā.
   Śukra, II, 139
2. Ashṭānāṁ mantriṇāṁ madhye mantraṁ rājopadhārayet.
   Mbh, XII, 85.
3. Sachivān sapta chāshṭau vā kurvīta suparīkshitān.
   Manu, VII, 54.
4. *A.S.*, I, Chap. 15.
5. *A.S.*, I, Chap. 15.
6. *A.S.*, I, 15.
7. *A.S.*, I, 15.
8. *Kāmandakā*, XI, 67-68.
9. Trayaḥ pañcha sapta vā mantriṇaḥ kāryāḥ.
   Nvk., Chap. 10
10. *Nvk.*, Chap. 10

recommends a ministry of ten[1] but refers to another view recommending a ministry of eight only. *Mānasollāsa*[2] refers to a ministry of seven or eight, as recommended by Manu.

Let us now see what was the cause of the difference of opinion among the political writers on this point. It appears very probable that the divergence of views arose due to the divergent needs of the different states. Kauṭilya states that the actual number of ministers should depend upon the needs of the state or the exigency of the situation.[3] If the state was a small one and if its activities were limited, a small ministry of four or five members would have been quite sufficient in carrying out its administration successfully. In the case of a bigger state, of course, the number of ministers would have been a large one, as its administrative requirements were extensive. The epigraphical evidence also shows that the foreign minister was assisted in his work by a number of assistants. Even in a small kingdom like that of the Śilāhāras,[4] we find that there were more than one foreign minister, each having full ministerial status. Now if a small kingdom like that of the Śilāhāra had two foreign ministers, it is very likely that the bigger states would have had even more foreign ministers. All this evidence clearly indicates that the strength of the ministry varied according to the extent and power of different states. Generally the ministry consisted of eight or ten members as is suggested by the evidence of the *Śukranīti* and the Mānasollāsa, whose opinion seems to be based upon the views of the *Mahābhārata* and the *Manusmṛiti*.[5] But if it was found that this number would not be sufficient to carry out the administration efficiently, then more persons were appointed either as ministers or as secretaries to the ministers.

1. *Śukra*, II, 70-71.
2. *Mānasollāsa*, II, 57.
3. Yathāsāmarthyāmiti Kauṭilyaḥ.
   A.S., I, Chap. 15
4. *I.A.*, V, 278.
5. The number eight for the council of ministers seems to have been followed by long tradition. When Shivaji wanted to revive the old Hindu administrative system in 1674 A.D., he also thought of a ministry of eight.

The jurisdiction of the ministry covered the whole field of administration. From the study of the functions of the different ministers given by Śukra, it appears that the ministry had to preserve law and order, to promote prosperity and avert disasters, to ensure proper administration of justice, to supervise the collection of revenue and sanction the necessary expenditure. It had also to take a survey of the socio-religious structure of society and to sanction the changes necessitated by new factors and circumstances.

The Smṛitis and most of the writers on Hindu polity do not inform us how the ministers used to discharge the above functions, and how the departments were distributed. Unfortunately the epigraphical records of our period also do not supply any information on these topics; they give us only a long list of officers without stating anything about their functions. It is the *Śukranīti*, the most comprehensive literary work on polity for our period, which throws considerable light upon this topic; earlier works including the *Arthaśāstra* are silent on the point. To judge from this work, it is clear that the ministry consisted of the Purohita, Pratinidhi, Pradhāna, Sachiva, Mantrī, Prāḍvivāka, Paṇḍita, Sumantra, Amātya and Dūta. It is important to note that many of the above ministers also figure in our records either with the same or equivalent titles, and hence it is very likely that ministers would have divided the departments on the lines suggested by Śukra.

Let us now survey the duties and functions of the different ministers.

PUROHITA

The *Purohita* or the Royal Priest was an important member of the ministry in early times. He figures prominently in the council of Ratnins in the age of the later Saṁhitās. Following the old tradition, Śukra[1] also includes him in the ministry and regards him as superior to all. But whether such was the case in the administrations of our

1. Purodhāḥ prathamaṁ śreshṭḥaḥ sarvebhyo rājarāshṭrabhṛit. *Śukra*, II, 74

period, may be doubted. The records of the Chedis, the Senas and the Gāhaḍawālas separate him from Mantrins or ministers in the list of royal officers.[1] He may therefore have not been included in the ministry in some governments. Śukra may be allotting him the first place out of the traditional reverence for him. Shivaji's ministry did not include him.

Besides having the knowledge of the technique of sacrificial rites and ceremonies, the Purohita was expected to be well-grounded in the different branches of learning; he had to master the three Vedas, the six Vedāṅgas, the Dharmaśāstra and the Nīti-Śāstra. He was also to be adept in the art of warfare.[2] This last qualification appears, no doubt strange, but it is more or less true, for even in the Vedic period we find him often accompanying the king to the battlefield in order to ensure his victory by his prayers, charms and incantations.

Under the Gāhaḍavālas, the royal priest had also to discharge the duties of the royal preceptor (Mahārājaguru). Thus Prahlādaśarman was both the Mahāpurohita and Mahārājaguru of the king Jayachandra.[3] Probably the same was the case with other dynasties also. Purohita became associated more with the rituals of the royal household than with details of administration; he therefore gradually lost his seat in the ministry, though he was honoured even more highly than a minister.

The Purohita was sometimes entrusted with the work of composing the text of the royal charters. Thus the Purohita Trivikramanātha was the writer of the Partapgarh inscription[4] of the Pāla king Mahendrapāla II. The royal priest Someśvara was also the composer of Dabohi inscription, dated 1254 A.D.[5] The selection of the royal priest for this work, that

1. *E.I.*, XVIII, p. 221.
2. Shaḍaṅgavit sāṅgadhanurvedavichchārtha-dharmavit
   Yat kopabhītyā rājāpi dharmanītirato bhavet
   Nītiśāstrāstravyūhādikuśalastu purohitaḥ
   Saivāchāryyaḥ purodhā yaḥ śāpānugrahayoḥ kshamaḥ.
   Śukra, II, 79-80
3. *E.I.*, IV, 121.
4. *E.I.*, XIV, 182-8.
5. *E.I.*, I, 31-32.

was sometime made, is not difficult to understand. He was usually a scholar and the charters were mainly religious in their character, as they recorded grants for Brāhmaṇas, temples, etc.

PRATINIDHI

The Pratinidhi or the Viceroy was the next important member of the ministry. He however does not figure in any of the records of the dynasties under consideration, probably because he was appointed only when the king was ill or absent from the kingdom. His main duty was to deputise for the king.[1] Shivaji's ministry of eight did not include a Pratinidhi; but later on when Rājārām had to leave Mahārāshṭra and take refuge in the fort of Ginji, a *Pratinidhi* was appointed. The status of the Pratinidhi family in the Kolhapur Durbar was higher than that of any other official or feudatory.

PRADHĀNA

The Pradhāna, or the PrimeMinister[2], was the most important member of the ministry. He is described as *sarvadarśī*[3] or the general supervisor over the entire administration. He figures very frequently but with different designations. Thus Brāhmaṇa Bhākamiśra, who is styled as the Mahāpradhāna of the Chedi king Yuvarāja,[4] Someśvara, who is designated as Mantrī-tilaka in one of the records of Chedi king Lakshamaṇarāja,[5] Mantrīndra Vatsarāja of the Chandella king Kīrtivarman,[6] Mahāmantrī, Mahāpradhāna Purushottamadeva of the Paramāra king Yaśovarman,[7] Rājā Ajayadeva, the Mahāpradhāna of the Paramāra king Jayavarman[8] II, the Mantrīmukhya Māladiva of the Chaulukya king

1. Kāryyākāryyapravijñātā smṛitaḥ pratinidhistu saḥ.
Śukra, II, 84.
2. The term Pradhāna denoted the prime-minister in the state of Jodhpur and Jaipur till modern times.
3. Sarvadarśī pradhānastu senâvit sachivastathā.
Śukra, II, 84
4. *E.I.*, II, 174.
5. *E.I.*, II, 174.
6. *I.A.*, VIII, 236; *E.I.* XIV, 324.
7. *E.I.*, I, 208-211.
8. *E.I.*, XX, 79.

Arjunadeva,[1]—these were probably all discharging the functions of the Prime Minister. In Kashmir, he was called Sarvādhikarin[2] and his status was lower than that of the king only. The same term was used for him under the Kalachūris of South Kośala, one of whose records refers to Purushottamadeva, the Sarvādhikarin under Ratnadeva II.

Several Mahāmātyas figure in the Chaulukya and Paramāra records, which expressly describe them as *Sakalamudrāvyāpārān paripanthayati*'- *i.e.* in charge of the issue of all the sealed documents. Thus the Kirādu inscription of Kumārapāla refers to Māhāmātya Mahādeva.[4] The Nādol grant, as well as the Udayapur stone inscription of Kumārapāla, mention Mahāmātyas Bahadadeva[5] and Yaśodhavala.[6] Mahāmātyas Ratnapāla[7] and Nagāda[8] appear in the Ṛoyal Asiatic Society's grant of the Chaulukya king Bhīma II and in the Kadi plates of the Chaulukya king Vīsaladeva. Mahāmātya Śrīkantha[9] figures in the Khokhrā stone inscription of Sāṛaṅgadeva. Probably all these Mahāmātyas were functioning as Prime-ministers.

As in modern times, so also during our period of survey the premier was in special charge of one department. Thus Madhusūdana, who was the premier of Sāraṅgadeva, was in charge of the foreign department also; he is described both as Mahāsandhivigrahika and Mahāmātya in one record.[10] Mahāmātya Śrī Ambā-prasāda was in charge of finance under Trailokyavarman[11]. It is very likely that other premiers may have taken other departments according to their choice.

The Prime Minister probably had several secretaries working under him. One of them is referred to in a Chedi record. Thus Mahāpradhānārthalekhi Thakkura Śrī Daśamūlika, who

1. *I.A.*, VI, 191.
2. *Raj.*, VII, 568; VIII, 560.
3. *C.L.I.*, IV, p. 532.
4. *E.I.*, 172-73.
5. *I.A.*, XLI, 202-3
6. *I.A.*, XVIII, 341-43.
7. *I.A.*, XVIII, 112-14.
8. *I.A.*, VI, 210-13.
9. *I.A.*, XXI, 276-77.
10. *I.A.*, 1912; 20-21.
11. *J.B.R.A.S.*, XXI, 322.

figures in the Jabalpur plate of the king Jayasiṁhadeva[1], was obviously a secretary (*arthalekhī*) to the Prime Minister. It may be noted that this arrangement corresponds to that of Śukra, who lays down that each minister should have a secretary under him.[2] It may be pointed out that in Shivaji's ministry, the Prime Minister was known as Pradhāna. In the states of Jodhpur and Jaipur, the same title was given to the same dignitary till the integration of the states with the Indian republic.

The status of the Prime Minister was naturally next only to that of the king only. His position probably resembled that of the Turkish Grand Vazier or the Mughal Vakil.

SACHIVA

Sachiva or the war minister was the next important member of the ministry.[3] It is important to note that Somadeva does not include him in the list of the ministers though Śukra does so. The epigraphical evidence both from the North and the South shows that he was given a place in the ministerial council. The war minister was expected to be well-grounded in the theory and practice of war and also in the art of organisation. It was his duty to keep all the branches of the army well-equipped and to see whether all the forts were properly provisioned.[4]

The records of our period designate the war minister by different names. Under the Gāhaḍavālas and the Chandellas, he is merely called Senāpati,[5] while the Pāla and Sena records give him the more high-sounding title Mahāsenāpati.[6] The records of the Chedi, the Chāhamāna, the Paramāra and the Chaulukya dynasties, however, do not mention him, though they refer to a number of military officers. The non-

1. *E.I.*, XXI, 95.
2. *Śukra*, II, 109-10.
3. In Shivaji's ministry, according to one authority (Chitnis), Sachiva denoted the chief secretary; according to another authority, he denoted the war minister (Jabata).
4. *Śukra* II, 91-95.
5. *E.I.*, XVIII, 221; *I.A.*, XXV, 205-8.
6. *E.I.*, XXVI, 7; *I.A*, XV, 306.

mention of his office may be accidental. It may be due to the Prime Minister being also the war minister, as was the case with the premier of the Chalukya ruler Jagadekamalla of the contemporary Deccan.[1]

The status of the war minister was very high. The contemporary South Indian records show that they were supplied with palatial buildings and were permitted to use elephants for riding and invested with brilliant robes and cunningly worked staffs, which were the insignia of their office. They had, like the Mahāsāmantas, the great musical instruments of their own office.[2] Whether such privileges were enjoyed by the war ministers in Northern India during our period cannot be stated with certainty, for our inscriptions do not throw any light on this topic.

MANTRĪ

The Mantrī or the foreign minister is the next important member of the ministry.[3] The records of our period invariably call him Mahāsandhivigrahika, the chief officer in charge of peace and war. According to Śukra, he was to be well grounded in the fourfold policy of *Sāma*, *Dāma*, *Daṇḍa* and *Bheda*, while according to Lakshmīdhara, he was to be adept in all aspects of the sixfold policy, a judge of opportunity and a past-master in diplomacy.[4]

The work of the foreign minister was very heavy and exacting. As a general rule, each state had a large number of feudatories and had to deal with several neighbouring states throughout our period. The foreign minister was assisted in his work by a number of sandhivigrahikas in the contemporary Deccan, each probably in charge of the foreign affairs relating to one or two particular regions in the empire. Thus under the Śilāhāras, we find that even though their kingdom was not a big one, there was one chief foreign

1. *I.A.*, VI, 139.
2. A.S. Altekar, *Rāshṭrakūṭas*, p. 168.
3. In Shivaji's cabinet, the foreign minister was known by this designation.
4. Shāḍguṇyavidhitatvajño deśakālaviśāradaḥ
Sandhivigrahikaḥ kāryo rājñā naya-viśāradaḥ.
Kkt. R., IV, 26.

minister and another foreign minister, working as his subordinate for Karnāṭaka affairs.[1] This would remind us of the minister of Kashmir affairs in Pakistan in modern times. The states in northern India also had probably several foreign ministers, though they do not figure in ourr ecords. If a small kingdom like the Śilāhāras had two foreign ministers, it is not unlikely that in big kingdoms like those of the Pratīhāras, the Pālas and the Chaulukyas, there would have been more than one foreign minister or at least several secretaries working under him.

A number of records show that the foreign minister was usually entrusted with the drafting of the copper plate charters, granting lands and villages to Brāhmaṇas and temples. Thus sandhivigrahika Mahīndaka was the writer of Haddāla grant of Mahīpāla;[2] sandhivigrahika Khelāditya of the Kiradu stone pillar inscription[3] of the Chaulukya king Kumārapāla; sandhivigrahika Vāmana of two Paramāra inscriptions;[4] sandhivigrahikas Nārāyaṇadatta and Śankaradhara[5] of the Govindapur and the India office plates of Lakshamaṇasena.[6] There is nothing strange in this procedure. The sandhivigrahika was entrusted with this work probably because it was rightly thought that he could usually give very reliable information about the genealogy and exploits of the grantor and his ancestors, which the charter had to describe at its beginning. It is interesting to note that Yājñavalkya also states that 'the drafter (of a copper plate charter) should be the foreign minister; he should draft the charter at the dictate of the king himself.[7]

The Mahā-sandhivigrahika not only drafted the charters, but was often appointed to deliver them to the grantees.

1. *I.A.*, V, 277
2. *I.A.*, XII, 190-95.
3. *E.I.*, IX, 63-65.
4. *E.I.*, XXI, 50.
5. *I.B.*, 92-98.
6. *E.I.*, XXVI, 7.
7. Sandhivigrahakārī tu bhavedyastasya lekhakaḥ
Svayaṁ rājñā samādishṭassa likhedrājaśasanam.
Yāj. I, 319-20

Thus sandhivigrahikas Bhīmaka Thakkura[1], Sudhā[2] and Vāhudeva[3] acted as Dūtakas in the Kadi plates of Bhīma II. The Dūtaka of the Radhanapur plate of the Chaulukya king Bhīma was the sandhivigrahika Chandraśarman[4] and that of the Suṇaka plate of the Chedi king Karṇadeva was Chāhīla.[5] Similarly Tripurinātha, the Dūtaka of the Śaktipur plate of Laskhamaṇasena,[6] Bhogāditya of the Pālanapur plate of Bhīma II,[7] Harighosha of the Naihati grant of Ballālasena,[8] Nārāyaṇadatta of the Anulia grant of Lakshamanasena,[9] and Kapivishṇu of the Madanapur plate of Vishwarūpasena,[10] were all sandhivigrahikas. The foreign minister had also to keep under proper control the numerous feudatories of the empire by summoning them to the capital for periodical visits and by stationing the representatives of the Imperial power at their courts.[11]

PRĀḌVIVĀKA

The minister Prāḍvivāka was in charge of the judicial department. While explaining the word, Śukra states that it denotes an officer, who first interpellates and then decides. More intelligible terms for the office were also current. This minister is for instance called Mahādharmādhyaksha under the Senas.[12] His non-mention in the records of other dynasties may be accidental. He was to be well-versed in the traditional and Smṛiti law and an expert in evaluating evidence.[13] Usually the king used to preside over the highest court, but if owing to ill health or pressure of work, he was unable to discharge this duty, the chief justice used to act

1. *I.A.*, XI, 71-73.
2. *I.A.*, VI. 194.
3. *I.A.*, VI, 199.
4. *I.A.*, VI, 193.
5. *E.I.*, I, 317.
6. *E.I.*, XXI, 219.
7. *E.I.*, XXI, 171.
8. *E.I.*, XIV, 168.
9. *J.A.S.B.*, XIX, 61-65.
10. *I.B.*, 132-39.
11. *Mānasollāsa*, II. 128.
12. *E.I.*, XII, 8.
13. *Śukra*, II, 97-98.

for him in the highest court of appeal and decide cases with the help of jurors.

PAṆḌITA

Śukra is the first writer to mention the portfolio of Paṇḍita; he is not mentioned in any earlier Smṛiti or Nīti works. His office came into prominence, probably because society was changing and old laws were becoming inoperative. The functions of the Paṇḍita resembled those of the *Parishad* of the earlier period. He was to be well-versed in Dharmaśāstras. His duty was to advise the king concerning the suitable changes that may become necessary in socio-religious matters owing to changed times and customs after surveying the whole situation.[1] It is perhaps likely that the Dharmamahāmātras under the Mauryas, the Śramaṇamahāmātras under the Sātavāhanas, the Vinayasthitisthāpakas under the Guptas, and the Dharmāṅkuśas under the Rāshṭrakūṭas were officers of this department, discharging similar but somewhat restricted functions in the earlier periods. This minister was included in Shivaji's ministry and was known as Paṇḍitrāo, a title almost identical with that of Śukra.

SUMANTRA

Sumantra or the treasurer was the next member of the ministry. His office seems to have existed since very early times. The Saṅgrahītā, who figures in the list of the Ratnins of the Vedic period, and the officer called Samāhartā in the *Arthaśāstra* were probably discharging functions similar to those of Sumantra. The Gāhaḍavāla records obviously refer to this minister as Bhāṇḍāgārika. It may be noted that during our period as in earlier days, land tax was usually collected in kind and so the title Bhāṇḍāgārika given to the minister in charge of treasury was quite appropriate. His non-

1. Mantrī tu nītikuśalaḥ paṇḍito dharmatatvavit.
Śukra, II, 85.
Vartamānāścha prāchīnā dharmmāḥ ke lokasaṅśṛitaḥ
Śāstreshu ke samuddishṭā virudhyante cha ke'dhunā
Lokaśāstraviruddhāḥ ke paṇḍitastān vichintya cha
Nṛipaṁ saṁbodhayet taischa paratreha sukhapradaiḥ,
Śukra, II, 99-100

mention in the records of other dynasties may be accidental. His duty was to find out what were the total collections and disbursements for the year and what was the balance at its end. He had to sell old corn and replace it by fresh stock every now and then, lest the contents of the stores should become useless.[1]

The term Sumantra was used to denote the foreign minister and not the treasurer in the ministry of Shivaji.

AMĀTYA

Amātya or the revenue minister is the last to be mentioned by Śukra. He however does not figure in the records of our dynasties under consideration. His duty was to keep a correct account of the income derived from forests, mines, villages, towns and the country and to keep correct records of the land under cultivation and the land lying fallow.[2] The minister of this title in Shivaji's ministry was performing almost identical functions.

(7) *Fuctioning of the ministry*

Unfortunately we have no epigraphical evidence to show as to how the daily business of the administration was carried on by the ministry. Early political writers also do not supply us sufficient information about the actual functioning of the ministry. It is very likely that the king usually presided over the council of ministers. He is advised not to lose his temper in the council meeting.[3] Manu asks the king to consult the ministers first individually and then collectively, and then to decide the point himself.[4] Kauṭilya also recommends joint consultation with three or four ministers, whose departments may be connected with the matter[5] under dis-

1. Iyaccha sanchitaṁ dravyaṁ vatsaresmin tṛiṇādikaṁ
   Vyayībhūtamiyachchaiva śeshaṁ sthāvara-jaṅgamam
   Iyadastīti vai rājñe sumantro vinivedayet.
   Śukra, II, 101
2. *Śukra*, II, 103-5.
3. Mantrakāle na kopayed.
   Bārhaspatya, II, 53
4. *Manu*, VII, 57.
5. *A.Ś.*, I, Chap. 15.

cussion. Śukra, however, states that it is very likely that the ministers may hesitate in giving their free and independent views in the presence of the king in the council. He therefore asks the ministers to send their opinions in separate memoranda, explaining fully the grounds for the same.[1] Someśvara also is in favour of separate consultation with the ministers[2]. The *Rājataraṅginī* shows that the Kashmirian kings followed all these alternatives; the king Harsha is seen to have consulted his ministers jointly in VII, 1043 and 1145, while in VIII, 3082-3, king Jayasiṁha is found to be consulting only a few ministers.

Consultations with the ministry must have been very frequent, but they are rarely referred to in epigraphical records. We get one reference to it in a Chāhamāna record. The Chāhamāna king Vigraharāja is stated to have consulted his Mantrī Śrīdhara as to the course of conduct on the impending struggle.[3] This is a solitary example one has of the consultation of the king with his minister in Northern India, though we get a similar case under the Śilāhāras of the Deccan.

Let us now discuss the routine working of the ministry. Here also we have to note that not a single writer on Hindu polity except Śukra has discussed this topic in detail. It is only from the *Śukranīti* that we learn that the minister should be assisted by two or more secretaries according to the magnitude of his work.[4] If, however, the work was not exacting, the minister was to do it alone.[5] A secretary was often promoted to the position of the minister in due course, if he had proved his capacity by his work and achievements; Śukra recommends a regular system of promotion to successively higher posts leading ultimately to the ministership.[6] He

1. Rāgāllobhādbhayādrājñaḥ syurmūkā iva mantriṇaḥ
Na tānanumatān vidyān nṛipatiḥ svārthasiddhaye
Pṛithakpṛithak mataṁ teshāṁ lekhayitvā sasādhanam
vimṛiśet svamatenaiva tat kuryād bahusammatam.
Śukra. I, 363-64
2. *Mānasollāsa*, II, 692.
3. *I.A.*, XX, 211.
4. *Śukra*, II, 109-10.
5. Adhikāribalaṁ dṛishṭvā yojayeddarśakān bahūn.
Adhikāriṇamekaṁ vā yojayeddarśakairvinā.
Śukra, II, 116
6. Yathāyathā Śreshṭhapade hyadhikārī yadā bhavet
Anukrameṇa saṁyojyo hyante taṁ prakṛitiṁ nayet.
Śukra, II, 290

further suggests the transfer of a minister from one department to another. That such transfers were often taking place in actual practice is also evident from epigraphical evidence. The Mau inscription of the time of Madanavarman informs us how Gadādhara, who was at first discharging the duties of Pratīhāra, was promoted to the post of a minister by Pṛithvīvarman.[1] Ananta, who held various responsible posts under the Chandella king Kīrtivarman, later on became the Prime Minister during the reign of Sallakshaṇavarman.[2] Śaṅkaradhara, who was at first a foreign minister of Lakshmaṇasena, was subsequently promoted to the post of Chief Councillor.[3]

As in modern times, a capable minister was often put in charge of two departments in ancient India. This would have happened only when the minister was very efficient and was able to discharge the duties of both the offices. Thus under the Paramāra king Dhaṅga, Yaśodhara was acting both as his Purohita and chief justice.[4] In the Chedi ministry under king Sāraṅgadeva, Madhusūdana was discharging the duties of both the Prime Minister and foreign minister.[5] The inscriptions of our period do not give us many such instances. It is therefore probable that this practice was not very common, and normally a minister was put in charge of only one department.

The king is advised to consult his ministers, while executing a particular policy. He is also required to keep carefully all the confidential records of business of the council. Even early writers like Manu and Kauṭilya, recommend that the consultation with ministers should be held in a guarded place. Somadeva, the writer of our period, also states that the deliberations in the council should be conducted in utmost secrecy. He advises the king not to hold council meeting in places which echo human voices. This advice about secrecy must obviously have been followed in actual practice.

Let us now see how the actual business of the council

1. *E.I.*, I, 197.
2. *E.I.*, I, 197.
3. *E.I.*, XXVI, 12.
4. *E.I.*, I, 140-7.
5. *I.A.*, 1912, 20-21.

was conducted. Śukra recommends that the agenda and the minutes should be recorded in writing. The written document is the best guide, for oral orders are liable to be misunderstood or forgotten. The ministers therefore should not do anything without a written order; nor should the king issue any command orally on any matter, however unimportant.[1] Śukra expressly states that the seal is the king and not the person of the ruler.[2] Bṛihaspati is also in favour of business being conducted in writing. According to him a king or an officer, who does state business by oral orders practises fraud on the state.[3]

Each minister managed the affairs of his own department with the help of his assistants. He had to submit writtenreports of his work to the king either daily or monthly or yearly according to circumstances.[4] The king had to read the report and if approved, he was to put his signature on it. If, however, due to heavy work, he was unable to see the report personally, then the crown prince was asked to examine it and to put his signature on behalf of the king.[5] The report was then sent to the department concerned and then the order which it contained was given effect to.

Śukra gives us an interesting and detailed description of the different expressions to be used for the approval of the order by different ministers. The Mantrī, the Prāḍvivāka, the Paṇḍita and the Dūta were to give their consent by the expression *svāviruddham* (not opposed to our views). The expressions of approval to be used by the Amātya, the Sumantra, the Pradhāna, the Pratinidhi, the Yuvarāja and the Purohita were *sādhulikhitam* (well-written) *samyagvichāritam* (well-considered) *satyam yathārthamiti* (true) *aṅgikṛitam* (it is approved) *angīkartavyamiti* (it should be accepted) and *lekhyam*

1. Na kāryaṁ bhṛitakaḥ kuryānnṛipalekhādvinā kvachit
   Nājñāpayellekhanena vinālpaṁ vā mahannṛipaḥ
   Śukra, II, 290
2. Nṛipasaṁchihnitaṁ lekhyaṁ nṛipastanna nṛipo nṛipaḥ.
   Śukra, II, 292
3. *Bārhaspatya*, IV, 37 ff.
4. Dainikaṁ māsikaṁ vrittaṁ vārshikaṁ bahuvārshikam
   Tatkāryajātalekhyantu rājñe samyak nivedayet.
   Śukra, II, 295
5. *Śukra*, II, 368.

svābhimatam (opinion is acceptable) respectively. The order was lastly sent to the king and he had to express his approval by the expression *drishṭam* (seen).[1] It is thus clear that when any new policy was to be carried out or when any new order was to be executed, it was to be approved by the ministers. Whether the absent minister was expected to give his opinion is not known. Śukra is silent on this point. Kauṭilya, however, suggests that absent members should send their views in writing, as they may be helpful in assessing the situation.

We have now finished the discussion about the different problems connected with the ministry; let us now survey the relation between the king and the minister. It may be observed at the outset that during our period, there existed no popular central assembly; the ministers were therefore directly responsible for their work to the king and their influence largely depended upon personal factors and not upon the constitutional backing of a popular assembly.

It has been already stated in the beginning that ministers possessed large powers even in normal times. These powers tended to increase, when the king happened to be a minor or a weak ruler. There is also an actual instance to show that at such times, they even used to play the role of king-makers. Thus the Jabalpur copper plate of the Chedi king Yaśakarṇadeva informs us how Kokalla II was placed on the throne by the Chief-minister (Amātyamukhya) of Yuvarāja II.[2]

The picture would of course change, if there was a powerful and self-willed ruler upon the throne. He could disregard the advice of ministers as was done by the Paramāra king Munja, when he decided to launch his expedition against the Chaulukyas in the teeth of the opposition of his minister,

1. *Śukra*, II, 362-367.
This expression occurs in several Vākāṭaka records in the margin of their plates. *E.I.*, VI, 38.

2. *E.I.*, II, 3-4, V. 8.
It may be pointed out that in Kashmir history, ministers had often an effective voice in the selection of the successor. Thus Sugandhā had to accept Pārtha as her successor, as the ministers would not consent to accept her nominee Śūravarman.
Rāj. V. 253-5.

Rudrâditya.[1] He could even dismiss a minister giving bad advice. Śukra clearly states that the king should first rebuke and then dismiss him from his office.[2]

Normally speaking the relation between the king and the ministers was a cordial one. The ministers were no doubt the servants of the king, but they were also at the same time trustees for the people. We have already seen how kings normally had a high regard for their ministers. It was the duty of ministers to prevent the king from following a wrong path and to oppose measures against the interest of the people.[3] The kingdom is bound to perish, states Śukra, if the king does not follow the advice of his ministers.[4] *Kāmandaka*, as has been stated already, calls those ministers as the real friends of the king, who prevent him from following a dangerous path.[5]

1. *Prabandhachintāmaṇi*, 33.
2. Amātyamapi saṁvīkshya sakṛidanyāyagāminam
   Ekānte daṇḍayet spashṭamabhyāsātprakṛitaṁ tyajet.
   Śukra, I, 376-77
3. Hitaṁ rājñaśchāhitaṁ yallokānāṁ tanna kārayet
   Navīnakaraśulkādyairloka udvijate tataḥ.
   Śukra, II, 273
4. *Śukra*, II, 81.
5. *Kāmandaka*, IV, 41.

CHAPTER IV

SECRETARIAT AND THE CENTRAL GOVERNMENT DEPARTMENTS

We have discussed in the last chapter the powers and functions of ministers; we shall now survey the organisation of what in modern terminology might be conveniently called the Central Secretariat and its various departments. Here also it may be noted that the records of our period supply us no direct and detailed information about the machinery of the central government; and hence it is difficult to say, how the secretariat and its various departments were organised and how they used to function. The records of our period merely give us a long list of officers, but they do not throw much light upon their powers and functions. We can, however, form a general idea of the secretariat and its different branches on the basis of the list of officers, supplied by the records of the different dynasties of our period. The contemporary Nīti writers also help us a good deal in this respect.

(1) *Qualifications of Secretariat Officials*

The success of administration depends largely upon the efficiency and ability of the secretariat officers and the accuracy with which they draft the orders of the central government. Ancient Indian political writers have therefore advised the king to take great care in the selection of the Secetariat officers. Śukra states that the king should appoint officers in the secretariat only after examining their fitness for the work.[1] The Sercetariat officers were also expected to be well trained and were required to possess almost as high qualifications as ministers, as far as ability and reliability were con-

1. Parīkshakairdrāvayitvā yathā svarṇaṁ parīkshyate.
Karmmaṇā sahavāsena guṇaiḥ śīlakulādibhiḥ.
Bhrityaṃ parīkshayennityaṁ viśvāsyaṁ viśvaset tadā.
Śukra. II, 53

cerned. We have already seen in the last chapter, how our Nīti writers have attached great importance to the business of the government being conducted in writing; the officers in the secretariat were therefore expected to be expert in drafting.

(2) *Working of the Secretariat*

The secretariat was known as Śrīkaraṇa under the Chāhamānas and Chaulukyas.[1] Its head was usually a Mahāmātya. It had a big record office, where official documents were carefully kept. The account of Abdur Razak shows that the Diwānkhānā of the Vijayanagar ministry was a big hall of 40 pillars with a gallery of 90′×18′ for accommodating the secretariat.[2] We may presume that similar arrangements existed in our period. In its normal work the secretariat had to deal with a considerable amount of correspondence. It received the reports from the districts and replied to them. Śukra lays down that daily monthly or periodical reports were to be submitted.[3]

The secretariat had also its inspecting staff to control provincial and district officers and find out whether its orders were being properly carried out or not by the subordinates. The inspection machinery of the central government is but rarely referred to in the records of our period; so far we have come across only one such instance in Northern India during our period. The Partāpgarḥ inscription of Mahendrapāla refers to a touring officer called Mādhava designated as Tantrapāla.[4] He is stated to have made a tour to Ujjayini to investigate certain matters as desired by the king. It may be, however, added that the inspecting officers are referred to in the Vākāṭaka, Gupta and Chola records. Śukra also, while recommending tours of inspection, observes that the king or the higher officers should inspect the villages and towns in order to have a first hand information about the real condition and feelings of their residents.[5] The solitary reference

1. *E. I.*, IX, 64
2. Saletore; *Social and Political Life in the Vijayanagar Empire* I, 252.
3. *Śukra*, II, 294-5.
4. *E. I.*, XIV, 182-8.
5. Grāmān purāṇi deśāṁshcha svayaṁ saṁvīkshya vatsare,
Adhikariganaiḥ kāshcha rañjitāḥ kāscha karshitaḥ.
Śukra. I, 374.

to the inspection agency in our epigraphs may be accidental. Administration is hardly possible without an efficient inspecting machinery.

Our records are usually land transfer documents, and they frequently refer to the work of the secretariat in connection with land-grants. That some secretariats used to keep duplicate copies of at least some land grants is suggested by the epigraphical evidence. One Palimpsest plate, containing an original inscription of the Rāshṭrakūṭas and a later one of the Paramāras, has been found.[1] It is plausible to suggest that the plate was obtained by the Paramāras, when they looted the Rāshṭrakūṭa treasury at Malkhed. If such was the case, then it may be permissible to conclude that office copies of some charters were kept in some secretariats. The evidence however is very insufficient to arrive at a definite conclusion.

Sometimes the donees wanted to exchange the village granted to them earlier. Thus the Nagpur Praśasti of the Paramāra king Naravarman informs us that the king donated three new villages in lieu of the two assigned earlier by his predecessor.[2] This must have been done after consulting the original charter.

Sometimes when the letters of the grant used to become blurred due to lapse of time, steps were taken to replace the charter by a new one. This was done by the Chāhamāna king Ratnapāla, when he renewed the grant of the village in the Saptaśata Vishaya, originally made by Mahārāja Jindarāja to the Brāhmaṇa residents in that village, as its letters became blurred due to lapse of time.[3]

The central government used to take proper and immediate steps to annul fraudulent grants. Sometimes government officers themselves went astray, took bribes and issued false copper plates. When such things occurred, the central government used to punish such officers. Thus in the Tārāchaṇḍi inscription we find that when an officer of the Gāhaḍavāla king Vijayachandra made a certain unauthorised

1. *E. I.*, XXIII, 101.
2. *E. I.*, II, 183.
3. *E. I.*, XIX, 15-19.

land grant to some Brāhmaṇas after receiving from them some bribe, the local ruler of Jāpila at once declared it to be fraudulent.[1]

Sometime owing to anarchy also the donees could not enjoy their full rights given to them under the land grants; when however order was re-established, the land grants were re-examined and renewed. The Barah Copper plate of the Pratīhāra king Bhoja informs us that the possession of the village Vālkāgrahāra, lying in the Udumbara Vishaya of the Kālañjara Maṇḍala, which had been originally granted by Nāgabhaṭṭa, was disturbed by the prevailing anarchy in the reign of Rāmabhadra. When sufficient evidence was adduced, the grant was renewed.[2] From another inscription of the same king we learn that the king Bhoja revived a grant in the year 893 A.D. in Gurjaratrā-bhūmi, originally made by Vatsarāja and later confirmed by Nāgabhaṭṭa, but subsequently fallen into desuetude during the time of Rāmabhadra owing to anarchy.[3]

All these records clearly show how the central secretariat was very careful in revenue transactions.

In modern administration, the minister is an official different from the head of his department; in ancient times, the two posts were often held by the same individual. We often find an officer rising to the position of a minister. The cases of Pratīhāra Gadādhara and Ananta rising to the ministerial position have been already referred to. This procedure is in accordance with the practice recommended by Śukra, according to whom the king should promote an officer successively to higher positions leading ultimately to the post of a minister, when he proves himself fully qualified and competent.[4]

(4) *Number of Departments*

As regards the number of the departments of the secretariat, there is no unanimity among the writers on polity.

1. *E. I.*, XIV, 182-8
2. *E. I.*, XIX, 15-19.
3. *E. I.*, V, 213.
4. *Śukra*, II, 115.

The epics[1] and the *Arthaśāstra* usually refer to eighteen departments;[2] the latter however, shows that their number was often increased by five or six if necessary.[3] According to Śukra, there should be twenty departments in the secretariat;[4] supervised by the superintendents of elephants, horses, chariots, infantry, cattle, camels, deer, birds, gold, jewels, silver, clothes, parks, buildings, palaces, religion and charity. The records of our period however, disclose some further departments, which are referred to by neither the Smṛiti nor the Nīti writers. As it is difficult to enumerate them separately, we shall for the sake of convenience group them under the different heads of administration.

(5) *Royal Household Department*

Monarchy being the normal form of government, we shall at the outset discuss the royal household department. The royal palaces and buildings were[5] in charge of an officer called Saudhagehādhipa by Śukra and Āvasathika by Pāla inscriptions.[6] Probably he might have had an assistant to issue permits to the intending visitors. Under him worked Dvārapāla,[7] who used to check visitors' entry into and exit from the palace premises. The officer, who used to take the visitors to the royal presence, was known as Mahā-Pratīhāra.[8] His assistants were known as Pratīhāras. The position of Mahāpratīhāra was similar to that of the modern aid-de-camp. Besides having a fine personality, he was expected to possess tact, charm and suavity.[9] Mahāpratīhāras were assisted by Vetradharas, who used to instruct the visitors in the formality of the proper deportment. The king was always

1. *Rāmāyaṇa* II 100.36; *Mbh.* 5.38.
2. In the *Rāj* I. 118-28 Jalauka is said to have increased the number of departments to 18 from their original number of seven. It appears that 18 had become a traditional number.
3. *A.Ś.I.*, Chap, 8.
4. *Śukra*, II, 117.
5. *Śukra*, II. 119.
6. R.C. Majumdar, *History of Bengal*, p. 284.
7. *Kkt. R*, IV, 28.
8. *Śukra*, II, 273.
9. *Kkt. R*, IV, 28

guarded by his body-guards designated as Aṅgarakshakas by Pāla inscriptions[1] and Aṅganigūhakas by Chaulukya records[2]

Mahārājaguru or the royal preceptor is the next officer that we have to consider. He figures frequently in our records. In the Khajurāho inscription, Vāsavachandra appears as Mahārājaguru of the Chandella king Dhaṅga.[3] Being a very learned man, he was sometimes asked to compose the copper plate grants; probably it was thought that he would compose them elegantly. Thus under the Paramāras, the Bhopal plates of 1214 and 1215 A.D. were both composed by Rājaguru Madana with the consent of Mahāsandhivigrahikas Rājasalaṇa and Bilhaṇa.[4] Sometimes he used to act as a witness, when the king made a land grant. For instance, when the Paramāra king Devarāja made a grant in V.S. 1059, the witness was his *Guru* Matvāka.[5] Sometime the duties of the royal priest and preceptor were combined in the same person. In the Kamauli grant, king Jayachandra is stated to have granted the village of Ośia to his Mahāpurohita, who was also his royal preceptor.[6]

Besides the royal preceptor there was also a royal physician in the king's court. He has been called Bhishak[7] in the Gāhaḍavāla records and Antaraṇga[8] in the Sena ones. Lakshmīdhara describes him as Vaidya.[9] He was expected to be well grounded in the eight branches of the medical science.

The 'science' of astrology had become well-established during our period and we find the king's court usually having a court astrologer. He was called Naimittika[10] under the Gāhaḍavālas, and Jyotishi[11] under the Chāhamānas and

1. R.C. Majumdar, *History of Bengal*, p. 285.
2. *Bhavnagar Inscriptions*, p. 158.
3. *E. I.*, I, 136.
4. *J. A. S. B.*, V, 377-82; *J.A.O.B.* VII, 253.
5. *E.I.*, XXII. 196.
6. *E. I.*, IV, 120.
7. *E. I.*, XVIII, 221.
8. *E. I.*, XXI, 217.
9. *Kkt. R.* IV, 28.
10. *I. A.*, XVIII, 17.
11. (1) *E. I.*, II, 343.
    (2) Peterson, M. S. S., 887, 97.

Mahāmauhūrtika under the Chaulukyas. Lakshmīdhara calls him Ṛiju,[1] a word whose derivation is difficult to make out. He was not only expected to be a master of omens but also of medicine. It may be noted that even in modern times Ayurvedic physicians often start their treatment after satisfying themselves that the day is auspicious. Just as we now sometimes have physicians-cum-astrologers, in the past, there were probably astrologers-cum-physicians. Being a learned man, he was sometimes entrusted with the drafting of the land grants. The Delhi Śiwalik pillar inscription of the Chāhamāna king Vīsaladeva was written by the astrologer according to the orders of the king.[2]

Since verly early times, the royal courts used to have their own poet laureates. The practice was continued during our period also. Under the Chandellas, they were often given the title *Kavichakravartī*. The Khajurāho inscription of the Chandella king Dhaṅga refers to *Kavichakravartī* Nandana.[3]

The internal management of the royal palace was looked after by several officers. Sambhārapa was one of them;[4] his duty was to keep a proper stock of the things necessary for the maintenance of the royal household. Under him worked the superintendent of kitchen,[5] who had to take particular precaution to see that no attempt was made to poison the king.

The royal harem was put in charge of an officer designated by Śukra as Antaḥapurayogyapurusha.[6] Lakshmīdhara calls him Antaḥpurādhyaksha.[7] He was to be sexless, truthful and sweet-tongued. The officer called Śayyāpāla,[8] mentioned only in the Chaulukya records, was probably in charge of the king's bed; he must have worked under the Antaḥapurādhipa.

1. Nimitte śakunajñāne vettā chaiva chikitsite.
Kṛitajñaḥ karmaṇāṁ śūrastathā kleśasaho ṛijuḥ.
Kkt. R., chap. IV, p. 28
2. *I.A.*, XIX, 218.
3. *E. I.*, I, 140-7.
4. *Śukra*, II, 162.
5. *Śukra*, II, 157.
6. *Śukra*, II. 185.
7. *K.Kt. R.*, chap. IV, 29.
8. *A.S.I.W. C.*; 1907-08, 55.

Besides him there were also maid-servants or Parichārikās, working in the inner apartments. They were expected to be skilful in serving and to take part in the diverse work of the royal harem allotted to them.

MILITARY DEPARTMENT

We shall now consider the different departments of the state administration. Among these the military department was the most important one. The commander-in-chief, who was in charge of this department, was known by different designations under different dynasties. The Gāhaḍavāla[1] and the Paramāra[2] records call him by the simple name Senāpati, while those of the Pālas[3] and Senas[4] give him the more high-sounding title of Mahāsenāpati. The title Kampanādhipati was in use in Kashmir[5]. The commander-in-chief was usually a member of the ministry also, as shown in the last chapter. His duty was to organise the fighting forces and to maintain them at maximum efficiency.

The Senāpati was assisted in his work by a number of subordinate military officers. The fighting force during our period had three main arms; infantry, cavalry, and elephant corps--each being in charge of one separate commander. The Pāla kingdom, which had the sea coast, had a naval arm as well. We do not know whether the Chaulukyas maintained a navy to protect their coast.

The superintendent of infantry was probably called Balādhipa[6] under the Chāhamānas and Balādhyaksha under the Pālas.[7] He had under him a number of officers of lower rank, who are referred to by Śukra. The Pattipāla[8] was the lowest among them; he was in charge of five or six foot soldiers and corresponded to a modern lance Naik. The next officer,

1. *E.I.*, IV, 121, XVIII.
2. *I.A.*, XXV, 205-8.
3. *I.A.*, XV, 306.
4. *E.I.*, XXI, 217.
5. *Rāja*, I, 232
6. *E.I.*, XI, 308.
7. R.C. Majumdar, *History of Bengal*, p. 285.
8. *E.I.*, IV, 248.

called Gaulmika[1] was in charge of thirty foot soldiers according to Śukra; he corresponded to the modern Jamadar. He appears in the Pāla and Sena records also, but unfortunately they do not throw any light upon his functions. Dr. R.C. Majumdar suggests that Gaulmika was an officer in charge of a military squadron called Gulma consisting of nine elephants, nine chariots, twenty-seven horses and forty-five foot soldiers.[2] Dr. U.N. Ghoshal takes him to be a collector of customs duties and refers to the term Gulmadeya[3] used in the *Arthaśāstra* in the sense of dues paid at the military or the police stations. While justifying his interpretation, he points out that in the Pāla records, Śaulkika is immediately followed by Gaulmika and hence he must be an officer connected with the revenue department.

Dr. R.C. Majumdar, however, does not agree with Dr. U.N. Ghoshal and he, while criticising the latter's view, argues that in the Sena records, Gaulmika immediately follows the military officers and hence he must be a member of that category. It is difficult to say which of the above views is correct, for neither in the Pāla records nor in the Sena epigraphs are the functions of Gaulmika referred to anywhere. It would appear that the functions of the Gaulmika may have differed in different administrations. However, it may be pointed out that Dr. R.C. Majumdar's view is supported by Śukra, who definitely states that he was a military officer.[4]

The next higher officer mentioned by Śukra is Śatānīka.[5] He was the head of one hundred foot-soldiers. He was expected to be well-grounded in the art of warfare and its different tactics. His duty was to train the soldiers both in the morning and evening and supervise military parades. He was assisted in his work by an officer called Anuśatika.[6] who was also of the same rank as that of Śatānīka.

The next higher officers referred to by Śukra were

1. *Śukra*, II, 140.
2. R.C. Majumdar, *History of Bengal*, p. 285.
3. R.C. Majumdar, *History of Bengal*, p. 286.
4. *Śukra*, II, 140.
5. *Śukra*, II, 141
6. *Śukra*, II, 141.

Sāhasrika[1] and Āyutika[2] in charge of a thousand and ten thousand foot soldiers respectively.

The bow, the spear and the sword were the main weapons of the age and soldiers used to fight generally with them. Lakshmīdhara, while describing the army, refers to Dhanurdhāris and Khaḍgadhāris[3] The swordsman and the bow-man had to fight sometimes on foot and sometimes from the back of the horse or the elephant. Lakshmīdhara therefore insists that swordsmen and bow-men should be able to manage the horse as well as the elephant. Probably the same was expected of the spearmen, though they are not referred to in this connection in the Rājadharma Kāṇḍa of *Kṛityakalpataru.*

Among the minor weapons of the army referred to in the *Mānasollāsa* (II. 681-83) may be mentioned clubs (*mudgara*), battle-axes, knives (ksurikās), tridents and machines to throw missiles (*yantramuktāyudhāḥ kechit*). The work also refers to *sellachakra*, whose nature is not clear. Śukra refers to fire arms and artillery (IV, 7, 213) but these passages are later than our period, as already pointed out. There is no evidence so far forthcoming to show that fire-arms were used by the Hindus before *c.* 1370 A.D.

The superintendent of cavalry is called Aśvapati[4] by Śukra. He was to be adept in military parades and was expected to know how to guide, train and treat the horses. Mahāsādhanika mentioned in some Chaulukya records[5] and Mahāśvasādhanika[6] figuring in some Chedi inscriptions were the designations of cavalry officers working under Aśvapati. Sāhaṇi[7] of the Chāhamāna epigraphs was perhaps the master of stables.

The Mahāsādhanika appears to have been an important officer, for sometimes he is seen enjoying the revenues of a town or a village without the power of alienation. Thus Āśni, the wife of Mahāsādhanika Māhāika, owned a plot of

1. *Śukra*, II, 142.
2. *Śukra*, II, 142
3. Kt. R., Chap. IV, 26.
4. *Sukra*, II, 130.
5. *I.A.*, XVIII, 341.
6. *E.I.*, 11, 309.
7. *E.I.*, XI, 29.

land in Semvalapuraka Grāma, which was enjoyed by her husband, but she had to supplicate for the permission of the Paramāra king Vākpatirāja[1] when she wanted to alienate a portion of it.

The superintendent of the elephant corps was designated as Mahāpīlupati[2] by the Sena records and Pīlupati[3] by the Pāla ones. Śukra describes him as Gajapati.[4] He was expected to have the knowledge of differentiating the three kinds of elephants and also of nourishing them properly; when they were ill, he was to make adequate arrangements to treat them. The officer called Nāyaka,[5] who used to be in charge of twenty elephants, worked under him.

The superintendent of chariots does not appear in the records of our dynasties under survey, probably because the chariot corps had ceased to be a part of the fighting force. But it appears that the army still used to require some chariots, probably for the use of high officials on ceremonial occasions. It therefore had a chariot superintendent. Śukra calls him Rathādhyaksha[6] and states that he should be skilled in moving, turning and controlling the chariots. He was also expected to know how to manufacture strong and durable chariots.

The officer called Mahāvyūhapati,[7] who is referred to only in the Pāla and Sena inscriptions, was one of the highest officers of the military department. His position was similar to that of the chief of the military staff in modern times. Unfortunately the precise nature of his work is not described any where in inscriptions, but there is no doubt that he had to study the different kinds of battle arrays, which formed an important part in military strategy.

The officer called Mahāgaṇastha[8], appearing in the Sena records was probably a military officer, for according to Śukra

1. *I.A.*, XIV, 159.
2. *E.I.*, XXI, 217.
3. *E.I.* IV. 248.
4. *Śukra*, II, 127.
5. *Śukra*, II, 147.
6. *Śukra*, II, 131-32.
7. *E.I.*, IV, 248.
8. *E.I.*, XXI, 217,; *E.I.*, XXVI, 7.

Gaṇa denotes a body of troops consisting of 27 chariots, as many elephants, 81 horses and 135 foot. Unfortunately we are not in a position to ascertain how and what functions this officer used to discharge, for the inscriptions throw no light upon the point.

Forts as units of defence were very important in our age, and the army had to supply the personnel for their garrison. Each fort was in charge of a capable and experienced officer. He was known as Koṭṭapāla[1] under the Pratīhāras. Śukra calls him Durgādhyaksha.

The warden of the marches called Maryādādhurya[2] by the Pratīhāra and Prāntapāla by the Pāla records was an important military officer. His duty was to watch over the frontier and to prevent undesirable or hostile persons from entering the kingdom. In Kashmir, he was known as Dvārapāla. He worked in close cooperation with the superintendents of forts in his vicinity.

Sometimes government used to appoint the same individual in charge of a fort and the adjoining frontier. Thus under the Pratīhāra dynasty, Gwalior, which was a very important fort, had only one officer, who was discharging the duties of both the Koṭṭapāla and Maryādādhurya.[3] This would have happened only when one officer was found efficient enough to discharge both the duties.

The military department had its own store of weapons. Under the Imperial Guptas, there used to be a separate office called Raṇabhāṅḍāgārādhikaraṇa, which was in charge of the stores and weapons. Whether such an office existed during our period also, we do not know, for there are no references to it in any of the records of our dynasties. It is, however, natural to assume that a separate officer was put in charge of stores of weapons during our period also, though he is not mentioned in the inscriptions.

The military department also looked after the distribution of the army in the different territories. It is important to note that as the means of communications were poor, the big

1. *E.I.*, I, 154.
2. *E.I.*, I, 154.
3. *E.I.*, I, 154.

empires in ancient India used to have battalions of their army stationed in the different directions. Thus under the Pratīhāras, we find that there was a southern army to watch over the Rāshṭrakūṭas, an eastern army to check the Pālas and a western army to oppose the Muslims.[1] Not only in the North but in the South also during our period of survey there were provincial headquarters for the army. It is interesting to note that even today our army has its different commands like the southern, the northern and the eastern ones.

Most of the kingdoms of our period were land bound and hence had no navy. The Pālas and the Senas, however, were maritime powers, and we find them maintaining a navy. Their records frequently refer to navy or *naubala*.[2] The officer known as Nākādhyaksha also appears in the Pāla records; according to Dr. R.C. Majumdar this title is a corrupt form of Nāvādhyaksha or Naukādhyaksha.[3] It is not possible to say how the navy was organised and how its administration was carried on, as both the literary and epigraphical sources are silent on the point.

FOREIGN DEPARTMENT

The Foreign Department was another important department at the centre. The minister in its charge is generally called Mahāsandhivigrahika in the records of our period. There were a number of subordinate officers in the foreign department to help the foreign minister whose work, as we have already seen in the last chapter, was very heavy, as he had to look after the feudatories and neighbouring powers. His work in connection with the former has been described in an interesting manner by Someśvara in the *Mānasollāsa* (II. 128). He was to summon the different feudatories at proper time to have discussions with them and then to dismiss them.

The officer called Mahāmudrādhikṛita appearing in the

1. Elliot, I, p. 23.
2. *I.A.*, XV, 306, *IOA.*, XXI, 217.
3. R.C. Majumdar, *History of Bengal*, p. 286.

Sena records probably worked in this department.[1] His duty was probably to grant passports to foreigners for entering the country. The Pāla records refer to another officer called Dūtapreshaṇika,[2] who seems to have been in charge of the dispatch of the envoys to other states on diplomatic business. The next officer concerned with this department was Gamāgamika.[3] Gamāgamika literally means one, who comes and goes. It is also n ot unlikely, as suggested by Dr. U.N. Ghoshal, that he would have been carrying out functions of an urgent character in connection with the diplomatic department of the state, requiring frequent visits to the neighbouring kingdoms or to the dominions of vassals.

POLICE DEPARTMENT

The police department may be conveniently considered at this point. Unfortunately the records of our period do not clearly distinguish between the police and military officers. It it likely that Daṇḍanāyakas of our period were both military and police officers. Sometimes the military officers did the duty of the police officers and *vice versa*. They had a number of subordinate officers like Daṇḍapāśikas, Chauroddharaṇikas, Dāṇḍikas, Daṇḍaśaktis, Chāṭas and Bhaṭas, who are frequently referred to in our records.

The Daṇḍapāśika,[4] who is referred to only by the Pāla and Sena records, was probably of the status of the modern district superintendent of police. As his designation indicates, his duty was to catch the thieves. Sometimes he was entrusted with the important work of discharging the functions of a Dūtaka[5] in connection with the delivery of a land-grant.

The Chauroddharaṇikas[6] were mainly concerned with the detection of thefts and the punishment of the concerned thieves. The Kālavān plates of Yaśovarman refer to an officer called

1. *E.I.*, XXI, 217.
2. *I.A.* XV, 306.
3. *I.A.*, XV, 308.
4. *E.I.*, XXVI, 7; *E.I.*, XXIII, 290.
5. *E.I.*, XIX, 58.
6. *E.I.*, XXI, 217.

Chaurika, but he was probably not different from Chaurod-dharaṇika.

The duty of the officer called Daśāparādhika[1] was most probably to collect fines for the ten traditional criminal offences. Some of these crimes were serious like murder, adultery, abortion, etc., while others were relatively lighter like defamation, obscene speech, etc.

Daṇḍaśakti and Dāṇḍika figure only in the Pāla records. Dr. R.C. Majumdar[2] is of opinion that Daṇḍaśakti was responsible for his duties to the military department, but this view does not seem to be a convincing one. The Daṇḍaśakti may as well have been in charge of the execution of punishment imposed upon criminals. It is important to note that this officer figures only in the Khalimpur plate of Dharmapāla. His place in the lists is taken by Dāṇḍika in other Pāla inscriptions. It is therefore very likely that Daṇḍaśakti and Dāṇḍika were not two different officers. Probably the same office was denoted by both the expressions.

The functions of the officer called Mahādauhasādhasādhanika[3] are difficult to determine. Most probably officers of this cadre were entrusted with specially difficult tasks. The Jabalpur plates of the Chedi king Jayasiṁhadeva refers to an officer called Dushṭasādhya;[4] he is probably the same as Dauhasādhasādhanika.

The state in ancient India controlled the institution of prostitution since very early times and it is not unlikely that the officer entrusted with this work, who is called Gaṇikādhyaksha by Kauṭilya, worked under the police department. It was his duty to have full information about the persons who used to visit prostitutes. This was often useful to detect persons who were of bad character and to watch their movements and activities. Very probably these officers worked under police department; it is however not improbable that in cities they may have worked under city superintendents.

1. *Śukra*, IV, 5, 83-4.
2. R.C. Majumdar, *History of Bengal*, p. 286; *Ancient India*, p. 445.
3. *I.A.*, XV, 306.
4. *E.I.*, XXI, 95.

The functions of the officer called Khola[1] have not yet been correctly ascertained. The meaning of this term, as revealed by Sanskrit dictionaries, is a lame person; it can hardly have any thing to do with this officer. If the term is connected with Khala (wicked person), he would be an officer working under the police department; if it is connected with *Khalaka*, he would be an officer under the revenue department.

REVENUE DEPARTMENT

The revenue department was in charge of the income of the state from taxes and state properties and concerns. Lakshmīdhara in his *Kṛityakalpataru* mentions an officer called Aksharakshita,[2] who had to keep a comprehensive account of income and expenditure of the state. He must have been the right hand man of the revenue minister. As we have already seen in the last chapter, the revenue department had to supervise the collection of taxes and revenues, which were usually paid partly in kind and partly in cash. It is therefore but natural that his office had to make elaborate arrangements for the proper administration of government granaries. He was probably keeping the duplicate copies of the land grants; for sometimes it so happened that people showed forged charters in their own names. When such frauds took place, the revenue department used to consult the original documents and arrive at a decision about the genuineness of the disputed records. The steps taken by the government in this connection have been already referred to earlier.

The revenue department had a large number of officers. The Mahākshapaṭalika, who was in charge of records, was an important one among them. During our period of survey, he is often seen composing copper plate charters. Thus Mahākshapaṭalika Thakkura Vosarin,[3] Mahākshapaṭalika Thak-

1. *E.I.*, IV, 248.
2. Āyavyayajño lokajño deśotpattiviśāradaḥ, Kṛitākṛitājño bhṛityānāṁ jñeyaḥ syādakasharakshitā. *Kkt. R.*, chap. IV, p. 28.
3. *I.A.*, VI. 194.

kura Kumyāra,[1] Mahākshapaṭalika Thakkura Govinda[2] and Akshapaṭalika Kāyastha Somasiṁhadeva[3] were the writers of the different documents known as Kādi plates of the Chaulukya king Bhīma II. The writer of the Lucknow Museum plate of the Gāhaḍavāla king Jayachandradeva was Akshapaṭalika Śrīpati,[4] while that of the Suṇak grant of the Chedi king Karṇadeva was Akshapaṭalika Kekkaka.[5] We have already seen in the last chapter that in some administrations, the Sandhivigrahika was also doing this duty. It is not unlikely that the historical part of the grant was drafted by the Sandhivigrahika and the details about land and taxes were supplied by Akshapaṭalika. For convenience sake, drafting of the document, though done by two persons, might have been ascribed to one of them.

The next officer of this department, who was in charge of collecting the revenue, was known as Mahākaraṇika under the Chedis.[6] He and his assistants Karaṇikas were stationed in the different provinces, towns and cities. The Karaṇikas are sometimes seen as the writers of copper plate charters. Thus the writer of the Gohrwa grant of the Chedi king Karṇa was the Karaṇika Sarvānanda.[7] Karaṇika Dhīra was the writer of the Bilhari stone inscription of the Chedi king Yuvarāja I[8]. Karaṇika Jaddha was the writer of the Khajuraho inscription of the Chandella king Dhaṅga.[9] Karaṇika Śrīśakti was the writer of the Bayānā inscription of Chitralekhā.[10] Sometimes the post of Karaṇikas used to be hereditary.

It is important to note that in Mahārāshṭra, the village revenue officer was till recently known as Kulkarṇī—a name derived from Kula-karaṇika—*i.e.*, an officer in charge of the land revenues of different families in a village.

1. *I.A.*, XI, 71.3.
2. *I.A.*, VI, 210.
3. *I.A.*, VI, 199.
4. *E I.*, XXIV, 291.
5. *E.I.*, I, 317.
6. *E.I.*, II, 309.
7. *E,I.*, XI, 139.
8. *E.I.* II, 174,
9. *E.I.*, I, 123-135.
10. *E.I.*, XXII 122.

The Chedi records refer to another officer called Mahāpramātā,[1] who was probably assisted by an officer known as Pramātṛi[2] under the Pālas and Senas. The functions of both these officers are difficult to determine. Some scholars take them to be judicial officers in charge of recording evidence, while others take them to be judges concerned with civil cases only.[3] Both these conjectures, however, do not seem to be probable. The term Pramātṛi is derived from the root *mā* to measure. Pramātṛi therefore should be taken as a land measuring officer working under the Mahākshapaṭalika. He was thus similar to the Rajjukas of Aśokan inscriptions. The Jabalpur grant of the Chedi king Jayasiṁhadeva refers to an officer called Pramattavāra.[4] The term may be a Prakrit derivative from Pramātṛi.

Another officer of the revenue department was Kshetrapa.[5] His function is difficult to determine; it is not improbable that he might have been in charge of some matters concerning cultivated lands. Probably he was keeping an account of every holding paying taxes to the king, and as such his activities were correlated to those of the Mahākshapaṭalika and his staff. He figures only in the Pāla inscriptions.

The Pāla records mention an officer called Shashṭhādhikṛita.[6] We have no information about his jurisdiction. Whether he was a Tāluka or district officer, we do not know. Most probably he worked under the revenue department. Land tax was traditionally to be one sixth of the produce and so the officer Shashṭhādhikṛita might have been in charge of collecting it from the cultivators.

Besides the Shashṭhādhikṛita, there was another officer called Bhogapati,[7] who probably collected the tax known as Bhoga, which was most probably a periodical supply of fuel, fruits, firewoods, flowers and the like, which the villagers

1. *E.I.*, II, 309.
2. *I.A.*, XXI, 266.
3. R.C. Majumdar, *History of Bengal*, p. 286; *Ancient India*, p. 445.
4. *E.I.*, XIX, 95.
5. *E.I.*, XXIII, 290.
6. *E.I.*, IV, 248.
7. *E.I.*, XXI, 217.

had to furnish to the king. This officer is called Mahābhogika[1] in the Sena records.

The term Bhoktri abbreviated into Bho was often used to denote a certain class of officers in Rajasthan under the Chāhamānas.[2] They had often octroi dues assigned to them. Whether they were the same as Bhogapatis, it is difficult to say.

Taxes, as we already know, were paid both in kind and cash during our period. Tax in cash was called Hiraṇya under the Pālas and the Senas and it was perhaps levied upon certain special kinds of crops. The officer, who was entrusted with the work of collecting taxes in cash, was known as Hiraṇyasāmudāyika in Bengal.[3]

Cattle-breeding was an important element in the economic life and the state did not neglect it. The officer, who was in charge of the herds, was known as Gokulika[4] in the Paramāra and Gāhaḍavāla kingdoms. Śukra also refers to officers in charge of camels, cattle, deer and birds;[5] They were expected to be skilled in breeding and rearing them.

Royal parks and forests were an important item of state property. The superintendent of parks was known as Ārāmādhipati.[6] One of his duties was to develop the resources by supplying proper manure at the suitable time. He was also expected to know the medicinal properties of the trees and plants. The forests also had a superintendent, though he does not figure in our records. He had a suitable staff to assist him.

TREASURY DEPARTMENT

The treasury department was in charge of a superintendent, who is called Koshādhyaksha both by Kauṭilya[7] and Śukra.[8] Paramāra records call him Koshādhikārī. He was

1. *E.I.*, XXI, 217.
2. *E.I.*, XI, 36.
3. R.C. Majumdar, *History of Bengal*, p. 277.
4. *E.I.*, XVIII, 221, *E.I.* XIX, 71.
5. II, 117
6. *Śukra*, II, 158
7. *A.S.*, 11, chap. 34.
8. II, 118.

expected to be well-versed in financial administration. The work of this department was onerous; it had to look after the government balance in kind and cash and to keep it in safe custody. It naturally engaged a number of officers. Among them the superintendent of granary, who is called Dhānyādhyaksha[1] by Śukra, was the most important one. Gāhadavāla inscriptions refer to him as Bhāṇḍāgārādhikṛita.[2] His duty was to store properly the corn collected as tax in the government granary and to replace it periodically by new stock. He was expected to know how to store corn and how to dispose it off at profit at suitable time.

FINANCE DEPARTMENT

Unfortunately there is hardly any reference to the finance department in the records of the dynasties surveyed by us. In the Chaulukya administration only, we come across an officer in charge of the expenditure known as Vyayakaraṇamahāmātya,[3] who probably belonged to this department. It is very likely that the work of this department was being discharged by the treasury department and hence there are no frequent references to the officers of finance. The superintendent of treasury himself would have looked after the allotment of revenue and expenditure of the state. In this connection, it may be noted that the Smritis also rarely refer to the officers working under the finance department.

COMMERCE AND INDUSTRY DEPARTMENT

There were several officers working under this department. The first among them was the superintendent of markets; he was called Drāṅgika[4] in Kathiawad and Haṭṭapati in Bengal. According to Kauṭilya, his duty was to fix the rates of different articles and to put the government products in the market under favourable condition. He also organised imports

1. *Śukra*,, II, 156.
   The designation Gañjeśa used for the treasury officer in the *Rāj.* VII, 266, does not occur in the Northern India inscriptions.
2. *E.I.*, XXIII, 229.
3. *J.B.B.R.A.S.*, XXV, 322.
4. *E.I.*, IX, 4-6.

of goods required in the locality and supervised their sales at reasonable rates.[1]

Another officer, who worked under this department, was the toll superintendent, who is designated as Śaulkika[2] in the Pāla records. He was to collect the octroi duties from the merchants at the gate of a town before they imported their articles for sale.

The third officer working under this department was Tarika or Tarapati.[3] He figures only in the Pāla records. He was probably in charge of ferry service. He had also to look after the construction of ferries, their repairs and upkeep.

Mining, spinning, weaving and Jewelry-making seem to have been the principal industries of the age. The state paid great attention to the mining industry, as the mines produced a large part of the wealth of the country. The superintendent of mines is called Ākarādhipati[4] in the Gāhaḍavāla records. His duties must have been similar to those described in the *Arthaśāstra*, *i.e.*, to exploit the resources of existing mines and to carry out operations, which might lead to the discovery of new ones.

Cloth industry was another flourishing industry of our period, and government took keen interest in it. The superintendent of this department is designated as Sūtrādhyaksha by Kauṭilya and Vastrādhipa by Śukra.[5] He was expected to have the knowledge of the fineness and roughness of texture of the cotton, woollen and silken cloth as well as of their durability. According to Kauṭilya, the employees of this department used to send cotton to the homes of weak and destitute persons and get the yarn spun through them at agreed rates;[6] whether this was being done in our period, we do not know.

1. *A.S.*, II, chap. 16.
2. *I.A.*, XV, 306.
3. *E.I.*, IV, 248.
4. *E.I.*, XVIII, 221.
5. *Śukra*, II, 119.
6. *A.S.*, II, chap., 25.

Sometimes, the state used to give licence to goldsmiths for the manufacture of silver and golden wares and ornaments. The officer, who was entrusted with this work, is called by Śukra as Suvarṇādhyaksha. He was expected to have the knowledge of distinguishing the values of different metals by their weight, lustre and colour.

Slaughter houses were also under strict state control, their superintendent is called Śaunika[1] in the Pāla records. According to Kauṭilya, it was the duty of this officer to prevent the outsiders from killing the animals in the game forests. How he discharged his duty during our period, we do not know.

JUDICIAL DEPARTMENT

The administration of justice was also carried on with the help of a number of officers. The king was at the head of this department and he administered justice, when he was present at the capital. If, however, due to ill health or the pressure of other work, he was unable to discharge this duty, the chief justice or Prāḍvivāka presided over the court at the capital. It is rather strange that the records of the dynasties under consideration do not refer to him. The non-mention of his office may be accidental.

The chief justice was assisted in his work by a number of judges known as Mahādharmādhyakshas[2] under the Senas and probably Dharmapradhānas[3] under the Chedis. It is difficult to say whether the Dharmalekhins,[4] who figure in the Chandella and Chedi records, were the pleaders, who wrote the complaints or judicial officers, who wrote the judgments. Probably they were state judicial officers, since they are sometimes seen as drafting the copper plate charters. Thus under the Chandellas, the writer of the Banda plate of Madanavarman was the Darmalekhī Dāsisūdha,[5] and that

1. *E.I.*, IV, 248.
2. *E.I.*, XII, 8.
3. *E.I.*, XXI, 95.
4. *E.I.*, XV. 205; *I.A.*, XVI, 208.
5. *I.A.*, XVI. 208.

of the Semra plate was the Dharmlekhī[1] Pṛithvīdhara. The writer of the Pacher plate of the Chandella king Paramardi was Dharmalekhī Shubhananda[2] and of Mahoba plate was Dharmalekhī Pṛithvīdhara.[3] The writer of the Kharhā grant of the Chedi king Yaśakarṇa was the Dharmalekhī Vacchuka.[4]

The chief justice used to have his own office in charge of an officer named as Mahādharmādhikaraṇika under the Chedis.[5] He was probably in charge of the records of the office, where all documents concerning important cases were kept. The officer called Daśāparādhika,[6] who collected fines imposed upon criminals, probably worked under the chief justice or his assistants.

The judicial department probably looked after the management of jails also. The epigraphs of our period, however, do not refer to the jail officer and hence we do not know how he used to function. The non-mention of the jail officer may be probably due to the fact that imprisonment was only one of the ten modes of punishment in our period.[7]

ECCLESIASTICAL DEPARTMENT

The last department that we have to consider is the ecclesiastical department, which was in charge of an officer called Paṇḍita by Śukra. An officer with this title does not figure at all in any of the records of the dynasties under consideration; it is unlikely that his function might have been discharged by the Purohita or Rājaguru, who figures in some of our records. His duty as we have already seen, was to advise the king in religious matters. He must have been assisted in his work by a number of subordinate officers, though they do not appear in our records. Their duty was to supervise all

1. *E.I.*, IV, 160.
2. *E.I.*, X, 47.
3. *E.I.*, X, 47.
4. *E.I.*, XII, 205.
5. *E.I.*, II, 309.
6. R.C. Majumdar, *History of Bengal*, p. 285.
7. According to Śukra, the methods of punishment were (i) Rebuke, (i) Degradation, (iii) Imprisonment, (iv) Beating, (v) Confiscation (vi) Banishment from the city, (vii) Branding, (viii) Shaving in a ridiculous fashion, (ix) Amputation and (x) Death. VI. 1.47.

religions and sects. These officers were called Dharmamahāmātras under the Mauryas, Vinayasthitisthāpakas under the Guptas and Dharmāṅkuśas under the Rāshṭrakūṭas.

The superintendent of religious establishments, institutions and charities is described as Dānādhyaksha by Śukra.[1] It is very likely that the donation made on the recommendation of this officer to the Brāhmaṇas and temples would have been utilised by them in organising schools, colleges, hospitals and poor-houses. The officer called Dharmādhikārin appearing in the Chedi records probably discharged similar functions.[2]

An officer called Agrahārika, appearing in the Pāla records, might have worked under this department. He probably looked after the administration of the villages granted to temples and Brāhmaṇas. It was his duty to see that there were no difficulties created in the enjoyment of grants given to the donees.

1. *Śukra*, II, 163.
2. *E.I.*, XXI, 165.

Chapter V

ADMINISTRATION OF ARMY

The higher directorate of the army has been already discussed in the last chapter; we shall now review the army organisation and its administration. It is important to note that the army was regarded by all the political writers of our period as an important constituent of the state organisation. "The army" states Śukra, "is the chief means of overpowering the enemy ; the king should, therefore, maintain a formidable force."[1] He gives us a beautiful simile, while emphasising the importance of the army. "What mind is to the human body, the army is to a state."[2] It is only by maintaining the army that the treasury and the kingdom prosper and the enemy is destroyed.[3] Kāmandaka, while recognising the importance of the army, states that the king with a strong fighting force rules the earth unhampered and even the foes of a king possessing an efficient army are turned into friends.[4]

Kauṭilya includes the army among the seven constituents of the state. He, however, does not regard it as the most important element. For, while discussing the relative importance of the army and the treasury, he holds the latter to be more important than the former. "The army", states Kauṭilya, "may go to the enemy or murder the king himself and bring about every kind of trouble, but the treasury is the chief means of performing virtuous acts and fulfilling desires."[5] The king should pay first attention to the preservation of an overflowing treasury. The writers of our period like Kāmandaka

1. Balameva ripornityaṁ parājayakaraṁ param
Tasmād balamabhedyaṁ tu dhārayedyatnato nṛipaḥ.
Śukra, IV, f, f

2. *Śukra*, I, 62.
3. Sainyādvinā naiva rājyaṁ na dhanaṁ na parākramaḥ.
Śukra, IV, f. 4
Balasaṁrakshaṇāt kośarāshṭravṛiddhirarikshayaḥ.
Śukra, IV, 5, 14

4. *Kāmandaka*, XIII, 37.
5. *A.S.*, VIII, Chap. I.

and Śukra, however, appear to have regarded army as more important than treasury.

Most of the writers of our period like those of the earlier age do not throw any light upon the army organisation, nor upon its administration. It is only Śukra, who gives us an interesting and detailed account about the army, its constituents and its administration.

As has already been pointed out, the commander-in-chief was the head of the army. He was expected to be skilled in the science and tactics of warfare and to be familiar with the use of all kinds of weapons. He was also expected to be well-grounded in forming the different kinds of battle-arrays demanded by the occasion. "If there be danger ahead" states Śukra, "the commander should normally march in crocodile array, if there be danger behind, in the *Sakaṭa* array, if on the sides, then in the *Vajra* array; if on all sides then in the *Sarvatobhadra* or *Chakra* or *Vyāla*[1] array. In these arrays, the strength of the army was concentrated at points, where danger was most apprehended.

Under the commander-in-chief each section of the army had its own sub-commanders. They were the commanders of infantry, cavalry and elephant corps. Their duties and functions have already been discussed in the last chapter (pp. 116-117).

UNITS OF THE ARMY

Subordinate to the above commanders, were other officers of different grades. They were the Pattipāla,[2] in charge of five or six foot-soldiers,[3] Gaulmika, in charge of thirty foot-soldiers, Śatānika, the officer over a hundred foot-soldiers, Sāhasṛika,[4] the leader of one thousand foot-soldiers and Āyutika,[5] the commander of ten thousand foot-soldiers. The head of twenty horses or twenty elephants was known as

1. *Śukra*, IV, Sect. VII, 279-284.
2. *Śukra*, II, 140-46.
3. *Śukra*, II, 140-46.
4. *Ibid.*
5. *Ibid.*

Nāyaka.[1] The functions and duties of these officers have already been described in the last chapter. It is quite likely that these official designations were not used in all the administrations, but we can well presume that an organisation of somewhat similar type prevailed in all the governments.

The army had its own record office, where all the important documents concerning the military administration were kept. The officer in charge of this office was called *Lekhaka* according to Śukra. He kept a regular record of soldiers actually serving in the army and also of those, who had been discharged.[2] His duty was to keep a correct account of the amount paid to the soldiers by way of salaries and rewards after taking regular receipts for the payments made.[3] The caste, the stature, the age, the province and the residence of the soldiers were recorded, as also their scales of pay.[4]

CONSTITUENTS OF THE ARMY

Our records do not refer to the traditional Chaturaṅga army, which was an important feature of the military forces for a long time. They mention only the three arms of the fighting forces namely, the infantry, the cavalry and the elephant corps; the chariot forces and the chariot officers are altogether omitted in our epigraphs. Even the contemporary Muslim writers are silent about the chariot forces. Śukra no doubt refers to an officer called Rathādhyaksha. But as has already been stated, he was probably an officer in charge of the chariots used as military insignia by distinguished generals, military officers and ministers. The use of the chariot was allowed to military officers above the grade of the commander of a thousand troops.[5]

In IV. 7. 194 ff. Śukra refers to matchlockmen and artillery

1. *Śukra*, II, 147.
2. Sainikāḥ kati santyetaiḥ kati prāptantu vetanam
   Prāchīnāḥ ke Kutra gatāśchaitān vetti sa lekhakaḥ
   Śukra, II, 147
3. Kati dattaṁ hi bhrityebhyo vetanaṁ pāritoshikam
   Tatprāptipatraṁ gṛihṇīyāddadyādvetanapatrakam.
   Śukra, IV, Sect. VII, 389.
4. *Śukra*, IV, Sect. VII, 388.
5. *Śukra*, IV, Sect V, 389.

as forming part of the fighting forces. He refers to small and big fire arms; the former were about two and a half feet in length and were carried on their shoulders by soldiers; the latter were much bigger and were moved on carts and could be turned on a fulcrum. Śukra also gives details about the preparation of the gun-powder.

For reasons already explained we have to conclude that fire-arms were not known before *c.* 1300 A.D.; the above was one of the passages added to the book at the time of its latest redaction. We, therefore, do not include the artillery as a part of the army of the period under review.

In Bengal, the government during our period maintained naval forces in addition to the army. The records of the Pālas clearly show that they utilised the nautical aptitude of people in building up a regular fleet for fighting purposes. Contemporary records refer to this fleet as Naubala[1] or Nauvātaka and to the admiral in command as the Naukādhyaksha.[2] The Khalimpur plate of Dharmapāla describes this royal fleet as "proceeding on the path of the Bhāgīrathī", and thus making it "seem as if a series of mountain tops had been sunk to build another causeway to Rāma's bridge."[3] The force is here referred to as operating in the Gaṅgā and not in the sea. The reason probably was that the enemy was an Indian state in Bengal itself and not any external invader. The Sena records also refer to naval units of Bengal. In the Deopārā inscription of Vijayasena, the Bengal fleet is described as proceeding on a conquering expedition "up to the whole course of the Gaṅgā.[4] Their records, however, show a change in the nomenclature of admiral. The title Naukādhyaksha of the Pāla period was replaced by the designation Nauvyāpṛitaka or Naubala-Vyāpṛitaka in the Sena period.

STRENGTH OF THE ARMY

The *Śukranīti* throws some light upon the relative strength of the different constituents of the army. Infantry was to be

1. *I.A.*, XV, 306.
2. *E.I.*, IV, 248.
3. *E.I.*, I, 299.
4. *E.I.*, I, 305.

four times as numerous as the cavalry, the bull and the camel corps were to be one-fifth and one-eighth the size of the cavalry; the elephant corps was to be one-fourth the size of the camel corps, and the chariot corps was to be half the size of the elephant corps; the artillery was to be twice the size of the chariot corps.[1] That is to say if the infantry was 6,400 strong, the cavalry should 1,600, the bull, the camel and the elephant corps to be 320,200 and 50 respectively; the chariot corps was to be only 25 and the artillery 50. The reference to the artillery in this passage would raise doubts as to whether it gives a correct picture of the relative constituents of the army during our period. They may have also differed according to local circumstances; the elephant corps of the Pālas might have been stronger than that of the Pratīhāras; the camel corps of the latter might have been more numerous than that of their contemporaries. We may perhaps conclude that the infantry in our period used to be four or five times the cavalry. The strength of the elephant and camel corps might have varied with their availability and necessity. The bull corps was probably intended for transport purposes. The small number of the chariots would confirm our conjecture that they were in use as ceremonial conveyances for higher officers in the army, rather than as a fighting arm.

Epigraphs of our period are silent about the actual strength of the fighting forces of the different dynasties. Muslim writers sometimes give us some information, but it is not always reliable. Al Masudi says that his contemporary Pratīhāra king of Kanauj maintained four armies "according to the four quarters of the wind" and each of them numbered seven to nine lakhs.[2] The Pratīhāra empire was no doubt an extensive one including practically the whole of Northern India excluding Sindh, the Punjab, Kashmir and Bengal. But it is difficult to say whether it could have maintained an army of thirty six lakhs. Even the great Mauryas had not maintained so large a force. Probably each territorial army of the Pratīhāras could be increased to seven or

1. *Śukra*, IV, Sect., VII, 19-20.
2. *Elliot*, I, 23

eight lakhs, when a serious danger was apprehended in the area concerned. The total fighting force of the Gurjara-Pratīhāras may perhaps have been a million and a quarter.

The Chandella army might have been relatively a smaller one, but here again our authorities do not agree. Both Nizamuddin Ahmad[1] and Firishta[2] state that the cavalry under the Chandella king Gaṇḍa was 36,000 strong at the time of the invasion of Mahmud in 1011 A.D. But as regards the strength of the infantry, both give different statements. According to Nizamuddin Ahmad there were one lakh forty five thousand foot soldiers, while according to Firishta they were only forty five thousand. The normal strength of the infantry is likely to have been 45,000 in the army of Gaṇḍa but it might have been strengthened to the number of 1,45,000 by the contingents of his feudatories, advanced to meet the invader" as has been pointed out by Mahammad Nazim.[3] The normal strength of the cavalry may also have been less than 36,000.

As regards the elephant force of the Pālas there is no unanimity among the writers. Sulaiman and Al Masudi observe that it consisted of fifty thousand elephants[4] but Ibn-Khurdadba states that it was only five thousand strong.[5] It is important to note that Al Masudi adds that the reports in these matters were exaggerated. It is not unlikely that the strength of the elephant force of the Pālas was 5,000 rather than 50,000 though this number also seems to be a little exaggerated. Even Chandragupta Maurya, whose empire included practically the whole of India, had an elephant force of 9,000· It may well be doubted whether the Pāla elephant corps was really 50,000 strong.

The available evidence thus gives us only scanty and inconclusive information regarding the strength of the fighting forces maintained by the different kingdoms. In this connection we should note that according to the views of Śukra,

1. *Tubquat-i-Akbari*, Biblioth. Ind. p. 12.
2. *Briggs*, 64.
3. Muhammad Nazim, *Life and Times of Sultan Mahmud of Ghazna*, p. 111.
4. *Elliot*, I, p. 5.
5. *Ibid.*, p. 14.

fifty per cent of the state income was to be spent on the army[1]. This renders it very likely that the Chedis, the Chandellas, the Chaulukyas, the Chāhamānas, the Pratīhāras, the Gāhaḍavālas, the Pālas and the Senas might have maintained fairly big armies costing a good deal to the exchequer. If the strength of the army of the Pratīhāra empire was about a million and a quarter, the peace time strength of the armies of the smaller kingdoms into which it was eventually split, might well have been about a lakh.

RECRUITMENT OF THE ARMY

Śukra gives us interesting information about the composition, efficiency and recruitment of the army. We are told that the army consisted of permanent forces known as *Maula-bala*, which were hereditary in character. In times of need, the army was augmented from the battalions of the allies. Very often, fighting forces were borrowed from the feudatories also. This reminds us of the method of British Government, which allowed the feudatories to have their small forces, which could however be commandeered by the paramount power, when necessary. Sometimes soldiers from the army of a defeated enemy were also recruited. The army was usually supplied with weapons by the state itself. Sometimes soldiers themselves used to bring their weapons with them. We thus see that the armies of the different states of our period were far from homogeneous. Coherence and efficiency were therefore bound to be not very high, as is evident from the success scored by the Muslim invaders.

It may be noted that though Śukra refers to several varieties of the fighting forces of the army, like Kāmandaka, he regards the *Maulabala* among them as the best force. He advises the king to proceed against the enemy with an army mainly consisting of *Maula-bala*, as its members do not leave the king in the battlefield even at the point of death. The Muslim writers probably refer to *Maula-bala*, when they state that the troops in India are not paid by Indian kings, but maintain themselves without receiving any thing from them.[2] It is very likely that the *Maula-bala* was paid by land

1. *Śukra*, 1, 316, 7
2. *Elliot*, I, 7.

assignments rather than by pay in cash.

In addition to the *Maula-bala,* which was naturally local in character, soldiers were recruited from outside the state also. From the Bhagalpur plate of Nārāyaṇapāla we learn that under the Pālas the army was not merely composed of the troops from Gauḍa but it had recruits from Mālavā, Khasa, Karṇāṭa and Lāṭa countries.[1] The *Rājataraṅgiṇī* also informs us that the kings of Kashmir recruited mercenaries not only from Rajasthan, the Salt Range in the Punjab and distant Rājagṛiha in Magadha but also from the Yavanas and Turushkas.[2] The Chachnāmā reveals that the king Dāhior of Sindh had in his employ as many as 500 Arab troops under the leadership of Muhammad Allafi.[3] Mercenary soldiers were known as *bhṛita* bala.

Both the literary and epigraphical evidence show that the recruitment was thrown open to all classes. Śukra clearly states at one place that the soldiers may be selected from among the Śūdras, Vaiśyas and Kashtriyas and Mlecchas or from mixed castes,[4] provided they are brave, well built, devoted to their master and scrupulous in obeying the orders.[5] Even the Brāhmaṇas were admitted in the army. The Brāhmaṇa, who fights bravely in this world, says Śukra, gets fame; for the virtue of a Kshatriya is also derived from Brāhmaṇa.[6]

The records of our period reveal the names of a number of Brāhmaṇas, who actually served as soldiers and commanders in the armies. Thus from the Mahoba inscription we learn that a Brāhmaṇa general named Gopāla under the Chandella king Kīrtivarman vanquished the Chedi monarch Karṇa and reinstated his master on his ancestral throne.[7] Madanapālaśarman was another Brāhmaṇa general under the

1. *I.A.*, XV, 306.
2. *Rāj.*, VII, 168.
3. *Elliot.*, I, 156.
4. Raj. VIII. 727 shows that in Kashmir the recruitment was made from cultivators, artisans and carters on several occasions.
5. *Śukra*, II, 139.
6. *Śukra*, IV, Sect., VIII, 304
7. *E.I.*, I, 220

Chandella king Paramarddideva.[1] The Icchāwar plates, dated 1171 A.D., inform us that his father Thakkura Māheś-vara was a Brāhmaṇa of the Kṛishṇātreya Gotra, who studied the Śākhā of Chāndogya. Vaidyadeva, the Brāhmaṇa minister of the Pāla king Kumārapāladeva, had won two battles for his master; one in the southern part of Vaṅga and the other in the east.[2] Gauravamiśra, the Brāhmaṇa minister of Nārāyaṇapāla, is also stated to have shown bravery in the battlefield.[3]

The contemporary south Indian records also disclose the names of a number of Brāhmaṇa soldiers. Thus under the Rāshṭrakūṭa king Kṛishṇa III, Brāhmaṇa Gaṇaramma is stated to have laid down his life in a valiant manner, while defending his village.[4] The Kalas inscription of Govinda IV describes the glorious achievements of two Brāhmaṇa generals, namely Ravidāsa Dīkshita and Visottara Dīkshita, who are expressly described as *Somayājins* and ornaments of the Brāhmaṇa race.[5] Under the Gaṅga king Rāja-Rāja, his Brāhmaṇa general Māṇḍalika Vanapati is stated to have led an expedition against the Chola king Rājendra Chola, winning a victory[6] over him. Kholeśvara, a Brāhmaṇa minister and general of the Yādava king Siṅghaṇa, is said to have humbled the Gurjaras and Mālavas and destroyed the race of the heroic Ābhīra king.[7] Brāhmaṇa Krishṇarāma, served as a commander-in-chief under the Chola kings Rājarāja the great and Rājendra Chola.[8]

These examples will show that the view of Śukra, who was in favour of recruitments from all classes including the Brāhmaṇas was followed in our age. In the Deccan even Jains figure among the generals.

1. *I.A.*, XXV, 205-8.
2. *E.I.*, I, 348.
3. *E.I.*, II, 106.
4. *Ibid.*, XIII, 334
5. *Ibid.*, XIII, 189
6. *Ibid.*, IV, 314.
7. *A.S.I.W.C.*, III, 86.
8. *S.I.I.*, Vol. II, pt. 1, 139.

DISCIPLINE AND RULES

The soldiers in the regular state forces had to observe strict discipline. Military orders were communicated to them on every eighth day.[1] They had to keep the arms, the weapons and the uniforms quite bright.[2] They were not allowed to enter a village without a royal permit[3] and were forbidden to harass the villagers. They were, however, permitted to camp near the village, but outside[4] it. This clearly shows that soldiers, while on march, used to encamp on the outskirts of villages and towns and were not usually allowed to enter them except with the permission of the authorities.

PAY, GIFTS AND REWARDS

The soldiers other than those of the Maula-bala were regularly paid during our period. The *Agni-Purāṇa* states that a regular payment to troops is a factor of great importance in building up a strong army. Kāmandaka points out that a force, which is given its wages without delay, will fight with greater enthusiasm than a force, which is not properly paid.[5]

The records of our period show that the generals and officers were sometimes given land grants probably in lieu of cash salaries. The Icchawar plates inform us that the Chandella king Paramarddideva granted the village of Nandini in the Nandāvana Vishaya to his general Madanapāla-Śarman.[6] A rock inscription of the time of Bhojavarman states that the Chandella king Kīrtivarman appointed one Maheśvara as the Viśiṣa (commander ?) of Kālanjara and endowed him with the grant of the village of Pipalāshikā.[7]

1. *Śukra*; IV, Sect, VII, 381
2. *Śukra*, IV, Sect., 385.
3. Nṛipājñayā vinā grāmaṁ na viśeyuḥ kadāchana.
   Śukra, IV, Sect., VII. 383.
4. Grāmādbahiḥ samīpe tu sainikān dhārayet sadā.
   Śukra, IV, Sect., VII, 379.
5. *Kāmandaka*; XIII
6. *I.A.*, XXV, 205.
7. *E.I.*, I, 336.

Similarly another officer named Vāśe or Vāska on being appointed as the commander of the Chandella king Trailokyavarman, received the revenues of the village Vaibhari.[1] The system of making assignments to military chiefs was responsible for the rise of a military landed aristocracy. Members of the Maula-bala probably received the salaries in the form of land assignments. As far as ordinary soldiers were concerned, they were probably given salaries in cash. Śukra advises that full pay should be given to trained soldiers and half to soldiers under training[2].

Besides the regular pay, soldiers sometimes received special rewards. Śukra states that gifts should be given to soldiers according to importance of their achievements.[3] The army, which is well rewarded by gifts and honours and also well supplied with war provisions leads to victory. Śukra points out how a well rewarded army remains loyal even to an unrighteous and low-born king.[4] Kāmandaka also states that the king should give rewards to the soldiers after they succeed in the venture.

The epigraphical evidence shows that successful generals were sometimes rewarded with the assignments of land. The Charkhāri plate of the Chandella king Vīra-Varmadeva mentions the grant of a village in the Dāhi Viśaya to one Rauta Ābhi in recognition of a special deed of valour performed by him in the battle of Sondhi[5].

The contemporary South Indian records show that the practice of giving land grants to the officers in recognition of their valour prevailed there also; for instance, an inscription of the Eastern Chalukya king Amma I describes how the general Mahākāla more than once annihilated the enemy's army and how the gratified king rewarded him

1. *E.I.*, I, 337.
2. Sainīkāḥ Śikshitā ye ke teshu pūrṇā bhṛitiḥ smṛitā
   Vyūhābhyāse niyuktā ye teshvardhāṁ bhṛitimāvahet.
   Śukra, IV, Sect., VII, 390.
3. Pratyagrekarmaṇi kṛite yodhairdadyāddhanaṁ cha tān.
   Pāritoshyanchādhikāraṁ kramato'rhaṁ nṛipaḥ sadā,
   Śukra, IV, Sect, VII, 366.
4. *Śukra*, IV, Sect. VII, 462-63.
5. *E.I.*, XX, 132.

with the grant of the village Druffuru in the Pennātavādi Viśaya.[1] Another inscription of the same king refers to the gift of village Gonturu together with twelve hamlets to a general named Bhāṇḍanāditya, who had a glorious record of service to the state.[2]

Besides the salaries and gifts of land, officers and troops in Kashmir were occasionally given special or additional allowances on the eve of an expedition.[3] Such an allowance is not mentioned in the epigraphical records, probably because there was no occasion to refer to it. In stead of an allowance, Śukra recommends an increase of 24 per cent in the pay on the eve of an expedition.[4] We may, therefore, well presume that the practice of sanctioning higher emoluments during an expedition was usually followed by the kings of our period.

The soldiers who displayed special pluck or courage in the course of a battle were duly honoured; they received special cash or land grants as stated in the *Nītivākyāmṛita.* Similar but higher honours and rewards were given to captains and generals also. Promotions usually followed a successful engagement.

PENSION TO SOLDIERS' DEPENDENTS

The Government in our period considered it as its prime duty to support the dependents of the soldiers killed in the war. The *Nītivākyāmṛita* states that the king incurs a sin, if he does not maintain the relations of an officer who died in the service of the state.[5] Epigraphical records also show that the dependents of the dead soldiers were actually supported by the state. Sometimes even land grants were made for their maintenance. Thus we learn from Gārrā plates[6] that the Chandella king Trailokyavarman granted two villages for the maintenance of a person, whose father had been killed in the

1. *E.I.*, I, 134.
2. *S.I.*, 1, 42-43.
3. *Rāj.*, VII, 1457, VIII, 157: 808-10.
4. *Śukra*, IV. Sect., VII, 351.
5. *Nvk.* Chap. 30
6. *E.I.*, XVI, 227.

battle with Turks. It is expressly stated in the plates that the grant was made by way of maintenance for the heirs of one who laid down his life on the battle-field. This practice prevailed in the Deccan also[1] and we may well presume that it was generally followed in our period. Pensions to the dependents of ordinary soldiers might have been usually in the form of cash payments rather than land assignments.

DRILL AND EXERCISE

The army had to go through daily exercises. "The untrained, inefficient, raw recruits" says Śukra[2], "are like bales of cotton". The king should, therefore, arrange for daily military parades both in the morning and in the evening[3], and should promote strength and valour among the soldiers by means of hunting and games[4]. Kāmandaka attaches great importance to the daily exercise of troops. "By constant exercises," says he, "one becomes adept in the use of chariots, horses, elephants and boats and a past-master in archery."[5] He further states that even when the army is in camp, the daily drill should not be discontinued.[6]

Even earlier writers on polity have recognised the importance of drill and exercise of the army. Kauṭilya states that one can infuse spirit and enthusiasm even in the timid by means of discipline and training. The king should therefore not only arrange for the daily exercises of soldiers but should himself watch and encourage them.

1. *I.A.*, XII, 30.
2. *Śukra*, IV, Sect., VII, 180.
3. *Śukra*, IV, Sect., VII, 387.
4. *Śukra*, IV, Sect., VII, 16.
5. Rathāśvanau-kunjarayānayogyo nitya-kriyaḥ syāddhanushi pragalbhaḥ
   Sumedhasām karmaṇi dushkare'pi nityā kṛiya kauśalamādadhāti.

   Kāmandaka, XV, 50
6. Nirvriksha-kshapa-pāshāṇa-sthāṇu-valmikanirdravaiḥ
   Kārayetkāraṇaiśchitraiḥ sainyavyāyāmamanvaham.

   Kāmandaka, XVI, 18.

THE AMBULANCE CORPS

The ambulance arrangements for the army are not referred to in our inscriptions, but they are mentioned by *Rājataranginī*[1] The Arthaśāstra also refers to them.[2] We may well presume that they were common in our period.

1. *Rāja*, VIII, 741.
2. *A.Ś.*, BK. X. Chap. 3.

CHAPTER VI

TERRITORIAL DIVISIONS AND ADMINISTRATION

Let us now discuss the scheme of territorial divisions in vogue in Northern India during our period. It has to be observed at the outset that it was not at all uniform and it differed with different dynasties. Several kingdoms flourished in Northern India during our period of survey; out of these, some were fairly big, but others were very small. Under these circumstances we should naturally find a variety in the dimensions and nomenclature of the different territorial and administrative divisions in the various kingdoms. It may be noted that even in a unitary state like the Indian Republic, we have Tehsils in some states and Talukas in others; similarly there are Commissioner's Divisions in some states and Boards of Revenues in others.

The biggest administrative division under the Pratīhāras,[1] the Pālas[2] and the Senas[3] was known as Bhukti.[4] It was usually presided over by an officer called Uparika under the Pālas, as was the case under the Imperial Guptas. Under the Senas, he was given a more high sounding epithet, namely Bṛihaduparika.[5] We do not know whether there were ordinary Uparikas working under him.

Bhukti usually comprised a number of Vishayas and thus corresponded to the size of a Commissioner's Division in modern times. Thus under the Pratīhāras, the Śrāvastī-Bhukti and the Kānyakubjabhukti in U.P.[6] were divided into Maṇḍalas and the latter into Vishayas. Under the Pālas and the Senas, the Śrīnagara-Bhukti in Bihar included Patna and Gaya

1. *I.A.*, XII, 140.
2. *E.I.*, XXIII, 290.
3. *E.I.*, XXI. 218.
4. The term Rājya, which denoted the province in Kashmir, was not in use in that sense in the rest of Northern India. The Kashmir valley was divided into three *rājyas* Kramarājya, Maṇḍavarājya and Lohārarājya (*Rāj.*, II, 87).
5. *E.I.*, XXI, 217.
6. *I.A.*, XV, 112-3, *E.I.*, XIX, p. 18.

districts.[1] The Tīrabhukti was obviously identical with modern Tirhut division in Bihar; it may probably have consisted of four districts, Saran, Champaran, Muzaffarpur and Darbhanga, as it does now.[2] The Pauṇḍravardhana-bhukti in Bengal, comprised Dinajpur, Bogra and Rajashahi districts.[3] The Kaṅkāgrāma-bhukti embraced a considerable portion of the valley of the Mor River and included parts of the Birbhum and Murshidabad districts.[4] The exact dimension of the Vardhamāna-bhukti[5] cannot be definitely ascertained. It embraced the valley of the Damodar river and is known to have included Uttararādhā and Daṇḍabhukti Maṇḍalas.

Under the Gāhaḍavālas, however, the biggest administrative division was called Deśa, which also corresponded to the modern commissioner's Division, and is thus identical with the Bhukti of the Pālas, the Senas and the Pratīhāras. Thus Pāñchāla is referred to as a *deśa*[6] and may have included most of the modern Rohilkhand.

The next administrative term that we come across is Maṇḍala. It is referred to in the Pratīhāra, the Paramāra the Chaulukya and the Sena records, but not in the same sense. In Bengal under the Senas, it is sometimes used to denote an area wider than a Vishaya but sometimes also to an area smaller than it. Thus in the Khalimpur plate of Dharmapāla, Vyāghrataṭamaṇḍala is used to denote an area wider than a Vishaya, as it included Mahantaprakāśa-Vishaya.[7] The Bāngarḥ grant[8] of Mahīpāla, on the other hand, refers to Gokulikā-maṇḍala as being comprised in the Koṭivarsha-Vishaya. Similarly the Manhali grant of Madanapāla[9] and the Amāgacchi[10] grant of Vigrahapāla IV refer to Halavartta-maṇḍala and Brāhmaṇigrāma-maṇḍala as included in the Koṭivarsha-Vishaya. The term Maṇḍala, when used to denote an area larger

1. *E.I.*, XXIII, 290.
2. *I.A.*, XV, 307.
3. *I.A.*, XXI, 99.
4. R.C. Majumdar, *History of Bengal*, p. 28.
5. R.C. Majumdar, *History of Bengal*, p. 28.
6. Pāñchāladeśe śrī jiavati pattalāyāṁ usithā grāme. *E.I.*, II, 359.
7. *E.I.*, IV, 252.
8. *E.I.*, XII, 328.
9. *J.A.S.B.*, 1900, LXIX, p. 66-73.
10. *I.A.*, XV, 166-68.

than a Vishaya, may perhaps have been used to denote a sub-division of Bhukti larger than Vishaya.

Under the Pratīhāras, Maṇḍala was used to denote a territorial division larger than a Vishaya but smaller than a Bhukti. Thus Kālañjara-maṇḍala was a division of Kānyakubja-Bhukti and included Udumbara Vishaya[1] in it. Similarly Śrāvastī-maṇḍala was a division of Śrāvastī-Bhukti and included Valayika-Vishaya[2] in it.

Under the Paramāras and Chaulukyas, Maṇḍala was apparently used for a district.[3]

In one of the Gāhaḍavāla records, we get a reference to the term Pathaka in between Deśa or the Commissioner's Division and Pattalā or Taluka.[4] It may therefore be taken as corresponding to the modern district and ancient Vishaya.

Under the Pālas, Vishaya was used in the sense of a modern district, being a division of Bhukti. Under the Senas, however, it is sometimes stated to be a division of Bhukti and sometimes a division of Maṇḍala. Under Gāhaḍavālas and the Paramāras, Vishaya was used to denote a Taluka and not a district.

The exact dimension of a Vishaya cannot be definitely ascertained. We get the names of several administrative divisions in between the Vishaya and Grāma or village, whose natures and dimensions varied with different dynasties. The Pāla and the Sena records usually refer to Vīthi after Vishaya or Maṇḍala. Thus from the Naihati grant we learn that Svalpadakshiṇā Vīthi was a sub-division of Uttararādhā-maṇḍala.[5] In the Śaktipur copper plate of Lakshamaṇasena, the largest division is no doubt Kaṅkāgrāma-bhukti, but it is difficult to say, which of the two other sub-divisions, the Madhugirimaṇḍala or the Dakshiṇā-vīthi was the larger one.[6] If we assume that the names of the different units are given in this record in an ascending scale in regard to their jurisdiction, then it is clear that the Madhugiri-maṇḍala was smaller than Dakshiṇāvīthi.

1. *E.I.*, XIX. p. 18.
2. *I.A.*, XV, 112-113.
3. *E.I.*, XI, 182.
4. *E.I.*, V, 114.
5. *E.I.*, XIV, 156-63.
6. *E.I.*, XXI, 211-19.

The Nālandā grant[1] of Dharmapāla shows that a Vishaya was a division bigger than a Vīthi, as in that record the Jambunadī-vīthi is stated to be included in the Gayā-Vishaya. Similarly the Kumudasūtra-vīthi was included in the Gayā-Vishaya in the Nālandā grant of Devapāla.[2]

Besides Vīthi, there were many other sub-divisions in Bengal between Vishaya and village known as Khāṭikā, Vṛitti and Chaturikā. The exact dimensions of the sub-divisions, however, cannot be definitely ascertained. The Govindapur grant of Lakshmaṇasena refers to Valadda-Chaturika as situated in the Pashchima-Khāṭikā of the Vardhamāna-bhukti, from which it will appear that a Khāṭikā was a larger area than Chaturikā.[3]

As regards the relation between Vṛitti and Chaturikā, the Madhiānagar grant of Lakshmaṇasena refers to Khaṇḍa-Vṛitti in Varendṛi in Puṇḍra-vardhana-Bhukti, without showing any relation of it to other units prevalent at that time.[4] The Sahitya Parishad grant refers to Madhukshirikā-vṛitti placed under Nānya (Maṇḍala?), which again was situated in Vaṅga.[5] This grant, however, shows that a Vṛitti was larger than a Chaturikā, the latter containing a number of Pāṭakas.

Under the Gāhaḍavālas, the terms Pattalā and Vishaya seem to have denoted a division of the dimension of the modern Tāluka. As both these terms do not figure simultaneously in one and the same inscription, one may probably be taken as the variant of the other. Under the Chedis also, the Taluka was denoted by the term Pattalā.[6]

The Pattalā was divided into Paraganās under the Paramāras. They are sometimes denoted by the term Pathaka and sometimes by the term Pratijāgaraṇaka. As both these terms do not figure in one and the same record, one may be taken to be a variant of the other. Under the Pratīhāras also, Paraganā is denoted by the term Pathaka.

1. *E.I.*, XXIII, 240.
2. *E.I.*, XVII, 310-17.
3. *I.B.*, 92-98.
4. *J.A.S.B.*, Vol. V, 467.
5. *I.B.*, 140-48.
6. *E.I.*, XIX, 18; *I.A.*, XVII, 226.

The Pathaka was sometimes divided into two parts. Thus Daśapur Pathaka under the Pratīhāras, had two divisions, namely eastern and western Pāthakas.[1] Under the Paramāras also, Nāgadraha and Ujjayini were both divided into Eastern and Western Pathakas.[2] This reminds us of the present division of eastern and western Khandesh or of Northern and Southern Satara district in Maharashtra State.

The Pratijāgaraṇaka or the Paraganā consisted of a number of groups of villages. Thus under the Paramāras, Nyāyapadraka group contained 17,[3] Makhāla 42,[4] Varakheṭaka 63,[5] Bhaillasvāmī 12[6], Muktāpali 84,[7] Bṛimgāri 64,[8] Voḍasira 48[9], Tinispadra 12,[10] and Savasisole 16.[11] Under the Chaulukyas, Makhulagāmva group contained 42[12] villages and that of Dhadhārika 12.[13] Under the Chandellas, Khaṭauḍa group contained villages, Haṭa 18 and Tānla 12.[14] Under the Chāhamānas, Tānukūpa, Ghaḍahaḍika and Khattaṇḍā were the headquarters of 12 villages.[15] These units seem to have been known after the name of the important towns or villages situated in them. Śukra[16] refers to officers over 10 and 100 villages, and Mānasollāsa to officers over 10, 20 and 100 villages. In actual practice this decimal system seems not to have been followed and there were groups of all kinds of odd number of villages like 12, 16, 17, 18, 42, 63, 64, etc.

The village was the lowest unit of administration. It however consisted of several Pāṭakas or small settlements under the Gāhaḍavālas. Thus Kailāśa-grāma had 8 Pāṭakas[17]

1. *E.I.*, XVI, 182.
2. *I.H.Q.*, VIII, 311-313; *I.A.*, VI, 53.
3. *E.I.*, XVIII, p. 322.
4. *E.I.*, III, 48.
5. *I.A.*, XIX, 350.
6. *I.A.*, XVIII, 344-48.
7. *E.I.*, XIX, 71.
8. *I.A.*, XVII, 243.
9. *I.A.*, XVI, 252.
10. *I.A.*, XIV, 159-61.
11. *J.A.S.B.*, VII, 32.
12. *Ibid.*, XVIII, 80-85.
13. *I.A.*, VI, 193-94.
14. *E.I.*, IV, 157-60.
15. *E.I.*, II, 109; *I.A.*, VI, 193-4; *E.I.*, IV, 157.
16. *Śukra*, IV, 5. 76.
17. *E.I.*, IV, 131-133.

and Godanti-grāma had two Pāṭakas.[1] Similarly Kusuphaṭa-grāma and Bhādapa Nāndapa Grāma had also several Pāṭakas.[2] The term Pāṭaka may probably correspond to the term Vadi current in Maharashṭra, denoting small settlements on the periphery of a village.

PROVINCIAL ADMINISTRATION

Big provinces like the Uttarāpatha or Ujjayini under the Mauryas, the Antarvedi between the Yamunā and the Narmadā under the Guptas and Vanavāsi under the Rāshṭra-kūṭas were non-existent during our period in northern India. Pratīhāras had a fairly big empire stretching over a great part of northern India, but it had provinces in the modern sense of the term like Kathiawar, Mālwā and Jejākabhukti. These were under governors, and their charges were known as Maṇḍalas. Under the Chaulukyas, Saurashṭra and Narma-dātaṭa had the status of Maṇḍalas. The Governors of these Maṇḍalas often belonged to the military cadres. Thus Vīsaladeva, who later became Mahāmaṇḍaleśvara over Nar-madātaṭa was a Daṇḍanāyaka in the reign of Kumārapāla. Governors were often transferred. Thus Salaksha was earlier a Governor of Surashtra and was later transferred to Lāṭa in the same capacity.

The title Maṇḍaleśvara given to provincial governors would show that there was a tendency of their becoming feudatory rulers. Provincial governors were executive and revenue officers in charge of the revenue collection and were res-ponsible for maintaining law and order. They were the immediate controlling authorities over the Bhukti and Vishaya officers and were appointed by the king himself.

BHUKTI ADMINISTRATION

The next biggest administrative unit of our age was a Bhukti; its governor was known as an Uparika in the Gupta period; this title continued to be in vogue in Bengal in our

1. *I.A.*, XVIII, 134-36.
2. *E.I.*, XXVI, 272.

age. He must have had under him an *adhikaraṇa* or office, which dealt with the various branches of the Bhukti administration. Officers in charge of the Maṇḍalas, Vishayas and the Pāṭakas worked under his general supervision. Although our records are silent on the point, we cannot be far wrong in assuming that the governor of the Bhukti was in charge of collecting state revenues. Śukra points out that officers of a status equal to that of a Śāmanta were to collect the royal revenue[1]. A little later he observes that Sāmanta was a title of an officer over 100 villages.[2] We may, therefore, well presume that the revenue collection was one of the main duties of the heads of the Bhukti, district and lower administrations.

Although our records throw no direct light upon the functions of the officer of Bhukti, it is not unlikely that he had to maintain law and order, supervise over the administration of justice and to carry on the works of public utility. Probably he had a small fighting force under him to help him in the work of maintaining law and order. He was also expected to submit a periodical report to the central government relating to the work done by him or the condition of his division.[3]

MANDALA ADMINISTRATION

Maṇḍala was in charge of an officer called Maṇḍaleśvara. In Gujarat under the Chaulukyas he was assisted by officers known as Daṇḍanāyakas, who were subordinate to him. In one of the inscriptions of Ajayapāla, we find a Mahāmaṇḍaleśvara ordering a Daṇḍanāyaka. Besides discharging police and military duties, Daṇḍanāyakas were often in charge of tax collection.[4] Daṇḍanāyakas were in course of time often promoted to the position of a Maṇḍaleśvara. Thus Vijayaka, who was first merely a Daṇḍanāyaka of Nādula[5] later became a Mahāmaṇḍaleśvara ruling over Narmadātaṭa.[6]

1. *Śukra*; I, 181.
2. *Śukra*; I, 191.
3. *Śukrā*; II, 294-5.
4. *B.G.* I, II, p. 451.
5. Bali Inscription, *P.R.A.S.W.C.*, 1907-8, p. 55.
6. Bombay Secretariat Grant of Ajayapāla.

DISTRICT ADMINISTRATION

We do not derive much information about the district administration from our records. It was presided over by an officer, who was given the designation of Vishayapati[1] or Vishayika in Bengal. His designation under other dynasties, where he governed over a Maṇḍala, is not known. He may have received his orders usually from the officer in charge of Bhukti. His functions were similar to those of the head of a Bhukti; but were confined to his smaller charge.

Under the Guptas, the Vishayapati enjoyed the right of selling the waste land under his jurisdiction, on behalf of the central government. Whether the same practice prevailed during our period also, we do not know, for our records are silent on this point.

The district officers were often recruited from the military cadre. The Daṇḍanāyakas, who figure very frequently in the Chaulukya, Sena and Pāla records, were probably military officers of the status of colonels and were often in charge of the administration of the Vishayas as also of the Maṇḍalas. Thus under the Chaulukya king Ajayapāladeva in 1137 A.D., Daṇḍanāyaka Vaijalladeva was ruling over the entire Narmadāṭaṭamaṇḍala.[2]

The district officer, like the Bhukti governor, was probably assisted in his work by police and C.I.D. officers such as Daṇḍapāśikas and Chauroddharaṇikas, whose duties were to apprehend criminals and to send them to the law courts for trial. Chāṭas and Bhaṭas, also worked under their supervision.[3]

It is difficult to say whether there existed judicial courts in the districts, for the records of our period do not refer to them. During the Gupta period, we find that there were the courts of justice in the districts, administered by specially appointed officers with the assistance of jurors trained in law. The same was probably the case during our period also, as

1. *I.A.*, XV, 306.
2. *A.S.I.W.C.*, 1907-8, 55.
3. R.C. Majumdar and A.S. Altekar; *The Age of the Vākāṭakas*, p. 285. For Chāṭas and Bhaṭas see p. 299.

is indicated by the seals of Dharmādhikāriṇs and Dharmaśāsanādhikaraṇa found at Nālandā.

During the Gupta period, we find that the Central Government could not sell the waste land owned by it before securing the concurrence of the district councils. Nay, there are even some copper plates, which, while making the grants of the waste land, actually bear the seal of the district administration as a proof of its approval.[1] Whether such powers were enjoyed by the district administration during our period is not revealed by our inscriptions.

Whether the district officers during our period were guided by any non-official council, as was the case under the Guptas, cannot be stated due to want of evidence. The contemporary Deccan records show that the Vishayapati was not the only governing authority. There was also a non-official district council, the members of which were known as Vishayamahattaras. Unfortunately the records do not give us any information about the existence and functioning of any district councils The districts were divided into Talukas, Vīthis, Pratijāgaraṇakas, and the latter into groups of villages as already indicated. But we do not get any details about their administration. They probably had a revenue officer to supervise and direct the revenue and executive functions.

TOWN ADMINISTRATION

The inscriptions of our period do not give us detailed information about the town administration. It was probably carried on by an officer appointed by the central government. Unfortunately due to the absence of epigraphical evidence, it is difficult to say by what name the head of the town administration was known; in the contemporary Deccan, under the Rāshṭrakūṭas and the Śilāhāras, he was designated as Purapati or Nagarapati. In Kāshmir the term Nagarādhipa was in use[2] Probably a similar term was also current in northern India.[3]

1. *E.I.*, XI, 107.
2. *Raj.*, VI, 70.
3. The Siyadoni inscription refers to an officer called Mahara, perhaps meaning the chief. But the record being fragmentary does not

The Purapati or Nagarapati was the most important officer of the town. Unfortunately satisfactory epigraphical evidence being not available, it is difficult to say what were the qualifications expected in him. Very often he was a military officer; Luṇapāsaka, who was in charge of the town of Udaipur under the Chaulukya king Ajayapāladeva, was a Daṇḍanāyaka.[1] Whether more importance was given to the military ability than to the administrative experience we do not know. Probably both were given due consideration. The contemporary Deccan records also show that very often the governor of the town was selected from among the military captains. Thus Rudrapayya, who was once a bodyguard of the Rāshṭrakūṭa king Kṛishṇa III, was acting later as a prefect of the town of Saravatura in Karnāṭaka.[2] Mahādeva and Pātāladeva, who were the Daṇḍaṇāyakas of the Chaulukya king Jagadekamalla, were also appointed as the joint prefects of Bādāmī in 1140.[3] Sometimes the heads of the town had literary predelictions, the twelve officers in charge of Teridal in Southern Maratha country are all described as promoting the everlasting six systems of Philosophy.[4] All this evidence clearly shows that the Purapati was sometimes selected for military ability, sometimes for administrative experience and sometimes for their learning, both in the Deccan and in Northern India.

When a place like Gwalior happened to be both a town and a fort, we come across slightly different administrative arrangement. The Gwalior inscription of the Pratīhāra king Bhoja refers to Allā as Koṭṭapāla, the commander of the fort, appointed by the emperor and to Tattaka as Balādhikṛita, the commander of the forces. It also refers to a committee consisting of two Śreshṭhis (guild presidents) and one Sārthavāha (caravan-leader) apparently selected or elected. In such cases, the commander of the fort and commander of the

enable us to state whether he was the Governor of the town or whether he was one of the officers. (*E.I.*, I, 173-9).

1. *I.A.*, XVIII, 347-8.
2. *I.A.*, XII. 258.
3. A.S. Altekar, *Rāshṭrakūṭas*, p. 182.
4. *I.A.*, XV, 15.

army were obviously in charge of military administration, whereas the civil administration was perhaps entrusted to a committee probably presided over by Purapati. This inscription does not refer to Purapati or Nagarapati. Can it be that the Koṭṭapāla himself might have exercised Purapati's powers and may have presided over the above committee? His duty was to maintain the internal peace and to collect the royal revenue.

The city affairs were managed by the Purapati with the help of a non-official committee, which was called by different names in the different parts, of the country. At Ghalop in Rajasthan, it was called Chaukaḍikā,[1] while under the Chandellas and Chaulukyas it was known as Pañchakula.[2] In the Gupta age, the term Pañchamaṇḍalī seems to have been common. The town committees existed in the Deccan of our period also; we find one functioning at Guṇapura.[3]

The inscriptions being silent, it is difficult to state as to who were eligible to become the members of the town committee. Whether the members were selected by the government or whether there was an election is not revealed by our records. It appears very probable that the people of the town themselves selected elderly and experienced persons of good and noble character as the members of the town committee.[4] Functional considerations may have often governed their choice. One Bhinmal inscription of Kṛishṇarāja Paramāra, dated 1067 A.D., informs us, how the committee consisted of persons of different castes and professions, one being a Sauvarṇika or a goldsmith, one being a Śreshṭhī or a prominent merchant and so on.[5] The com-

1. *E.I.*, XI, 39.
2. *E.I.*, I, 173.
3. *E.I.*, III, 260.
4. There is no direct evidence for the statement, but it is rendered very probable by the circumstance that the members of the village council were described as *grāmamahattaras* or *grāmamahattamas*. Mahattara indicated either a person of high status or an elderly person (Apte's Dictionary) but in ancient times high status was not usually associated with young age.
5. *B.G.*, I. 473.

mittee at Guṇapura consisted of one Brāhmaṇa, one merchant and two bankers.[1]

Sometimes the town was divided into several wards, each of which used to send its own representatives to the committee. Thus the Nāḍol stone inscription of the king Rājyapāla informs us that the town of Ghalop was divided into eight wards, known as Wāḍas, each of which used to send two representatives.[2] The Pañchakula thus did not consist of five members only, as may be suggested by the term *pañcha*, but of a large number of representatives sent by different wards. The term *Pañcha* in words like *pañchakula* or *panchamaṇḍalī* had no exact numerical significance ; the modern pañchanāmā has only two witnesses. The strength of the town committee was 16 at Ghalop and 30 at Uttaramerur. It seems to have varied according to the size of the towns.

How the members of the wards were elected or selected cannot be stated with certainty for want of evidence. It is, however, certain that some kind of election or selection took place for constituting the town committee, since these members were non-officials. It may be that lots also were drawn from among the eligibles, as was done in the Tamil country during our period of survey. The election by lots no doubt now looks odd, but it was not unknown to ancient Greek democracy also.

It was the duty of the town committee to maintain peace and order in the town and to apprehend the law-breakers. The Nāḍol stone inscription informs us that if a theft took place in any ward, it was the duty of the committee to apprehend the thief, no doubt with the cooperation of the representatives of wards. The Central Government of the day also used to help it in tracing the lost articles by supplying it with money, weapons and watchmen.

The Town Committee also looked after routine adminis-

1. The earlier practice, as indicated by the Dāmodarpur plates, often favoured functional representation; bankers, traders and writers were represented at Puṇḍravardhana by the most senior members of their guilds or professions.

E.I., XII, 130.

2. *E.I.*, XI, 39.

trative work such as the collection of taxes,[1] the maintenance of records and the correspondence with the Central Government. It also supervised the markets through the officer called Kauptika.[2] It probably carried out the different works of public utility such as repairing and constructing roads and maintaining gardens, temples and educational institutions, as was the case in the contemporary South India.

Whether the Town Committee was divided into sub-committees for the convenience of work, is not revealed by our records. In the Mauryan period, we find that the town committee of big cities like Pāṭaliputra was divided into sub-committees, each being entrusted with a particular function. A similar state of affairs prevailed at Uttaramerur in south India during our period. We have, however, no evidence as to whether it prevailed in Northern India during our age.

The Town Committee had its own executive, which used to carry on the business of the town administration. It was called Vāra in Rajasthan and central India under the Chāhamānas and Pratīhāras.[3] Under the Chāhamānas, the executive was changed annually, for the Bhinmal inscription of 1067 A.D. clearly refers to one Jogachandra as the member of the executive for the current year.[4] In the Siyādoni inscription, however, we find one Aśvānarasindhu functioning as a member of the committee once in 967 and then again in 969 A.D.[5] It appears that the members of the executive committee were elected for more than one year at Siyādoni, unless we assume that Aśvānarasindhu was being annually 're-elected'.

The strength of the executive committee varied according to the needs of the situation. If the town was a big one, its executive committee would naturally have consisted of a larger number of members; while in case of small towns, there would have been only a few members in the executive. The

1. *E.I.*, I. 188.
2. *E.I.*, U, 188.
3. *E.I.*, I, 178-79, *E.I.*, I. 188
4. *B.G.*, I, 473.
5. *E.I.*, 173-79,

Gwalior inscription of the Pratīhāra king Bhoja informs us that there were three members of the executive committee at Gwalior.[1] The Bhinmal inscription of 1067 A.D. on the other hand informs us that the executive consisted of 4 members.[2] At Siyādoni however, there were only two members in the executive.[3]

The Vārikas, or the members of the executive committee, carried on their work in an office known as Sthāna in Rājapūtānā, where all important charters were deposited and a careful record of important documents was kept. The Pehoā inscription clearly informs us how the horse dealers at Pehoā, after having executed a deed of voluntary cess from buyers and sellers, passed a formal resolution and deposited its copy in the office (Sthāna) of the town-committee in order to enable it to collect the dues in future according to the agreed scheme.[4]

The executive of the town committee used to have its own Karaṇika or writer, whose post was probably permanent. Unfortunately due to the absence of epigraphical evidence, we are not in a position to state whether he was appointed by the Government or by the committee. It appears very probable that he was a local resident and was appointed to the post with the approval of the members of the town committee. His duty was to maintain the office records in the proper order. He was, if necessary, assisted in his work by some assistants, though they are not referred to in our records.

Besides the secretary, there was also another officer called Kauptika, whose duty was to collect the market dues, which formed one of the important sources of income of the town administration.

Let us now briefly survey the different sources of revenue of the town committee. The tax on shops and houses was one source of the town revenue. The second source was the octroi duties collected within the jurisdiction of the town. Probably the town committee also received a portion of the

1. *E.I.*, I, 154-60.
2. *B.G.*, I, 473.
3. *Ibid.*, I, 173-79.
4. *E.I.*, I, 188.

fines. The central government often helped the committee with funds in carrying out the different works of public utility, if they were of considerable magnitude.

VILLAGE ADMINISTRATION

Village has been the most stable unit of administration from early times. As usual, village administration was presided over by the village headman. He was called by different names under the different dynasties. In Bengal under the Pālas, the headman was known as Grāmapati,[1] while under the Paramāras, he was designated as Paṭṭakila.[2] Under the Gāhaḍavālas in U.P. the title of the village headman was Mahattaka.[3]

The post of village headman was usually hereditary. The Paramāra records often refer to hereditary Paṭṭakilas. One of them shows that Janha and his father Cahila were both Paṭṭakilas.[4] It is however not unlikely that if the succession of the son was not approved by the government, it might be appointing a colateral in his place.

There were some villages assigned to scholars, some to pious Brāhmaṇas, some to military captains and some to high government officers. Unfortunately we do not know whether these donees were only entitled to the enjoyment of the income of the villages or whether they supervised over their administration also. In the South, however, the donees were only entitled to enjoy the income. This clearly indicates that the assignment of villages to Brāhmaṇas and military captains did not interfere with the normal scheme of administration and the headman continued to function in all villages, whether alienated or unalienated.

Normally there was one headman for each village in Northern India during our period. Such was not, however, the case in the Deccan. Under the Raṭṭas of Saundatti and the later Chālukyas of Kalyāṇi, we find a village being

1. *I.A.*, XV, 306.
2. *I.A.*, XIX, 349.
3. *E.I.*, II, 359-61.
4. *Pr. Rep. A.S.I.W.C.* 1913, p. 56.

governed by several headmen. The five Raṭṭa records of Saundatti inform us that there were twelve headmen in each of the three villages, namely Sugandhavatī, Elerava and Hasudi, while the village of Hirayakummi had six.[1] One of the recdrds of the Chālukya king Vikramāditya VI shows that the village Teridal had twelve headmen.[2] It is difficult to say whether in reality there were so many headmen in one village. It is very likely that under the Chālukyas and the Raṭṭas, there might be a custom of allowing the senior representatives of the main branches of the original headman's family to officiate simultaneously. Even today we find in Mahārāshṭra two headmen representing the two main branches of the original stock functioning in several villages, one in charge of the revenue work and the other of the police duties. It is very likely that the same principle might have been followed there during our period of survey also.

The village headman was the most important officer of the village administration. He was in custody of the village records. A number of epigraphs show, how even the king used to consult formally the village headman at the time of granting a piece of land in the village. Thus from one of the Gāhaḍavāla grants of 1109, we learn that Govindachandra consulted the village headman called Śrī Gāṅgeya, when he made a grant of one Seerā of land measuring four ploughs.[3] The Kamauli grant of the same ruler informs us that, while granting the village of Usithā in the Jiāvatipattala in the Pāṅchāla-deśa to the Brāhmaṇa Vithākeyadīkshita, Govindachandra took the 'consent' (*sammati*) of not only the Purohita, the queen and other members of the ministry but also of the Mahattaka Vālhaṇa.[4] From the Basāhi grant, we learn that the views of the same Mahattaka Vālhaṇa were ascertained by the king Govindchandra, when he granted the village of Vasabhi to the Brāhmaṇa Ālheka.[5] All this evidence clearly indicates that under the Gāhaḍavāla ruler,

1. *J.B.B.R.A.S.*, X, 283; A.S. Altekar, *Rāshṭrakūṭas*, 189.
2. *I.A.* XIV, 14.
3. *I.A.*, VIII, 15-17.
4. *E.I.*, II, 359-61; See p. no. 3.
5. *I.A.*, XIV, 103-4.

the views of the village headman were ascertained, when the king proposed to make any land grant. The village headman was a custodian of records and had an accurate information about the revenue of the village and of the ownership of the different pieces of land situated in it. It was therefore but natural that he should have been consulted at the time of land grant. The consultation was probably to ascertain whether there were any administrative difficulties; it does not suggest that the consent of the headman was a *sine-qua-non* for the grant of a village or a piece of land by a king.

DUTIES OF THE HEADMAN

The most important duty of the village headman was to preserve law and order in the village; for this purpose he used to have a local militia under him. During our period, the rebellions of feudatories were frequent. Sometimes the peace of villages was also disturbed by the rivalries of adjacent villages. The headman, on such occasions, had to discharge the duties of a military captain and often to lay down his life, while defending the homes of the fellow villagers. Unfortunately the North Indian inscriptions of our period do not give us any specific instance of a village headman giving his life, while fighting for the protection of his village. Śukra, however, says that the headman should protect the villagers from thieves and dacoits,[1] suggesting thereby that it was the duty of the headman to preserve law and order and apprehend bad characters and robbers. He must have discharged this duty with the help of village police or militia.

In the contemporary Deccan records we come across a number of instances of the village headmen fighting and dying for their villages. A number of inscriptions of the Rāshṭrakūṭa kings Krishṇa II, Krishṇa III and Karkka II inform us, how in the skirmishes caused by the cattle-lifting propensity, number of village headmen gave up their lives.[2]

1. Ādharshakebhyaśchorebhyo hyadhikārigaṇāt tathā.
Prajā-saṁrakshaṇe daksho, grāmapo mātṛipitṛivat.
Śukra. II, 171.

2. *E.C.*, VIII, Sorab No. 234.

In Northern India, during our period of survey, as observed already, there were constant wars going on between the different dynasties; the villagers therefore could not have enjoyed complete peace. They had to be self-reliant in defence and to be expert in the use of arms, as owing to communications being slow, it was not possible for the central government to help them by providing military or police aid at the nick of time, when there were sudden raids of bandits and robbers.

The next duty of the village headman was to collect the village revenues and to pay them into the royal treasury. This is evident from a number of inscriptions, which, while referring to village and land grants, generally mention the name of the village headman. Even in the extreme south in the Tamil country, where village councils had become permanent bodies, meeting regularly and functioning methodically, we find the village headman collecting the village revenues.

When the government wanted to make any extra demand from the villagers, it was the village headman, who used to carry on negotiations on behalf of the villagers. According to Śukra,[1] he was to protect the village against the government officers. This would suggest that it was his duty to resist unfair demands.

We do not know whether the headman was assisted in his work of the collection by other officers also, for our inscriptions do not throw any light on this point. As far as the small village is concerned, it is very likely that the headman himself would have collected the revenues, but in case of big villages, it is not improbable that he would have been assisted in his work by other village officers.

Settlement of village disputes was also another important duty of the village headman. Being the village magistrate, he had the right of trying petty criminal cases. Civil cases were probably settled by the village Pañchāyat, meeting under the chairmanship of the headman.

Besides the setttlement of village disputes, the headman had to look after the works of public utility. He had also to entertain and make arrangements for the boarding and lodg-

1. *Śukra*, II, 171.

ing of the officers of the central government, when they paid their visits to the villages.

The headman was remunerated for his services in various ways. It is difficult to say whether in Northern India, he was given rent-free land for his services; the records so far discovered are usually silent on this point. In the Deccan, however, the headman used to have his own rent-free land. One of the records of the Raṭṭas of Saundatti clearly states, how Govinda of Kadole alienated 200 *mattars* of cultivable land, which was enjoyed by him as his rent-free land.[1] This record clearly shows that the headman not only enjoyed rent-free land but had also the right of alienating it. Whether all the headmen of the Deccan during our period enjoyed this right, we do not know.

The headman was entitled to a number of petty dues in kind, which consisted of articles like *Guṛa*, *Ghee*, betel leaves, etc. These were described as *Maulika-arhaṇas* or requisites of hereditary officers in Kalachūri records.[2] Our inscriptions further refer to *Bhogakara*, which probably represented petty taxes in kind on fruits, vegetables, etc., paid by the villagers as a government tax. It is important to note that as the king could exact these taxes only when on tour, they were usually assigned in practice to the village headman, most probably as a part of his pay.

The village headman was not usually a Brāhmaṇa by caste, as is evident from the nature of his duties and also from the evidence of a number of inscriptions. It is no doubt true that Śukra states that a *grāmapa* should be a Brāhmaṇa; perhaps it may have been the case in some places. The duties of the headman are more appropriate for a Kshatriya than for a Brāhmaṇa. The six copper plates of the Gāhaḍavāla king Jayachandra record grants to a Kshatṛiya hereditary Rauta Mahāmahattaka.[3] Sometimes he was selected even from lower castes. One of the Paramāra records informs us that in 1186 A.D. in the Banwāsa state in Rajasthan, the Paṭṭakila Jahṇa belonged to the *Tailika* family. His post was also hereditary,

1. *J.B.B.R.A.S.*, X, 260.
2. *I.A.*, IV, 276.
3. *I.A.*, XVIII, 136.

for his father Chāhil is also described as Paṭṭakila in this record.[1]

The village headman exercised great influence over the villagers. His influence with the government also was as great as that with the people, for as already shown, he was often consulted at the time of making village or land grants. There is no doubt that he was responsible for his work to the central government; but still he remained a man of the people. Śukra observes that he was like father and mother to the villagers taking full care for their economic prosperity and happiness,[2] and protecting them against government officials.

VILLAGE OFFICE

The village headman must have carried on the administrative business in a suitable office building in the village, where all the records relating to the rights to and transfers of the village lands as well as the documents connected with the government dues were carefully kept.

VILLAGE ACCOUNTANT

It is important to note that our records nowhere refer to the village accountant. The contemporary South Indian records show that under the Cholas, the accountant was an important officer of the village administration, whose duty was to keep an account of the land and other taxes, noting the amount paid by each villager. Why he does not figure in the records of Northern India of our period, we do not know. Whether his post had disappeared, or whether his omission is accidental cannot be stated with certainty. Śukra, whose work sums up the general condition of our age, however, refers to the village accountant and calls him by the name Lekhaka; it is therefore very likely that he would have been a member of the village administration. He was to be skilled

1. *A.S.I.W.C.*, 1913, p. 56.
2. Prajāsaṁrakshaṇe daksho grāmapo mātṛipitṛivat.
Śukra, II, 171.

in account keeping.[1] Like modern village accountants, he also used to keep accounts of the income and the expenditure of the village and received the Government revenue in cash or kind, after making proper entries in the registers.

Besides village headman and the village accountant, there were also some other officers, who are referred to by Śukra but do not figure in the inscriptions. One of them was Sāhasādhipati, whose position was probably similar to that of the modern magistrate. Other officers were Bhāgahāra or the revenue collector, Śulkagrāha or the toll collector and Pratīhāra or the gate-keeper. It is very probable that these separate posts existed only in the big villages or towns; in the normal village, however, the headman himself would have discharged the functions of these different posts.

The Pratīhāra and Pāla records refer to some other officers namely, Yuktas, Niyuktas, Āyuktas and Viniyuktakas. The precise nature of the functions of these officers is still uncertain, but it is not unlikely that they would have belonged to the village administration. If so, may it not be that the duties of these officers corresponded to those of Bhāgahāra, Śulkagrāha and Pratīhāra mentioned by Śukra? Probably they also existed only in bigger villages.

THE VILLAGE COUNCIL

The village headman carried on the village government with the help of a village council, known as Pañchakula in Rajasthan under the Chāhamānas. What its name was under other dynasties is not known. It was an important body in the village administration; for we find that even royal grants made for the works of public utility were often made in its presence. Thus when princes Lākhaṇapāla and Abhayapāla made a grant of one *haraka* of barley from the village Bhādiyannva, conjointly with the queen Mahābaladevī, it was made in the presence of the Pañchakula.[2] The grant of 40 *drammas* by Vibhāka was also made in the presence of the

1. *Śukra*, II, 173.
2. *E.I.*, XI, 49-51.

Pañchakula.[1] The Bhinmal stone inscription of 1249 A.D. also records a grant of 50 *drammas* to the treasury of the God Jayasvāmī in the presence of the Pañchakula.[2] The grant made by Kāyastha Subhaṭa for the worship and services of the Tīrthaṅkara Mahāvīra was made in the presence of the village Pañchakula.[3] Even small donations intended for providing for the offerings of Naivedya were often made in the presence of Pañchakula.[4] All this evidence clearly indicates that the Pañchakula was an inportant body of the village administration under the Chāhamānas.

The Gāhaḍavāla records, however, do not refer to a Pañchakula. They only mention the village elders or Mahattaras. The non-reference may be accidental. It is also likely that the members of the Pañchakula were also known as Mahattaras. The president of the village council was usually the headman.

It is somewhat strange that the Pañchakula or the village council should not figure in the records of the Pratīhāras, the Paramāras, the Chedis, the Chandellas, the Pālas and the Senas. This silence is rather difficult to explain. It is hardly likely that the village council was unknown to the administration of these dynasties.

Let us now see who were eligible to become the members of the village council. It appears that there was no caste restriction and people from all the castes could become its members. One Chāhamāna inscription, dated 1153 A.D., informs us that in Nādula kingdom, the village administration was carried on by one Bhan (Bhaṇḍāri), one Rā (Rauta), one Vaṇika and one Vipradha.[5] They were probably members of the village council and obviously belonged to different castes.

Village revenues were usually collected in kind; the Bhaṇḍāri, whose duty was to collect it, played an important

1. *B.G.*, I, 474, No. 7.
2. *B.G.*, I, 1 p. 475.
3. *B.G*, I. I, 479.
4. *B.G*,, I. I, p. 475.
5. *E.I.*, XI, 35.

part in the village administration and would have been included in the council.

We have no information as to how the village councils were constituted. Our records nowhere refer to any election or selection of the members of the village councils nor to their qualifications. The contemporary South Indian records from Tamil country give us detailed rules in this connection; candidates were required to have certain property and educational qualifications along with a blameless character.

In Northern India also, probably the same would have been the case. Equal importance was probably given both to the moral, educational and property qualifications, while selecting the members of the village council. Whether there was any age restriction for the candidates seeking the membership of the council in Northern India during our period, as was the case in the Tamil country, is not revealed by our records. Nor do we know whether a person once 'selected' as the member of the council could again stand for 'selection'.

Whether elected or selected there is clear evidence to show that the village council under the Chāhamānas was constituted periodically. In one of the Bhinmal Inscriptions, we find the members of the local community making a religious grant and observing that though they have made the donations, all the members of the future council will enjoy its merit.[1] This instance not only indicates that the village council was constituted periodically, but it also shows that the grant made by the earlier bodies could be modified or cancelled by the later committees. It appears that, it was open for the subsequent Pañchakulas or village councils, as for later kings, to stop, to continue or to vary the grant.

The contemporary records from Tamil country show that there were a number of sub-committees of the village or the town council, each being in charge of a particular department like the adjudication, tanks, temples and roads. Apparently such was not the case in northern India, for the work in connection with temples, well construction and other works of public utility, is seen to be in charge of special committees known as Goshṭhis. Our records do not suggest that these

1. *B.G.*, I.I, 480.

Goshṭhis were sub-committees of the town or village committee. It is also doubtful whether they were connected with them. Thus one of the Chāhamāna inscriptions informs us that Valaṇadeva, who was a feudatory of Jaitrasiṁha, levied a cess from ploughs and oil mills for the management of a well in 1215 A.D. at a village in Jodhapur state, the management of which was entrusted to a Pratipālikā Goshṭhi.[1] The Bhaduṇḍa inscription of the Paramāra king Pūrṇapāla, dated 1145 A.D. refers to the construction of step-well in the village of Bhūmipadra and the work done by the Goshṭhikas in its charge. The Pehoa inscription of the Pratīhāra king Bhoja refers to the Goshṭhikas of horse dealers, who were entrusted with the collection of agreed cesses and contributions for the upkeep of a local temple and its worship expenses.[2] The Āhar inscription refers to a Goshṭhi managing the Kanakadevi temple and looking after the investment of its funds.[3] The management of a Jain temple was also carried on by the members of a Goshṭhi.[4] The Pārśvanātha temple at Jalor was also administered by a Goshṭhī, the members of which are stated to have been in charge of the collection of the rent of a building for Pañchamī-bali ceremony.[5] Another inscription informs us that the members of a Goshṭhi acted as witnesses at the time of a grant made by a Jain *śreshṭhi* for a *maṇḍapa*.[6]

The above evidence tends to show that there were non-official committees of respectable members formed for the purpose of organising and managing works of public utility and arranging for the needs of temples and other centres of religion and culture. How they were constituted, we do not know. It is possible that the members of these committees acted like trustees in modern days.

1. *I.A.*, XII, 87-88.
2. *E.I.*, I, 188.
3. *E.I.*, XIX, 45.
4. *E.I.*, VIII, 219-22.
5. *E.I.*, XI, 61.
6. *E.I.*, XI, 54.

It is difficult to say whether the village council under the Chāhamānas discharged the functions of trustees and bankers as was the case in the Tamil country during our period; nor can we say whether it looked after the management of schools and poor houses (*sattras*). Our inscriptions are all silent on these points. It is probable that the village councils in Northern India did not enjoy considerable powers like those of the Chola councils.

ADJUDICATION

Both the literary and epigraphical evidence shows that the settlement of village disputes was one of the most important functions of the village council. Somadeva informs us how king's court did not entertain any case at first instance and how the village council used to try them first. If, however, the parties felt dissatisfied with the decision of the village council, then alone they could appeal to the king's court.[1] Śukra expresses the same view.[2] Our records also indicate the same; for village grants usually assign to the donees not only the right to receive the land revenue, but also the fines and other sums due from the villagers in connection with their disputes and crimes. If all the cases were tried directly by the king's court or at the headquarter of district, the donees of our copper plate grants, residing in distant villages, could have hardly found it convenient to collect the fines imposed by the royal courts in towns and cities. It was because the lighter criminal cases were usually tried at the village itself, that the assignment of fines to the grantees of village grants was found practicable. The village councils could not try all the criminal cases. There were, however, usually no limitations on their civil jurisdiction.

PROCEDURE OF THE VILLAGE COUNCIL

Unfortunately the records of our period give us no clue about the precedure of the meetings of the village council. It is, however, not unlikely that the village headman would have presided over the meetings, which were probably held

1. Grāme pure vā vṛitto vyavahārastasya vivāde tadā rājānamupeyāt. *Nvk.*, XXVII, 22.
2. *Śukra*, IV, 5, 74.

in the village office. The other officer, who used to be present at the meetings was probably the accountant, who used to keep the records of the proceedings in the village office.

SOURCES OF REVENUE

The tax on shops and houses, the fines imposed by the local courts, extra taxes for special works, voluntary cesses levied for important works[1] were the main sources of the income of the village councils. The state was entitled to free service for one or two days in the month from the skilled and unskilled labourers; this right was usually transferred to the village communities, which found it very useful for digging wells, constructing dams and similar works. Probably a percentage of the land revenue was also assigned to the village communities.

1. *E.I.* I, 159-62 refers to voluntary cesses agreed to by horse dealers, gardeners etc.

CHAPTER VII

REVENUE AND EXPENDITURE

Ancient Indian political thinkers regard the treasury as a very important limb of the body politic. The *Mahābhārata* advises the king to protect his Kośa (treasury) with great care and effort, since it is the very root of the state.[1] Writers like Manu,[2] Yājñavalkya[3] and Kauṭilya[4] also express the same view. They all declare that the kingdom can never prosper without an overflowing treasury. The king should therefore pay first attention to Kośa.

The same is the view of the writers of our period. The *Agni-Purāṇa* emphasises the importance of a full treasury, for, it says that without treasury, the realization of one's objectives can never be ensured.[5] The *Vishṇudharmottara* points out how the treasury is the very root of sovereignty.[6] The same is the view of Kāmandaka,[7] who naturally insists that proper attention should be given to the treasury department. According to Somadeva,[8] it is the treasury which is the breath of the king's existence, and not the air he breathes. In fact it is the treasury and not the person of the king, who is the sovereign. The king, whose treasury is full is always victorious; otherwise even his security is in danger. In short a kingdom can never be safe, if its treasury is not prosperous. Śukra states "The treasury is the root of the army, and the

1. Kośamūla hi rājānaḥ kośo vṛiddhikaro bhavet.
   Mbh., XII, 119, 16.
2. *Manu*. VII. 65.
3. *Yaj*. I. 327-28.
4. Kośamūlaḥ kośapūrvāḥ sarvārambhāḥ tasmātpūrvaṁ kośamavekshetа.
   A.Ś., II, 2.
5. Shastri, J.L., *Political Thought in the Purāṇas*.
6. *V.P.*, II. 61.17.
7. Kośamūlo hi rājeti pravādaḥ sārvalaukikaḥ.
   Kāmandaka; XIII, 33.
8. Kośo hi mahīpatīnāṁ jīvanaṁ na prāṇāḥ.
   Kośo hi rājochyate na śarīram.
   Nvk., p. 81.

army is root of the treasury. The king should therefore personally look into the income and expenditure everyday."[1] The *Rājataraṅgiṇī* informs us how the king Kalaśa of Kashmir watched the income and expenditure and had a clerk by his side to take down his instructions.[2] All this evidence clearly indicates that ancient Indian political thinkers regard the treasury and ample reserve funds as the most essential for the welfare of the state. They have clearly declared that any deterioration in this connection would lead to the most serious national calamity.

PRINCIPLES OF TAXATION

The principal sources of state income during our period were the different kinds of taxes and fines, income from government properties and tributes from the feudatories. Among these the income from taxes was the most important one. We shall therefore discuss at the outset the general principles of taxation, as evolved by our political writers.

From very ancient times, great emphasis was laid by our political writers on the necessity of the taxation being reasonable and equitable. Both the *Mahābhārata* and the *Manusmṛiti* point out that excessive taxation will lead the king to ruin and hatred.[3] Śukra, while expressing the same view, states that the best king is he, who following the practice of a garland maker (who takes flowers without rooting out the plants), protects his subjects, makes the enemies tributaries, and increases the treasure by their wealth.[4] In short, it is only by moderate and timely collection of taxes that people will become attached and loyal to the king, thus ensuring a continuous payment of taxation.

Kāmandaka advises the king to recover taxes at proper time and proper place.[5] The Śāntiparva also advises the

1. *Śukra*, IV, 2 14.
2. *Raj*. VII, 507-8.
3. *Mbh.*, XII, 87-19.
4. Mālākārasya vṛityaiva svaprajārakshaṇena cha
   Śatruṁ hi karadīkṛitya tatddhanaiḥ kośavardhanam.
   Śukra, IV, 2, 18.
5. *Kāmandaka*, IV, 83-84.

king to levy taxes at the proper time and place, which may be convenient to the subjects.[1]

In the case of trade and industry, the king should levy taxes on net profits and not on gross earnings. The king, says Śukra, should not realise duty from the seller, when he receives what is less than or just equal to the cost. Under such circumstances the duty should be realised from the buyer.[2] In case of peasants also, the king should levy taxes upon them after ascertaining the amount of profits.[3]

An article should be taxed only once and not twice. The duty, says Śukra, should not be realised more than once by the king under one excuse or the other.[4]

Articles of very small value should not be taxed.[5]

The criterion of equitable taxation was that the state on the one side and the agriculturist and the trader on the other should both feel that they have got a fair and reasonable return for their labours. The king, says Śukra, should receive the rent from the peasant in such a way that he may not be destroyed.[6] He should behave like a weaver of garland, who plucks only full blown flowers from the tree and leaves the remaining untouched, as also the trees. He should not follow the example of a coal manufacturer, who entirely consumes the wood once for all.[7]

The last principle of taxation was that the king should impose extra taxes only in times of crisis. Śukra says that it is only at the time of national calamity that the king should receive from the people special grants and contributions.[8] In

1. *Mbh.*, Śāntiparva, XXXVIII, 12.
2. Lābhaṁ dṛishṭvā haret-śulkaṁ kretṛitaścha sadānṛipaḥ.
   Śukra, IV, 2, 111.
3. Jñatvāpūrvaṁ bhāgamichchhuḥ paśchād bhāgaṁ Vikalpayet.
   Harechcha karshakādbhāgaṁ yathā nashṭo bhavenna saḥ.
   Śukra, IV, 2, 112
4. Vastujātasyaikavāraṁ śulkaṁ grāhyaṁ prayatnataḥ.
   Śukra, IV, 2, 109
5. Na mūlyaṁ guṇahīnasya vyavahārakshamasya cha.
   Śukra, IV, 2, 107.
6. *Śukra*, IV, 2, 112.
7. Mālākāriva grāhyo bhāgonāṅgārakāravat.
   Śukra, IV, 2, 113.
8. Daṇḍa-bhū-bhāga-śulkānāmādhikyāt kośavardhanam
   Anāpadi na kurvīta tīrthadevakaragrahāt.
   Śukra, IV, 2, 9.

normal times, however, the king is not permitted to increase the land revenue, nor is he allowed to levy extra duties or to make a levy upon the property of temples and other holy establishments. In short, extra taxation was regarded as only an exceptional remedy to be adopted, when there was no other alternative. Somadeva also permits the state to tax the temples, Brāhmaṇas and the wealth collected for sacrifices only in case of emergency to tide over great difficulties.[1] We thus see that our political writers have laid down excellent principles of taxation, which are generally sound and reasonable.

Ancient Indian political thinkers have also laid down equitable and sound principles for remissions in taxation. According to Śukra, people who undertake new industries or bring waste lands under cultivation, or who for the growth of irrigation, construct new canals or dig tanks or wells, should not be taxed until they realise profit equal to twice the expenditure.[2] It is interesting to note that this recommendation of Śukra is similar to but more specific than that of Kauṭilya, who also recommends five years remission in taxation in case of new construction, four years remission in case of repairs, three years remission in case of improving and extending water works, and two years remission to those who mortgage or purchase uncultivated land. Śukra further lays down that family necessities like milk, vegetables, cloth, etc., apparently when produced in the house itself, were not to be taxed[3].

Let us now tackle the problem whether Brāhmaṇas were exempted from taxation or not. Śukra[4] and Somadeva[5] no doubt state that a king should not tax Brāhmaṇas and temples except in times of stress. This no doubt suggests that in normal times they were not taxed. It is, however, doubtful whether the exemption was applicable to all the Brāhmaṇas, for most of the Smṛitis exempt only Śrotriyas from taxation[6]. Other Brāhmaṇas following the professions of trade and industry were not exempted from taxes. The epigraphical evidence

1. *Nvk.*, 82.
2. *Śukra*, IV, 2, 115.
3. *Śukra*, IV, 2, 127.
4. *Śukra*, IV, 2, 2, 9.
5. *Nvk*, XXI, 14.
6. e.g. *Manu*, VII, 133.

also shows that the claim of the Brāhmaṇa class as a whole for remission from taxation was generally not recognised by the state. The donees of the Brāhmadeya villages may perhaps have been exempted from taxes. But we are not sure even on this point; for the contemporary South Indian records inform us that when lands or villages were granted to the Brāhmaṇas or temples, they were usually required to pay a quit rent. Such might have been the case in the North also during our period of survey, though we have no specific epigraphical evidence to prove it. If Devadāya grants in South India were not exempted from taxation, ordinary Brāhmaṇas, who were following a number of non-Brahmanical professions, could hardly have received a better treatment. There is no doubt that the Mount Ābu inscription of Tejapāla of 1230 A D. reveals that the king Somasiṁha of the Paramāra dynasty remitted the tax upon the Brāhmaṇas,[1] but this statement should not be taken as literally true, for it is made in the course of that king's eulogy. It is further to be noted that the inscription does not make it clear whether all the Brāhmaṇas or only a section of them was exempted from taxation. The utmost we can say is that occasionally a king like Somasiṁha took this unusual step.

SOURCES OF REVENUE

Let us now see what were the sources of revenue of the different governments of the period under consideration. Smṛitis give us a regular list of taxes in this connection. The inscriptions do not do so; but the statements made in them about the immunities of the villages alienated in favour of Brāhmaṇas and temples help us to a great extent in having the knowledge of the principal sources of income. Accounts of the Muslim traders are also useful to some extent in this connection.

The principal sources of revenue may be classified under the following five heads:—

Regular taxes, (*kara* and *śulka*).[2]
Occasional taxes.

1. Muktvā viprakarān—*E.I.*, VIII, 208-13.
2. *Śukra*, II, 384.

Income from state properties (*ākara* of Śukra).

Tributes from feudatories.

Fines (*daṇḍa* of Śukra).

Of these items, the fourth one will be considered in the ninth chapter, where the position of the feudatories will be reviewed; the remaining will be considered here.

Let us now discuss the different sources of revenue one by one.

Regular Taxes : The close study of the inscriptions reveals that the following were the usual taxes levied in our period:—

Bhāga-kara

Bhoga-kara

Śulka

Vishṭi

Udraṅga and

Uparikara.

Among these taxes, the first four are referred to by the Smṛitis and also by the books on polity; the last two appear only in inscriptions.

Bhāga-kara :—Agriculture being the main avocation of the people, the land tax was naturally an important source of the state income. The Śmṛitis invariably call it as *Bhāga-kara*, i.e., a tax consisting of a portion (of the produce of land). Its incidence varied from 16 to 25 per cent according to the quality of the land. It was usually collected in kind, as the term *bhāga-kara* clearly suggests. That the term *bhāga* denotes a royal share of land produce is also evident from Sanskrit literature, where the king is very often described as subsisting on *ṣashṭhāṁśa-bhāga*, i.e., the sixth part of the produce of the land.[1] It is therefore certain that *bhāga-kara* of the inscriptions is nothing else but the land tax.

Bhoga-kara:—It represents petty taxes payable in the form of daily presents in kind such as fruits, flowers, vegetables, fodder, betel leaves, etc. As these taxes were paid in kind, they were generally assigned to the local officers of the villages, most probably as part of their pay. They were, however, utilised in providing for the provisions for the visit of the king

1. *Śakuntalā*, Act II, V. 13.

and officers when they happened to come there on the inspection tour.

Let us now consider the meaning of the terms *Udraṅga* and *Uparikara*. Unfortunately we are not still in a position to determine the meaning of these terms, for they are not referred to in modern Sanskrit dictionaries. Some Sanskrit Kośas, however, refer to the term Udraṅga. According to Trikhaṇḍaśeshakośa, *udraṅga* is the name of the celestial city of Hariśchandra.[1] But this meaning can hardly be considered in connection with the present enquiry. The *Śāśvata-Kośa* refers to a word *Uddhāra*, which is taken by some scholars as a synonym of *udraṅga* meaning a tax levied on the permanent tenants.[2] But as the word *uddhāra* means a special share in property given to the eldest son, it cannot be taken in connection with taxation.

Can we identify *udraṅga* with *draṅga*? The *Rājataraṅgiṇī* mentions the term *draṅga* in the sense of a frontier town.[1] It is therefore possible that the term *sodraṅgaḥ* may mean 'along with the octroi duties'. But against this view, it can be argued that if the term was used in the sense of octroi duties, it would not have been *sodraṅgaḥ* but *sadraṅgaḥ*. It is, however, important to note that our records refer to several variations of the fiscal terms, but none of them ever mentions *sadraṅgaḥ* as an alternative form of *sodraṅgaḥ*. The form of the term *sodraṅgaḥ* is constant in all the records of the different dynasties of our period of survey.

Let us now discuss the different interpretations of the terms *udraṅga* and *uparikara* offered by different scholars. According to Fleet, *udraṅga* means a tax on permanent tenants and *uparikara* a tax levied on cultivators, who have no proprietary rights in the soil.[2] This view is however untenable, for it is very unlikely that the government would have made any distinction between the taxes paid by the permanent tenants and temporary cultivators. Further there is no evidence to show that the government was imposing any extra or special taxation on such tenants, who had no proprietary rights in the soil.

1. A.S. Altekar, *Rāshṭrakūṭas*, p. 214.
2. *C.I.I.*, III, p. 98.

According to Dr. Ghoshal, the term *uparikara* means 'an irregular tax, which bore harshly on cultivators'.[1] In other words it was a tax on land, which had to be paid over and above (—*upari*) the normal land tax. It thus appears to be identical with Bhogakara as both the terms denote additional taxes.

Dr. Altekar takes the term *sodraṅgaḥ* and *soparikaraḥ* as identical with the terms *sabhāga-bhogakaraḥ*.[2] This view is supported by the fact that in none of our records the terms *sodraṅgaḥ* and *soparikaḥ* appear along with the expression *sabhāga-bhoga-karaḥ*. Where the expression *sabhāga-bhoga* is used, the terms *sodraṅgaḥ* and *sopairkaraḥ* do not figure and where *sodraṅgaḥ* and *soparikaraḥ* appear, the expression *sabhāga-bhoga-karaḥ* is not used. Further it is important to note that there is hardly any record, where neither set of taxes is mentioned. It is therefore probable that the terms *bhāga* and *bhoga* are synonymous with the terms *udraṅga* and *uparikara* and stand for taxes that were almost universally levied in connection with land.

The incidence of the land tax is not revealed by our epigraphical records. Several records from Bengal give us the amount of the tax collection from some villages, but as we do not know the gross produce of these villages, we cannot determine the incidence of the tax. Śukra in one place states that in the ideal state, the farmer should have as his net income an amount double the expenditure incurred including the state tax.[3] This ideal was rarely realised, for elsewhere he allows 16% taxation on poor land, 25% on ordinary dry land, 33% on well-irrigated land and 50% on river-irrigated fields.[4] It is true that the state was recommended to return 5% of the tax to the farmer;[5] but this does not conceal the onerous nature of the above scale of the land tax. The high percentage of the land tax was probably due to the high expenditure on the military establishment.

Was the land tax collected directly from the farmer or had the zemindari system come into existence is a question,

1. U.N. Ghoshal, *Hindu Revenue System*, p. 210-11
2. A.S. Altekar, *Rāshṭrakuṭas*, p. 214.
3. *Śukra*, IV, 2, 115.
4. *Śukra*, IV, 2, 116-1 f.
5. *Śukra*, IV, 2, 11 f.

which is difficult to answer. Alienation of villages, of which we get several instances, do not attest to the existence of the zemindari system; for the grantees usually got the right of receiving the state's dues and had nothing to pay to the state. The general instructions about the collection of the land tax given in Śukra[1] suggest that the tax was collected by the king through his officers. A little later, Sukra, however, states that a king may settle the amount of land revenue and collect it from one individual in advance. This obviously is the beginning of the zemindari system.

One is, however, inclined to think that the earlier account referring to the direct collection of the tax by the state represents the reality in our period and the later verses refer to innovations that were coming into vogue towards its close and had become common in the 13th and 14th centuries.

Land tax was collected both in kind and in cash.[3] The very term *bhāga-kara* denotes that it was paid as a part of what was actually produced in the field. The *Jātakas* describe how royal officers went to the farms at the time of harvest and collected the tax in kind.[4] The same was the case under the Mauryas also, for Kauṭilya lays down a fine of 53 *paṇas* for an unauthorised removal of corn from fields. Śukra refers to the officer called Koshṭhāgārādhyaksha, who was in charge of state granaries at different centres, where the corn collected in tax was stored. It was his duty to dispose of the corn before it started deteriorating on account of time or insects.

The records of the Senas indicate that in Bengal land tax was very often collected in cash. The Barrackpur grant of Vijayasena records the gift of four *pāṭakas* of land yielding 200 Kapardaka-purāṇas.[5] The Govindapur grant, in which the village Viddasasasan was donated, informs us that the village granted yielded annually 900 *purāṇas* at the rate of 15 *purāṇas* to a Droṇa[6]. The grant of village Velahisti in the

1. *Śukra*, IV, 4, 113.
2. *Śukra*, IV, 4, 124-6.
3. *E.I.*, XV, 278-286.
4. II, p. 378.
5. *E.I.*, XV, 278.
6. *I.B.*, III, 92-98.

Tārāpandighi inscription yielded an income of 150 Kapardaka-purāṇas annually.[1] The Madhiānagar grant records a gift of Dāpaniyapāṭaka yielding 100 purāṇas and 68 Kapardakas.[2] The village of Pinjokāshṭhi divided into two parts in the Madanapāda grant gave to the donee an income of 500 (Purāṇas).[3] In the Naihati grant of Ballālasena, one village yielding an income of 500 Kapardaka-purāṇas was gifted away.[4] The Śaktipur grant of Lakshmaṇasena records that Kshetrapāṭaka yielded an income of 500 Kapardaka-purāṇas.[5] The Sahitya Parishad grant refers to an income of 500 Purāṇas.[6] Under the Pratīhāras also the land tax was sometimes collected in cash. From one of the inscriptions of Mahīpāla I, we learn that he assigned 500 *drammas* for a temple out of the revenues of a certain village. It appears that cash collection was, however, not very common in all parts of Northern India, for the records of other dynasties under consideration do not refer to it.

Pratīhāras had issued fairly copious silver currency in *drammas* under Bhoja I and one can understand the collection of the land tax in cash under Mahīpāla I. Purāṇas used by the Senas have so far not come to light. Can it be that the Sena records refer to the Vigrahapāla-Drammas, which continued to be minted even after the death of that king ? Or can it be that Dramma was merely a coin of account and that the records convert the tax in kind into tax in cash and give the amount in Purāṇas ? Further discoveries alone can solve this riddle.

It is difficult to say whether land tax in kind was collected in more than one instalment, for our records do not throw any light on this point. The Begumara plates of the Rāshṭrakūṭa king Kṛishṇa II inform us that it was collected in three instalments, one in Bhādrapada, one in Kārtika and one in Māgha. The same would have been the case in the North also during our period of survey. If the land

1. *E.I.*, XII, 6-10.
2. *J.A.S.B.*, V, 467.
3. *J.A.S.B.*, 1896, *I.B.*, 132.
4. *E.I.*, XIV. 156.
5. *E.I.*, XXI, 211.
6. *I.H.Q.* Vol. II, No. 1, p. 76-86.
7. *I.A.*, XVI, 174-5.

tax is to be levied in kind as part of the field produce, it has to be collected as often as the crop is reaped.

Ownership of Land

Let us now discuss the question of the ownership of land, which falls under different categories, namely, the arable, barren, marshy and forest land. It may be noted at the outset that as far as ownership in forests, marshy and waste lands is concerned, there is overwhelming evidence to show that it was vested in the state. But as regards the arable land, there is a divergence of opinion. Early Anglo-Indian administrators were inclined to the view that the state was the owner of all the arable land. They were interested in advocating this view, because they were of the opinion that what the British government took from the tenants was not land tax but land rent.

Indian scholars, on the other hand, are generally seen advocating the view that the land was not the state property at any time and that its ownership was vested in private individuals. So what the government obtained was a land tax and not land rent.

There is no doubt that in the pre-historic times, the ownership of land was vested in the whole community and that no one could alienate it without the consent of the village residents. But later on, gradually the right of ownership of the person, who tilled the land, came to be recognised. This is quite clear from the Smriti and Nīti works of early and medieval periods. Kauṭilya also differentiates between the crown lands and the private lands. His law of sale recognises private property in the land.[1] According to *Pūrvamīmāṁsā* in the Viśvajit sacrifice, a king has to give every thing of which he is the owner, but not the land, because he does not own it; the commentator Śabarasvāmī points out that the ownership of the fields belongs to different private individuals.[2] Nārada states "A householder's house and his field are con-

1. *A.Ś.*, II, Chap. 23.
2. Na bhūmiḥ sarvānpratyaviśishṭatvāt. VI, 7, 3. The commentator says kshetrāṇāmīśitāro manushyāḥ dṛishyante.

sidered as the two fundamentals of his existence, therefore let not the king upset either of them; for that is the root of the householders.[1] The same is the view of many other writers like Kātyāyana,[2] Nilakaṇṭha[3] and Śabara.[4] All this evidence clearly indicates that the ownership of arable land was vested in the peasant proprietor and not in the state.

To turn to our period, it may be noted that when our records contain grants of villages to temples and Brāhmaṇas, they usually refer to the transfer of the land tax and other specified dues to the donee.

The state no doubt often possessed some lands in different localities, the ownership of which had become vested in it by purchase, forfeiture, escheat, etc; but they were not very extensive. For, when the ownership in fields is granted, our records usually refer to the alienation of small pieces of land by kings. Thus the Patan grant of the Chaulukya king Bhīma II informs us that the king granted four ploughs of land in Kaḍāgrāma to Brāhmaṇa Āśādhara.[5] The Augasī grant records a gift of ten ploughs of land to a Brāhmaṇa made by the Chandella king Madanavarman.[6] In the Mahoba grant, the king Paramarddi is stated to have granted a piece of land measuring 60 square *vāḍhas*, cultivable by five ploughs in the village Dhanaura to Brāhmaṇa Rāmaśarman.[7] The Paramāra king Bhojadeva granted 100 *nivartanas* of land at Vaṭapadraka to the Brāhmaṇa Bhallā.[8] The Chāhamāna queen Āṇaladevī granted one plough of land to the Tīrthaṅkara Mahāvīra.[9] Depālapur grant of Bhojadeva

1. Gṛihakshetre cha dve dṛishṭe vāsahetū kuṭumbinām.
   Tasmātte nākshipedrājā te hi mūle kuṭumbinām.
   Nārada XI, 42.
2. Quoted in Vīramitrodaya *Rājanīti*, p. 271.
3. *Vyavahāramayūkha*, svatvāgama chapter.
4. VI. 7, 3.
5. *I.A.*, XI, 71-73.
6. *I.A.*, XVI. 202.
7. *E.I.*, XVI. 9-15.
8. *E.I.* XI, 181-83.
9. *E.I.*, IX, 47.

informs us that he granted 34 Aṁśās of level land furnished with four ploughs at Kirikaika in the western Pathaka of Ujjaini to the Brāhmaṇa Vacchāla.[1] The Chaulukya king Bhīma I granted three ploughs of land at a village named Varaṇavādā to the Brāhmaṇa Janaka.[2] The Barrackpur grant informs us that the Sena king Vijayasena granted four Pāṭakas of land measured by *Samataṭīya-nala* to the Brāhmaṇa Udayakarṇadevaśarman.[3] The Bombay grant of the Paramāra king Naravarman informs us that he and his wife Mahādevī granted some pieces of land to the Brāhmaṇa Āśādhara.[4] All this evidence clearly indicates that when full ownership in land was transferred to the donee, not the entire land in the village but certain small pieces situated in it acquired by the state, by forfeiture, escheat, etc., were usually transferred.

It is further worth noting that when the state wanted to give considerable landed property, usually some fields scattered here and there were given and not a continuous and big piece of land. Thus the two Paramāra inscriptions state that the king Māṇḍalika granted to the temples of Maṇḍaleśvara some lands as well as a garden behind Nagnataḍāga and to the temple of Varuṇeśvarī, some rice fields along with some other pieces of land in the villages of Nattapāṭaka, Pānacha and Maṇḍaladraha.[5] Now if the state had the right over all the arable land, Māṇḍalika would not have given to the temple pieces of land scattered here and there. The contemporary South Indian inscription from Mūlugunḍa, in which the king Karṇa is stated to have given detached pieces of cultivable land situated in different corners of the village, clearly show that the state was not the proprietor of the entire land of the realm.[6]

1. *I.H.Q.*, 1932, 305-13.
2. *E.I.*, XXI, 172.
3. *E.I.*, XV, 278-86.
4. *A.S.I.W.C.*, 1921, 54.
5. *E.I.*, XXI. 49.
6. *J.B.B.R.A.S.*, X, 199.

Such was the case in the earlier period also. The Kadamba king Vishnu-Varman is said to have granted the village of Katallaka along with a specified plot of 100 *Nivartanas* situated in it. In another Kadamba grant issued by the king Mṛigeśvaravarman, hailing from Karnaṭaka the village Kadākalani is given to a Brāhmaṇa along with a plot of land for building a house in it.

That the grant of the village did not mean the transfer to the donee of the ownership in all the arable land situated within its boundaries is made further clear by some records where, along with the village granted, some land situated in that village itself is also given to the donee. Thus in one of the grants of the Gāhaḍavāla king Govindachandra, the village of Lelispāda along with the field named Tiyāyi situated in it was granted to the donee.[1] One of the Kādī plates of the Chaulukya king Bhīma II also informs us that a village was given along with twenty ploughs of land situated in it.[2] In the contemporary Deccan also we come across similar instances. Amoghavarsha I of the Rāshṭrakūṭa dynasty is stated to have donated the village of Taleyar and also a flower garden 530 × 150 cubits in dimension, situated in the same village.[3]

It is true that we also come across some cases where when the whole village is granted, an exception is made in the case of some plots of land situated in it. Thus from the Charkkhāri plate of the Chandella king Paramarddideva, we learn that he granted the village of Gaganda with the exception of 5 ploughs of land gifted to Buddha.[4] The Bānagarh grant of Mahīpāla records the donation of the village of Kurala with the exception of Chūta-pallikā situated in it.[5]

It is possible to argue from these cases that these grants are making exceptions in the case of particular plots of land because the ownership in all other plots of arable land was being conveyed to the donees. Such a conclusion would, however, not be a correct one in view of the other and overwhelming evidence that we have cited to prove individual ownership of land. It it likely that when small pieces of land were being granted to temples, they were exempted from the land tax or had to pay a quit rent only. The specific exception made in the above grants probably refers to such fields and would indicate that the new donee was

1. *E.I.*, VII, 203-4.
2. *I.A.*, VI, 203-4.
3. *E.I.*, VI, 29.
4. *E.I.*, XX, 130.
5. *E.I.*, XII. 328.

not entitled to any land tax or the full land tax from the plots of land previously given to temples or Brāhmaṇas. They do not show that he became the owner of the remaining arable land.

It is thus clear that during our period ownership in the arable land was not vested in the state. On the other hand, it belonged to private proprietors, who could not be dispossessed by the state at its own will as long as they paid regular land tax. If there was a default in this connection for two or three years, then this land was forfeited to the state. This, however, was a well-recognised limitation over individual ownership of land.

CUSTOMS AND EXCISE DUTY

We have finished the discussion about the problems connected with the land tax; we shall now have a glance at other taxes levied under the different governments during our period of survey. Among them the customs, octroi and excise duties were very important. The officer called Śaulkika, who used to collect the octroi duties from the traders and industrialists at the gate of a town or a village, figures in almost all the inscriptions of the Pālas of Bengal.[1] He is also included in the list of officers of the Paramāra administration.[2] His absence in the records of other dynasties is of no particular significance, because they often mention the octroi duties.

Duties were collected sometimes at the boundary of the state, sometimes on the road and sometimes at the entrance of a town or village.[3]

The expression *sanirgama-praveśa*, occurring in Chandella,[4] Chedi[5] and Sena[6] records, probably refers to the excise and octroi duties, levied on merchants by the state.

Śukra, while giving us an interesting and convincing

I.A., XV, 306.
E.I., XIX, 71.
Śukra, IV, 2. 18.
E.I., IV, 157.
I.A., XVII, 224.
E.I., XXI, 95.

explanation for the justification of these taxes, says that the king should levy duties on the merchants in order to maintain and protect the roads, which they use for the transport of their commodities.[1] It may be noted here that the state had to spend then as now a large amount of money for the upkeep and protection of the roads; it is therefore very likely that the income derived from the customs and excise duties would have been partly spent for this purpose. The epigraphical evidence also shows that there was a road tax. The Gāhaḍavāla records refer to a tax called *pravaṇikara*,[2] and the Chedi records mention a tax called *pravaṇivāḍa*.[3] It is very likely that both these taxes were identical. *Pravaṇi*[4] literally means a place, where four roads meet. And hence it may be an octroi duty imposed upon merchants at the important stages of roads.

It is difficult to say how the customs officer used to discharge his functions, and at what rate he levied the duties on different articles; for our inscriptions do not throw any light upon these problems. In the earlier period, under the Vākāṭakas, we find that the state used to demand the best article brought to the market by a merchant as a part of its tax upon him. Whether such was the case in our period also we do not know. It appears that in the normal course of events, a tax of a certain percentage, varying from 5 to 20, was levied on different kinds of goods.

Octroi and excise duties were collected both in kind and in cash. There is no doubt that the Smṛitis state that these duties were usually collected in kind, but the inscriptions of our period show that cash collections were also not un-known. The taxes on articles like ghee, milk, flowers, butter, vegetables were usually collected in kind. The reason for this is not difficult to understand. It is doubtful whether any government of our period issued currency in copper in copious quantity. Nor does the work appear to have

1. Mārga-saṁskāra-rakshārthaṁ mārgagebhyo haret phalam.

Sukra IV, 2, 129.

2. *E.I.*, XXIV, 295.
3. *E.I.*, XXI, 95.
4. Apte's Dictionary.

been undertaken by any private agency or corporation. Economic transactions, including payment of octroi duties, had therefore to be made in kind or on barter basis.

It is further to be noted that the taxes collected in kind were often assigned to the local officers. This is but natural. For in ancient India, when communications were very slow, it was difficult for the king to send his officers daily to the villages to collect these dues. Even if this had been organised, some of the articles like vegetables would have been rendered useless before they reached the central depot at the head quarters of a Pathaka or Vishaya.

Let us now survey the information given by our epigraphs about the octroi and customs duties. Some of these taxes were imposed by kings no doubt for temple service; but the fact that they could do so for the temple shows that they must have been levying similar imposts for the state also.

Under the Pratīhāras, a tax of fifty leaves was levied upon every *Chollikā*.[1] Under the Paramāras, a tax equal to one *māṇaka* was levied on every *bharaka* of cocoanuts and fruits.[2] Merchants who used to trade in grains had to pay one *bharaka* on twenty packs of loaded grain.[3] The traders of barley used to pay a tax equal to a *vāpa* on each *mūtaka* of barley.[4] People, who used to carry away the loads of cattle fodder were required to pay one *Vṛisha-Viṁśopaka* on each load.[5]

Duty was also levied on the cloth industry. In Rajaputana under the Chāhamānas, the cloth merchants had to pay one *rūpaka* as a tax on each *bharaka* of thread and cotton.[6] In Mālwā, under the Paramāra rule, the cloth merchants were taxed one and half *rūpakas* on each *Koṭikā* of cotton fabric.[7]

The precise meaning and implication of the terms *māṇaka, bharaka, chollikā, vāpa* and *koṭikā* is not known. The

1. *E.I.*, IX 130.
2. *E.I.*, XIV, 297-303.
3. *E.I.*, XIV, 297-303.
4. *Ibid.*
5. *Ibid.*
6. *Ibid.*, XIV, 309.
7. *E.I.*, XIV, 292.

Sanskrit and Prakrit dictionaries explain some of these terms as merely a measure without giving its precise quantity. The exact incidence of taxation on the above—mentioned articles, therefore, cannot be ascertained. As has been stated already, it may have varied from 5 to 20 percent.

Excise duty was levied on oil. From one of the Pratīhāra records we learn that a tax of two *pallikās* was imposed on every Ghaṭakakūpaka of clarified oil.[1] In Mālwā, the oilmen used to pay one *pāṇaka* on each *karsha* of oil and one *pallikā* on every *ghaṭaka* of oil.[2] Under the Chāhamānas in Rajasthan a tax of two *pallikās* of oil was imposed on each oil mill.[3] Another inscription from the same province mentions a tax of two *pallikās* from four *pailas* of oil paid by the oilmen from every *ghāṇaka*[4] or oil mill. Unfortunately dictionaries do not give the exact significance of the terms *ghaṭaka*, *kūpaka*, and *pallikā*. It is possible that *ghaṭaka* denotes a *ghaḍā* or a pot; but what was its exact quantum, we do not know.

We shall now discuss the excise duty that was levied on articles like butter, sugar, candied sugar and jaggery. It is important to note here that the incidence on these articles varied from place to place. Under the Pratīhāra dynasty, we find the butter merchants paying a tax of two *pallikās* on every *ghaṭaka-kūpaka* of clarified butter;[5] but under the Paramāras, only half of the above tax was imposed on every *ghaṭaka* of butter.[6] Traders of sugar had to pay one *dramma* on each *pailā* of sugar in Mālwā;[7] while in Rajasthan, a tax of one *varṇika* was levied on each *bharaka* of candied sugar and jaggery.[8] It is very likely that similar cess was levied upon the above-mentioned article under other dynasties under review.

1. *E.I.*, XIX, 5-10.
2. *E.I.*, XIV, 309.
3. *E.I.*, IX, 34-36.
4. *E.I.*, XI, 41-42.
5. *E.I.*, IX, 5-10.
6. *E.I.*, XIV, 309.
7. *E.I.*, XIV, 309.
8. *E.I.*, XIV, 309.

Apart from the above duties, tax was also imposed upon goods in transit. What was its exact rate we do not know. A Paramāra record refers to a contribution of one *viṁśopaka* per bull that passed on the road.[1] This was no doubt given to defray the expenses in connection with a Śiva temple, but it suggests a regular tax paid to the state also per pack-animal.

Apart from octroi and excise duties, the traders had to bear another burden of tax called the shop tax. It is important to note here that the early Smṛitis rarely refer to this tax; but it is expressly referred to by Śukra as *paṇyabhūśulka*, a tax upon the site of a plot in the market[2] Our epigraphical records, however, do not refer to shop tax paid to the state; they mention contributions by shop-keepers for charitable and religious purposes,[3] which probably presuppose a regular tax paid to the state also. But whether this was a shop tax or a general tax on merchants, we do not know.

The rate of shop tax varied under the different dynasties. One of the Pratīhāra records informs us that the shop-keepers used to pay two *Viṁśopakas* as a shop tax.[4] Under the Paramāras a tax of one *dramma* was imposed on every shop of braziers.[5] It is very likely that the shop-keepers dealing in other commodities also had to pay similar tax under different governments.

Cattle breeding was an important profession in ancient India; it had also to bear its own share of taxation. The exact rate of the tax, however, is not known. According to Manu, cattle breeders should pay 2% tax, on the herd.[6] This obviously means that the tax was levied on the corpus of the herd. Śukra, on the other hand, imposes a duty of 6% to 12%, which probably refers to the increase in the herd effected during the year.[7] The inscriptions of our

1. *E.I.*, XXI, 51.
2. *Śukra*, IV, 2, 129.
3. *E.I.*, XIV, 309.
4. *E.I.*, III, No. 36.
5. *E.I.*, XIV. 309.
6. VII. 130.
7. *Śukra*. IV, *Manu*, 2, 239-40.

period, however, refer to a third method of taxation at a certain cash rate per head, per cow, horse, bull, etc. The Bayānā inscription of Chitralekhā refers to a temple tax on the sale of articles. We are told there that a tax of one *dramma* per horse was levied for the God Vishṇu by the queen.[1] This was probably the normal tax imposed on the sale of horses. The Gāhaḍavāla records also invariable mention *Gokara*,[2] which was levied on cows. Unfortunately, its exact incidence cannot be determined, as the records are silent upon the point.

Trade in wine was usually under state control. The *Arthaśāstra* informs us that it was manufactured partly in state and partly in private distilleries; the wine prepared by the latter had to pay an excise duty of 5%.[3] Under the Paramāras, four *rūpakas* were levied as tax on each *vumvāka* of wine.[4] Unfortunately inscriptions give us no clue to the quantity of the measure *vumvāka* and hence the incidence of the tax cannot be determined.

Excise duty was levied on salt under the Pratīhāras,[5] the Gāhaḍavālas,[6] the Chedis[7] and the Chandellas.[8] Sometimes the state used to give licences to the manufacturers to work on salt wells. When such was the case, the latter had to pay one *māṇaka* as a tax on each *mūṭaka* of the salt under the Paramāras. The exact significance of the term *mūṭaka*, however, cannot be determined and hence it is difficult to say what was the actual rate of this tax. It is interesting to note that when villages were granted to the donees, they were also invested with the right over the excise duty on salt that could be produced from the salt water wells in the villages.

Most of the records of the dynasties under survey refer to a tax on mines. In ancient India, all the mines were regarded as state property, but as the government itself was often

1. *E.I.*, XXII, 120.
2. *E.I.*, XIII, 217.
3. *A.S.*, I. Chap. II. p. 25.
4. *E.I.*, X V, 309.
5. *I.A.*, XVIII, 39-5.
6. *I.A.*, XVIII, 57.
7. *E.I.*, XXI, 95.
8. I.*A.*, XVI, 205.

unable to work them, they were sometimes entrusted to private individuals. When such was the case, the lessee had to pay a fairly heavy excise duty. According to Śukra, it was to be 50% in the case of gold and diamond; 33% in the case of silver and copper and 16% to 25% in the case of other metals.[1] The proportion mentioned above was probably levied not on the gross but on the net value. The Smṛitis on the other hand refer to a tax of 2% on gold[2], but it was most probably a customs duty rather than an excise duty. Salt and iron mines and stone quaries were also state properties, as shown by the expressions *salohalavaṇākaraḥ* and *sapāshāṇakhani* occurring in several Chedi, Chandella and Pratīhāra records.[3]

All this evidence clearly indicates that customs and excise duties were collected both in kind and cash. Unfortunately we are not able to determine the exact incidence of taxation, as our records are generally silent on the point. We have seen above how they do not supply data in terms, which can be fully understood. Most of the Smṛiti writers lay down that the excise duty should be 16% in cash on articles like fish, meat, honey, medicines, fruits, pottery, fuel, etc.[4] It is very likely that the taxation may have varied in practice with different articles, but the average may have been in the vicinity of 16%. The *Arthaśāstra*, on the other hand, levies a light duty on articles like medicines, fuel, leather goods and earthen pots and a little higher duty on wine, silken pieces, etc., varying from 6%[5] to 10%. Śukra, however, recommends a duty varying from 3% to 6%.[6]

VISHṬI

The institution of compulsory or forced labour is very old in India. It is referred to in most of the Smṛitis and is also mentioned in several north Indian inscriptions of the dyna-

1. *Śukra*, IV. 2, 118-19.
2. *Vishṇu*, III, 24.; Manu, VII, 131-2.
3. *I.A.*, XVIII, 34-35. *E.I.*, XXI, 95.
4. *Manu*, VII, 131-32.
5. *A.S.*, II, 22.
6. *Śukra*, IV, 2, 110.

sties under consideration, which assign the right to exact it to the grantee of the village gifted away. The writers on polity of our period also lay down a rule that every citizen, whether he may be rich or poor, should pay something to the state by way of taxation in return for the protection received. The rich could afford to pay in cash or kind but not so the extreme poor; they were therefore required to pay their tax in labour.

Each labourer was expected to work for a certain number of days in the year for the state. Śukra recommends that the artists and artisans should work one day in the fortnight for the state.[1] This liability is two times the liability imposed by Manu, who asks the king to take free labour from artisans for one day in the month. This tax, being not a regular one, was generally imposed upon labourers when kings or their officers were on tours in villages or when public works in the villages like the excavation of tanks, wells, etc. were carried out or when the government granary was to be cleansed or taxes paid in kind had to be weighed or measured. The Gāhaḍavāla records refer to a tax called *Skandhaka*,[2] the meaning of which is rather obscure. *Skandhaka* may mean one who carries load on shoulders or the load carried on shoulders. It may therefore refer to the liability of the labourers to carry the luggages of the touring officers upon their shoulders.

MISCELLANEOUS TAXES

Let us now discuss the miscellaneous taxes imposed by the different dynasties. Under this head may be first mentioned a tax on houses. That the house tax was a common demand of the state would appear probable from the circumstance that very often we find the people agreeing to pay a contribution per house to the temple treasury for the temple expenses. Thus one of the Paramāra inscriptions informs us that a tax of one *dramma* was imposed by the king Māṇḍalika on every house for meeting temple expenses.[3] The

1. *Śukra*, IV, 2, 241.
2. *E.I.*, III, 266.
3. *E.I.*, XIV, 309.

same inscription also reveals that at the time of Chaitra festivals a tax of one *dramma* was levied on the house of every trader for the same purpose.[1] If the king in this way could impose upon the people a house contribution for temple expenditure, it follows that he could do the same for general administration also. It may be noted here that Śukra also imposes a tax on house sites[2]

Besides the house tax, there was an irrigation tax or *jalakara*, which was levied under the Gāhaḍavālas. This must have been an important source of income. Śukra also says that the king should realise 1/3, 1/4 and 1/2 of the produce from places, which are irrigated by tanks, canals, wells and rivers respectively.[3]

Inscriptions, however, refer to another method of taxation on irrigation. The Sevadi stone inscription of the Chāhamāna dynasty records a grant of one *Haraka* of barley from every one of the wells belonging to four villages for worship of Dharmanāthadeva in the temple of Semvipati.[4] Under the Paramāras, a tax of one *haraka* of barley was imposed on one water wheel.[5] This tax was probably in addition to the general land tax.

People indulging in gambling were also taxed. From one of the Paramāra records we learn that a tax of two *rūpakas* was levied on each gambling house in Mālwā.[6]

Under the Chāhamānas, tax was imposed upon dancing girls also. What was its exact rate, we do not know. The Nadol stone incription informs us that Bhanaṇa, a local chief, freed the dancing girls from Daśabandha, which was probably a kind of tax equal to one-tenth of their income.[7]

Articles accidentally found were also usually taxed. The Pratīhāra records refer to a tax called *mārgaṇaka*[8] and the Chaulukya epigraphs refer to *abhinavamārgaṇaka*.[9] Unfortunately the exact significance of these terms cannot be definitely

1. *E.I.*. XIV, 309.
2. *Śukra* IV, 2, 129
3. *Śukra*. IV, 2, 27-29.
4. *E.I.*, XI, 28-30.
5. *E.I.*, XIV, 309.
6. *E.I.*, XIV, 309.
7. *A.S.I.W.C.*, 1902-9, p. 45.
8. *E.I.*, XIV, 182; *E.I.* III, 266.
9. *I.A.*, XVIII, 83.

ascertained. Mārgaṇaka literally means what is obtained by search. It may therefore possibly refer to the treasure-troves found under ground. It seems to be the same as *navanidhāna*, mentioned in Chaulukya records.[1] Smṛitis recommend a levy of tax on treasure-troves and the state of our period must have followed the advice.

Dr. U.N. Ghoshal, however, holds that *Mārgaṇaka* was a tax of the nature of a benevolence levied upon the villages and that *abhinavamārgaṇaka* indicated an additional levy made, when the original imposition had become permanent. In the absence of any authority for this interpretation, it is diffcult to accept it.

Along with the tax *mārgaṇaka*, the Pratīhāra records refer to another tax called *Khalaka*[2] or *khalabhikahā*, which was probably a cess imposed upon a threshing floor. It may therefore stand for the demand for a portion of a crop over and above the usual grain share, that was collected from the grain heaped upon the threshing floor. It is also not unlikely that *khalabhikahā* may be the customary dues claimed by the village artisans for their services in the year to the village residents. This custom still prevails in Western India.

OCCASIONAL TAXES

In ancient India, the visits of the inspecting and detective staff were regarded to some extent as visitation. The expenses connected with their stay had to be borne by villagers. In the Deccan during our period we find that under the Yādavas, a special kind of tax was levied at the time of the halt or departure of the royal officers, so that they may be provided with free boarding and lodging. In the earlier period, under the Vākāṭakas, the villagers had to supply fodder to the horses of the visiting royal officers and supply labour, bulls and carts necessary for their transport. The records of our period are no doubt silent about such impositions; but this silence is probably accidental. The villagers

1. *I.A.*, XI, 71-2.
2. *E.I.*, III. 266.

and citizens of our period also had probably to pay an additional impost, when officers of the central government used to come for inspection. The Gāhaḍavāla records[1] refer to Paṭṭakiladāya, Vishayikadāya, Akshapaṭalikaprastha, Pratihārīprastha and Aḍhuprastha. Unfortunately we do not know what is meant by Aḍhuprastha, for Sanskrit dictionaries do not give us the meaning of this term; but the remaining four terms may probably indicate the dues given to the government officers called Pratīharī, Akshapaṭalika, Vishayika and Paṭṭakila, at the time of their visits to the villages. These dues were probably paid in kind. It is very likely that some corn measuring one *prastha* was supplied to Pratīhārī and Akshapaṭalika. As regards the dues given to Vishayika and Paṭṭakila, it is difficult to say what they actually used to be.

Chāṭa-bhaṭa-praveśa-daṇḍa is mentioned in several records. It obviously refers to a tax or impost levied at the visit of of *chāṭas* and *bhaṭas*. Who these persons were is however not quite certain. *Bhaṭa* obviously refers to soldiers, and the entire expression is usually taken to refer to the levies imposed at the entry of regular and irregular soldiers. There is however no clear authority for taking the term *chāṭa* as denoting irregular soldiers. It is not impossible that *chāṭa* may be a corruption of *Chhāṭa* and that the latter may stand for *chhatra*. If so, the term *chhatra* may by implication *lakshaṇā* stand for umbrella-bearer and may refer to attendants in general, who did umbrella-bearing and other menial work. *Chāṭas* may therefore be standing for peons and other menials, who attended the government officers, when they visited the villages for inspection. A third interpretation is also possible for the term *chāṭa*. On the authority of *Yājñavalkya* I, 355 *Pañchatantra*, I,390 and *Mṛichchhakaṭika* 78.13, *St. Petersburg Dictionary* suggests that *chāṭa* may stand for a cheat. *Chāṭabhaṭapraveśadaṇḍa* may therefore stand for.

(i) a tax levied upon villagers to meet the expenses connected with the visits of soldiers and officers with their peons and attendants.

1. *E.I.*, XXIX, Part 1, p. 5.

(2) a tax levied upon the villagers for meeting the expenses of soldiers quartered on the village and a fine imposed upon it for giving shelter to cheats and bad characters.

(3) a tax levied at the entry of regular and irregular troops.

The first interpretation seems to be probable. In contemporary south India, the villagers had to supply police and military officers with boiled rice, milk, vegetable, grass, fuel and other necessaries and luxuries of life.[1] In northern India also the same may have been the case. *Chāṭabhaṭa-praveśa-daṇḍa* therefore probably indicates the additional imposts levied to supply provisions for soldiers and peons and other attendants, when they had to stay in villages probably in connection with the visits of touring officers.

In India, it is a custom to offer a present to a person on occasions of festivity like the birth of a son or the marriage of any member of his family. This custom was followed by the subjects with reference to their king in ancient times and continued even in the 20th century. The Kumāragadiāṇaka[2] tax mentioned in the Gāhaḍavāla records was due to this practice. Gadiāṇaka is well-known to be a weight equal to 41 *guñjas*, or 70 grains; probably it denotes the gold coin current under the Gāhaḍavālas. It is therefore very likely that the subjects used to pay one gold coin to the king on the occasion of the birth of prince. This was undoubtedly a heavy demand and may have been paid only by the rich.

EMERGENCY TAXES

As already stated or discussed Hindu political writers have given the right to the king to levy extra taxes at the time of national emergency or foreign invasion. This is also evident from inscriptions. The Gāhaḍavāla records refer to a tax called Turushka-daṇḍa,[3] which was levied in their kingdom. The meaning of this term is very obscure. It may mean a tax collected by the Hindu Government for the

1. *I.E.* XI, 6.
2. *E.I.*, IV, 105.
3. *E.I.*, XXIII, 217.

payment of a tribute to Muslim invaders; or it may be a sort of poll tax imposed on Moslems. But more probably it refers to a special tax to meet the cost of extra military forces and preparations to meet the danger of the Moslem invasions.[1] So it was a measure of emergency taxation.

INCOME FROM STATE PROPERTY

Let us now consider the different sources of revenue other than taxation. These are not directly mentioned in our records; but the privileges and exemptions, given to the donees of the copper plate grants, help us to a great extent in getting some indirect idea in this connection. A close study of the records reveals that the donees were usually given the right to work salt and iron mines, appropriate buried treasures and use village pastures. This clearly indicates that normally the state claimed ownership over all the mines, treasure troves and the waste lands. The same was probably the case with forests also.

Waste, fallow and pasture lands were not regarded as private property and were naturally owned by the state. The expressions *Svasīmātṛinayūtigocharaparyantaḥ*,[2] *sagartosharaḥ*,[3] *sasthalaḥ*[4] and *sagochara*[5] occurring in many of our records transfer to the donees the right to utilise fallow lands, pastures and waste lands. These were used for grazing cattle; and when the villages were granted to the donee, the latter used to impose a fee on them. Sometimes the expression *svakāshṭhatṛiṇodakopetaḥ*[6] is also used, which means that all the trees, whether valuable or not, grass, fuel, etc. growing on the waste lands included in the boundaries of the village were granted to the donees.

It is interesting to note that in the Gupta period, though the state claimed ownership over the above mentioned lands,

1. A.S Altekar, *State and Government in Ancient India.*, p. 207.
2. *I.A.*, VI, 191-2; *I.A.*, XVI; 205-6; *E.I.*, XXIII, 292; *IA*, XVII, 224.
3. *E.I.*, XXVI, 9; *I.A.*, XVII, 224; *E.I.*, XXI, 95; *I.A.*, XV, 306.
4. *E.I.*, XXI, 216; *E.I.*, XVII, 321; *E.I.*, XXI, 95.
5. *E.I*, XXI, 95; *I.A.*, XVII, 224.
6. *I·A.*, VI, 191-2.

it did not enjoy the right of alienating them. It had to take the consent of the village conncils at the time of their disposals. The same was the case in South also during our period. The waste and fallow lands were administered by the village assemblies. They are often seen selling or mortgaging common land at the time of national calamities such as famines, floods, etc. There is no evidence so far forthcoming to show that village committees exercised similar right over waste lands in northern India.

Marshy land was also regarded as state property. The expression *sānūpajaṅgalaḥ*[1] occurring in the Pratīhāra and Chedi records, transfers to the donee the right to utilise marshy land, which was often converted into a tank in the rainy season and could be used for fishery.

The state claimed its ownership over mountains, hills and vales. Trees growing in these places were claimed by the state as its own property. The expressions *sanimnonnata*[2] and *saparvata*[3] occurring in the Chandella and Pratīhāra records authorise the donee to utilise the land consisting of mountains, pits and hills. The donee was also entitled to utilise temporarily abandoned land (*ūsharavāha-pratibaddha*).[4]

Rivers were an important source of state income. As pointed out already, cultivators, who used to irrigate their lands by the water of the river, had to pay 50% as land tax. Toll duties were also collected from the people on water ways, which yielded considerable income to the state. The expression *sajalaḥ*[5] occurring in the Gāhaḍavāla records is difficult to explain. Probably it refers to watersheets like those of tanks and rivers. It is interesting to note that as early as the period of the *Arthaśāstra* we find the state claiming its ownership over fish, aquatic animals and green vegetables from irrigation works and tanks in so far as these formed articles of merchandise. The expression *sajalaḥ* would suggest that the same was the case in our period.

1. *I.A.*, XVIII, 34-5; *E.I.*, XXI, 95.
2. *I.A.*, VI, 202-3.
3. *E.I.*, XXI, 95.
4. *I.A.*, XVI, 202-3.
5. *E.I.*, XIV, 193.

Ownership over the treasure-troves was also vested in the state. The records of our period frequently refer to treasure-troves. In ancient India there were no banks and hence people were mostly in the habit of burying their treasures. The donees of our copper plate grants are usually seen enjoying the right over treasure—troves that were discoverd in the villages or lands granted. The expression used in this connection is *nidhinikshepasahitaḥ*[1] meaning "along with the right to treasures and buried wealth". The state claimed its ownership over treasure troves either because it claimed to be the heir of heirless property or because it regarded them as similar in nature to the mineral yields, both being recovered from the bowels of the earth. Most of the Smṛiti writers state that the king was entitled to a fairly large share of the treasure—troves except when the discoverer was a Brāhmaṇa. They clearly lay down that the property discovered by a Brāhmaṇa should be regarded as his property. The king should not take even a single penny from it. If the property was discovered by a man other than a Brāhmaṇa, the king could claim his right over half of it; the remaining half was given to the finder.

Forests were also regarded as the Government property. From the *Arthaśāstra* we learn that the king used to reserve a portion of forests for breeding elephants and another for his game. The remaining area was utilised for fuel and timber. Most of the records of our age, while granting the villages, use the expression *savananidhāna* or *savṛikshamālākulaḥ*, which refers to the transfer to the donee of the state's right in the forest lands situated within the boundaries of village.

The records of the Gāhaḍavāla rulers declare their proprietary rights in mango and Madhūka trees. The grants of the Sena dynasty invest the donee with the proprietary right in the cocoanut and betel-nut trees. The Chandella kings claimed ownership in plants like sugarcane, cotton and jute. It is difficult to say whether the state ever claimed ownership in these plants growing in private fields. Can it be that expressions *śāmramadhūka*,[2] *sakarpāsa*[3] and *saguwākandāri-*

1. *I.A.*, XVII, 224.
2. *I.A.*, XIV, 103-4.
3. *I.A.*, XXV, 206-8.

kela[1] refer to the state's right in these plants growing on waste land and pastures ?

Under the Chandellas the donee was invested with the right over *mandira* and *prākāra*. It is difficult to state what is meant by the term *samandira-prākārān*.[2] Possibly it refers to some state-buildings, the ownership over which was sometimes transferred to the donee. In this connection it is interesting to note that Śukra includes rent as one of the state revenues. Very probably this rent might have accrued from state buildings.

The Chandella government also claimed its ownership in the birds flying in the sky, fish swimming in water and games roaming in the forest. The expression used in this connection is *samṛigavihaṅgama-jalacharam*.[3] This would probably indicate that the state used to impose a tax upon hunters and fisherman, the proceeds of which were often assigned to donees.

FINES

As in modern times, fines formed one of the items of state income in ancient India also. The expression *daṇḍadāyādi*[4] occurring in the Chandella records and *Sadanḍadaśāparādha* occurring in the Pratīhāra, the Chedi, the Pāla and the Sena records[5] transfer to the donees the right to receive the fines imposed upon criminals. In villages and towns not assigned to the alienees, these fines when imposed by popular courts, formed a part of the village income. In alienated villages, however, they were often assigned to the donor.

The fines imposed by the state courts, however, went to the central treasury. The officer called *daśāparādhika*, who figures in many of our records, was put in charge of collecting the fines imposed on persons found guilty of any of the ten traditional offences. In the Chedi records also we find

1. *E.I.*, XXI, 216.
2. *E.I.*, IV, 157.
3. *I.A.*, XXV, 206-8.
4. *I.A.*, XVI, 205-6.
5. *I.A.*, VI, 191-2.

a reference to the fines imposed upon fraudulent people. The officer who collected these fines was probably known as *Dauhasādhasādhanika*.[1] The Gāhaḍavāla records also refer to a term *Kūṭaka*, the exact significance of which is still uncertain. But as it is mentioned along with *daśabandha*,[2] it may be taken as a fine imposed upon fraudulent people

APUTRIKĀ-DHANA OR HEIRLESS PROPERTY

The state also claimed its right over heirless property. The donees of the copper plate grants are often seen invested with this right at the time of the gift of villages. It is important to note that in ancient India, for a long time, widows were not regarded as heirs to their husbands' property; and hence at the time of their husbands' deaths, the property was escheated to the state which gave only a maintenance to the widow. When, however, the right of the widow's inheritance was recognised, the state tried to compensate its loss by imposing a tax on the property of the widow, which was naturally known as *aputrikā-dhana*.[3]

EXPENDITURE

Let us now discuss the topic of state expenditure and see how far it was well-regulated. It has to be observed at the outset that neither the epigraphical records of our period nor any literary works on polity except the *Śukranīti* give us any information in detail about the various items of state expenditure. Kauṭilya, no doubt, deals with this topic, but the information which he supplies does not exactly bear on the entire state expenditure. He enumerates 14 items of expenditure, but as Dr. Altekar has pointed out, the information is neither systematic nor exhaustive. Kauṭilya deals mostly with the royal household, but does not inform us the exact percentage of the state income that was spent on it. The judiciary and the civil administration are not mentioned by him in the list of the items of state expenditure. The salaries of

1. *E.I.*, XXI, 95.
2. *I.A.*, XII, 103-4.
3. *E.I.*, III, 216.

the different ministers and officers of the ideal state are no doubt mentioned by him but it is difficult to state how far the emoluments received by different officers were reasonable, as he does not refer to the exact income of his ideal state. We thus see that the information, which Kauṭilya gives us about the state expenditure, is not sufficient for our purpose. Most of the subsequent writers do not at all enlighten us on this point.

Śukra,[1] the principal writer for our period, however, gives us detailed and definite information about the percentage of state income devoted to the different items. He divides the the state expenditure into the following six items and makes the following allotment.

Bala or Fighting forces	50%
Prakṛiti or high officials	$8\frac{1}{3}\%$
Dāna or Charity	$8\frac{1}{3}\%$
Adhikāriṇah or Civil Administration	$8\frac{1}{3}\%$
Ātmabhoja or Privy purse	$8\frac{1}{3}\%$
Kosha or Reserve fund	$16\frac{2}{3}\%$

Let us now see how far the above budget of state expenditure is satisfactory. There is no doubt that the percentage of income spent on the fighting forces was very high. But we should, however, not forget that during our period constant wars were going on between the different dynasties for the supremacy of power. Each state therefore probably felt it necessary to maintain a big force, which required a large amount of state expenditure for its proper maintenance. There is, therefore, nothing improbable in the military expenditure of the normal state having amounted to half of its revenues.

The Privy purse at 8 1/3% of the state income also seems to be reasonable. It is, however, not unlikely that the kings during our period would have taken a little more than what was permitted by Śukra. The Union Government of India allowed 10% of the revenue as the maximum privy purse, when the states were integrated in the Indian Union.

1. *Śukra*, I, 316-17.

The high officials '*prakṛitayaḥ*' and the civil administration (*adhikāriṇaḥ*) claimed 16 1/3% of the state revenue. This seems to be rather a high percentage, but very probably it included the pays of the central, provincial and local officers.

The banking of the modern type was unknown in ancient India and a prudent state was expected to have a reserve fund in cash equal to twenty times its annual revenue.[1] Hence it is that 15 2/3% of the annual revenue was transferred to the reserve fund.

The item of Dāna or charity, which was allotted 8 1/3% included not only religious gifts but grants for schools, colleges, hospitals and canals. This item thus partly helped the nation-building activities.

1. Daṇḍa-bhū-bhāga-śulkaistu vinā kośād balasya cha saṁrakshaṇam bhavet samyag yāvat viṁśati vatsaram.

Śukra, IV, 2, 13.

CHAPTER VIII

JUDICIAL ADMINISTRATION

The administration of justice is regarded as one of the most important functions of the state in modern times. Such was not, however, the case in the ancient period, both in India and elsewhere. A number of offences like murder, theft, etc., are referred to in the Vedic literature, but the king is not described as a judge deciding either civil or criminal cases. Nor do we get any reference to the king's court. The assemblies of tribes and clans known as Sabhā and Samiti used to settle disputes; it appears that the king had very little to do with the administration of justice.

When, however, the powers of the king increased, administration of justice became one of his important functions as will be clear from the duties of the king in the early Smṛiti period. Śukra, the principal writer for our period, says that the king should punish the wicked by administering justice, for otherwise the good will suffer and the wicked prosper.[1] Somadeva also expresses the same view, when he states that the king should always punish the sinners and criminals and all those, who are obstacles to the happiness of his people [2]

The king as the head of the judicial administration is required to be impartial in deciding the cases, in accordance with the sacred law and local customs; the latter were as important as the former. The king, says Śukra, who does not follow the local customs, becomes the cause of hatred among the subjects; he should therefore maintain and enforce the customs current in society.[3]

1. Dushṭanigrahaṇam kuryād vyavahārānudarśanaiḥ.

Śukra, IV, 5, 1.

2. Rājñāṁ maryādāṁ vātikrāman sadyaḥ phalena daṇḍenopaḥantavyaḥ,
Nahi durvṛittānāṁ daṇḍādanyo'sti vinayopāyaḥ,

Nvk.

3. Jātijānapadān dharmān śreṇidharmānstathaiva cha
samīkshya kuladharmāṁścha svadharmaṁ pratipālayet.
Deṣajātikulānāṁ cha ye dharmāḥ prāk pravartitāḥ.
Tathaiva te pālanīyaḥ prajā prakshubhyate'nyathā.

Śukra, IV, 5, 47-48

The Nīti writers of our period further advise the king to try the cases with the help of Sabhyas or jurors, and not only by himself.[1] Śukra states that if the king will act unrighteously, the enemies will soon overpower him.[2] He should, therefore decide the cases without being influenced by any passion, greed or anger; evidence was to be carefully studied in the light of logic and inference.[3]

Prāḍvivāka or the chief justice is the next important member of the judicial administration. He presided over the high court of the realm and deputised for the king in his absence. Somadeva calls him Sabhāpati.[4] In the epigraphs of the Chedis he is described as Mahādharmādhyaksha.[5] He was to be well grounded in the substantive law, the law of procedure and the sacred and customary law. Like the king, he was also required to decide cases impartially and according to the law with the help of the Sabhyas.[6] Śukra imposes upon him a fine of a thousand, if he decides a case contrary to law.[7]

Sabhyas or jurors also played an important part in the judicial administration. Both the king and the chief justice are advised by Śukra to decide cases along with three, five or seven jurors.[8] Somadeva also is of the same opinion, though he does not give the number of jurors. Great care was taken in the selection of the jurors.[9] The court, says

1. Lokavedajñadharmajñāḥ sapta pañcha trayo'pi vā.
Yatropavishṭa viprāḥ syuḥ sā yajñasadṛiśī sabhā.
Śukra, IV, 5, 26.
2. Yastvadharmeṇa kāryyāṇi mohāt kuryyānnarādhipaḥ
Achirāt taṁ durātmānaṁ vaśe kurvanti śatravaḥ.
Śukra, VI, 5, 9.
3. Dharmmaśastrānusāreṇa krodha-lobha-vivarjitaḥ.
Samāhitamatiḥ paśyed vyavahārānanukramāt.
Śukra, IV, 5, 5.
4. *Nvk*. p. 180.
5. *E.I.*, XXI, 217.
6. Bahusammatasaṁsiddhān viniśchitya sabhāsthitaḥ
Sasabhyaḥ prāḍvivākastu nṛipaṁ sambhodhayet sadā.
Śukra, II, 98.
7. Amātyaḥ prāḍvivāko vā ye kuryyuḥ kāryyamanyathā
Tatsarvaṁ nṛipatiḥ kuryyāttān sahatsrantu daṇḍayet.
Śukra, IV, 5, 282.
8. Lokavedajñadharmajñāḥ sapta pañcha trayo'pI vā.
Śukra, IV, 5, 26.
9. *Nvk*., p. 110.

Somadeva, will be like a desolate forest, if it will not consist of learned jurors.[1]

The jurors were to be truthful, virtuous and well-grounded in the Vedas and Dharmaśāstras.[2] They were further required to be strong enough to bear the strain of the judicial administration.[3] At the time of the trial of a case, they had to give their own frank opinion, even if it was in opposition to that of the king.[4] Śukra condemns a juror, who keeps silence in the court and calls him a sinner, if he does not speak out truthfully.[5] The juror was even deprived of his office, if he decided the case through greed or fear without studying it carefully.[6]

It is important to note that almost all the Smṛitis recommend that the Sabhyas should be Brāhmaṇas. The reason is not far to seek; the study of the Dharmaśāstra was usually cultivated in the Brāhmaṇical circles, and a thorough knowledge of the sacred law was necessary for the proper discharge of the duties and functions of the juror. This recommendation of the Smṛitis, however, does not seem to have been followed in all cases in actual practice. It may be pointed out here that even the Dharmaśāstra writers themselves recommend that the cases should be tried with the help of the jurors selected from the castes, or the professions of the parties themselves. Śukra, who sums up the practice of our age, also states that the Sabhyas should be selected from all the castes.[7] He further points out that the foresters are to be tried with the help of foresters, merchants with the

1. Sā sabha araṇyāni, yasyāṁ na santi vidvāṁsaḥ. *Nvk.*, p. 110.
2. Vyavahāravidaḥ prājñā vṛitta-śīla-guṇānvitāḥ
   Ripau mitre samā ye cha dharmajñāḥ satyavādinaḥ.
   Śukra, IV, 5, 16.
3. Vyavahāradhuraṁ voḍhuṁ ye śaktāḥ puṅgavā iva.
   Śukra, IV, 5, 25.
4. Adharmataḥ pravṛittaṁ taṁ nopeksheran sabhāsadaḥ
   Upekshyamāṇaḥ sanṛipāḥ narakaṁ yāntyadhomukhāḥ
   Śukra, IV, 5, 275.
5. Sabhā vā na praveshṭavyā vaktavyaṁ vā samañjasam
   Abruvan vibruvan vāpi naro bhavati kilbishī.
   Śukra, IV, 5, 29.
6. Rāgāllobhād bhayād vāpi smṛityarthe vādhikāriṇaḥ
   Sabhyādīn daṇḍayitvā tu hyadhikārānnivartayet.
   Śukra, IV, 5, 93.
7. Rājñā niyojitavyāste sabhyāḥ sarvāsu jātishu.
   Śukra, IV, 5, 17.

help of merchants, soldiers with the help of soldiers, making it clear that jurors were selected from all the castes.

It appears that pleaders emerged in society during our period. They are not mentioned by Nārada; his commentator Asahāya, however, refers to them. Śukra (IV, 5, 110) refers to Tajña-Pratinidhi, who was to plead on behalf of minors, women and old men. It would appear that if a party did not belong to any of these categories, the Pratinidhi or pleader could not be appointed. In some cases, however, parties regarded as incapable of defending their own cases, were allowed to have the Pratinidhi. The statements made by these Tajña-Pratinidhis were regarded as binding on their clients.

The clerical staff of the court consisted of an accountant and a *Lekhaka*. The former probably collected the court fees, and the latter recorded the statements of the parties. The *Lekhaka*[1] writing incorrect statements was punished as severely as a thief.

Let us now survey the fundamental principles followed by the Hindu jurisprudence. The first and the most important among them was that the trial should be held in public and no case should be heard in secret either by the king or by the chief justice or by the Sabhyas.[2]

Both the king and chief justice should try the case with the help of jurors. Smṛitis, whether early or late, are particular on this point.[3]

Judgment was to be in accordance with the rules of Dharmaśāstras. 'Even the king is a sinner', says Śukra, 'if he decides the case in an arbitrary manner; he should therefore administer justice in accordance with the spirit of Dharmaśāstra'.[4]

1. Anyaduktaṁ likhedanyadyo'rthipratyarthināṁ vachaḥ
   Chauravat trāsayedrājā lekhakaṁ drāgatandritaḥ.
   Śukra, IV, 5, 63.
2. Naikaḥ paśyechcha kāryāṇi vādinaḥ śṛiṇuyād vachaḥ.
   Rahasi cha nṛipaḥ prājñaḥ sabhyās'chaiva kadāchana.
   Śukra, IV, 5, 6.
3. Sabhyādibhirvinirṇiktaṁ vidhṛitaṁ prativādinā
   Dṛishṭvā rājā tu jayine pradadyājjayapatrakam.
   Śukra, IV, 5, 285.
4. Svatantraḥ sādhayannarthān rājāpi syāchcha kilbishī.
   Dharmaśāstrāvirodhena hyarthaśastraṁ vichārayet.
   Śukra. IV, 5, 274.

Cases should be tried as soon as possible; for if they will be delayed, there will arise great difficulties, which will lead to miscarriage of justice. Law's delays are also condemned by the Smṛitis.

Evidence was to be recorded in the presence of both the parties. Śukra advises the king not to record any evidence, if one party is absent.[2]

Cases should not be decided as far as possible with only one kind of evidence, *i.e.*, oral, documentary or circumstantial. Effort was to be made to have all available evidence.[3]

Cases were normally tried in the order of priority; but the gravity or importance of a case often led to its being taken up earlier.[4]

Amendment in the plaint was possible before the statement of the opponent was filed; but after the filing of the statement, no amendment was permitted.[5]

Retrial could be possible only after depositing a double stamp duty[6] (*daṇḍa*). Stamps did not exist in our period but the word stamp duty has been used here for the sake of convenience.

The judges were to act with ideal decency; during the pendency of a suit, they were not to have any private talk or communications with the parties.[7]

POPULAR COURTS

The epigraphical records of our period do not at all refer to the popular courts, which were a special feature of ancient

1. Na Kālaharaṇaṁ kāryyaṁ rājñā sādhanadarśane
Mahān dosho bhavet Kālātdharmavyāpattilakshaṇam.
Śukra, IV, 5, 167.
2. Arthipratyarthipratyakshaṁ sādhanāni pradarśayet
Apratyakshaṁ tayornaiva grihṇīyāt sādhanaṃ nripaḥ,
Śukra, IV, 5, 168.
3. Kevalena cha bhogena lekhenāpi cha sākshibhiḥ
Kāryyaṁ na chintayedrāja lokadeśādidharmataḥ
Śukra, IV, 5, 211-12
4. Kramāgatān vivādaṁstu paśyed vā kāryyagauravat.
Śukra, IV, 5, 156.
5. Śrāvayitvā tu yat kāryyaṁ tyajedanyad vadedasau.
Anyapakshāśrayād vādī hīno daṇḍyaścha sa'smṛitaḥ.
Śukra, IV, 5, 136
6. Dviguṇaṁ daṇḍamādhāya punastat kāryyamuddharet.
Śukra, IV, 5, 167.
7. Na kālaharaṇaṁ kāryyaṁ rājñā sākshiprabhāshaṇe.
Śukra, IV, 5, 1.93

Indian polity for a long time. The Nīti writers, on the other hand, reveal the existence of such popular courts knowns as *Kula*, *Śreṇī*, and *Gaṇa* during our period. Śukra clearly states at one place that the *Śreṇīs* should consider points passed over by the *Kulas*; the *Gaṇas* were to review the cases decided by the *Śreṇīs* and lastly the king and his officers were to be the higher courts of appeal.[1] The *Kula*, *Sreṇī* and *Gaṇa* were thus the three types of popular courts, each succeeding one being more important than the preceding one. When and where these three failed to administer proper justice, the king or his officers were to interfere.

Unfortunately Śukra does not explain the nature of the above three types of popular courts. But on the evidence of the Mitāksharā composed towards the end of our period, we can say that *Kula* court consisted of a group of relations, near or distant. It is important to note that in ancient India joint families were the order of the day and they were usually very large. When therefore a disagreement or dispute used to take place between two members of a family, it was usually settled by its elders. If they failed to bring about any compromise, the *Śreṇī* or the guild court used to intervene. It is important to note that *Śreṇīs* or guilds became a prominent feature of commercial life in ancient India from *c.* 500 B.C. They were well organised and had their own executive committees of four or five members. It is therefore not unlikely that these executive committees would have been entrusted with the work of the settlement of disputes among the members of the guild. The nature of Gaṇa court is difficult to ascertain. Probably it was identical with the Pūga court of Yājñavalkya, which consisted of persons of different castes and professions, but residing in the same place.[2] It was obviously the popular Pañchāyat court.

1. Vichāryya śreṇibhiḥ kāryyaṁ kulairyannāvichāritam,
Gaṇaiścha śreṇyavijnātaṁ gaṇajñātaṁ niyuktakaiḥ.
Kulādibhyo'dhikāḥ sabhyāstebhyo'dhyaksho'dhikaḥ kṛitaḥ,
Sarveshāmadhiko rājā dharmādharmaniyojakaḥ.
Śukra, IV, 5, 30-31.

2. Nṛipenādhikṛitāḥ pūgāḥ śreṇayo'tha kulāni cha
pūrvaṁ purvaṁguru jñeyam vyavahāravidhaunṛinām.
Bhinnajātīnāṁ bhinna-vṛittīnāṁ ekasthāna-nivāsināṁ samūhāḥ pūgāḥ
Yāj. II, 29-30.

Ample evidence exists to show that the village Panchāyat court continued to function efficiently even under the Muslim rule in the Deccan. We find the Muslim emperor Ibrahim Adil Shah of Bijapur refusing to entertain the appeal of Bapaji Musalman for the retrial of his case in the royal court. During the medieval period, we come across several Maratha kings, refusing to entertain any case at the first instance. Thus when the dispute about the *Patilkī-watan* of Ravet in Poona Pargana was taken to Shahaji, the father of Shivaji, he ordered that the Panchāyat of the place concerned should decide the case.[1] Shivaji also, while declining to entertain the case of one Ramaji Krishna, makes an interesting statement, which is very important. He said to the plaintiff "If you so wish, I shall send your case to your own village Panchāyat if that will meet your desire, or I shall refer it to the district Panchāyat, if that course recommends itself to you. Let me know what you like."[2] It is interesting to note here that though Shivaji puts before the plaintiff a number of alternatives, he nowhere refers to the possibility of the trial of the case by himself or by any of his officers. Shivaji's son Rajaram also followed the same practice. When a very important dispute involving the *Watan* right to more than twenty villages was referred to him, he immediately directed the local Panchāyat to decide it.

While there thus exists ample evidence to show that the Village Panchāyats and guild courts were actually functioning even under the Muslim rule in Maharashtra, we have no contemporary epigraphical evidence to show that they were actually functioning as suggested by Śukra. We have, however, to remember in this connection that these popular courts are first mentioned by Yājñavalkya and then by Nārada, Bṛihaspati, Somadeva and Śukra. These writers covered a period of about a thousand years, *c.* 250 to 1250 A.D., and they could not have mechanically referred to the popular courts if they were not actually functioning. A reference in the *Jñāneśvarī*[3] shows that cases were tried actually by the village *chāvaḍī* in the Deccan in *c.* 1300 A.D.

1. *Raj. Ait. Lekh.*, Vol. XVI, No. 82.
2. A.S. Altekar, *Village Communities*, p. 46.
3. *Jñāneśvarī* 18, 382; 16, 295.

It is important to note that Somadeva, who flourished in the 10th century, observes that the royal courts could be approached only after a case was decided by the town or the village court.[1] The village court, he refers to, must obviously have been the Gaṇa court of the Nārada and Śukra. Had it not been functioning, Somadeva could hardly have laid down that the royal courts should come in the picture only after a case was decided by the village court. It is also very unlikely that they could suddenly have sprung into existence in Western India under the Muslim rule as shown by the papers of Maratha history. We must therefore conclude that they were a reality in the body politic during our period though not mentioned by contemporary epigraphs. The silence of the latter was probably due to there being no occasion to mention them.

We thus see that the village Panchāyats played an important part throughout the long course of Indian history. They flourished in India, not due to anarchy as was propounded by Sir Henry Maine, but because the Central Government was itself refusing to entertain any suits at the first instance and was deliberately referring all of them back to the village Panchāyats. The village Panchāyats thus reduced the burden of the Central Government, helped the cause of justice and encouraged the principle of self-government.

1. *Nvk.*, XXVII. 22.

CHAPTER IX

FEUDATORIES

Feudatory states existed in India since very early times; they are not a new feature in Indian polity introduced by Lord Wellesely. From the very beginning of the historic period of Indian history, we find that a big empire was not directly administered by the emperor, however powerful he might have been. Some parts of the empire used to be under the direct control of the Central Government, while others were put in charge of chiefs, who had recognised the suzerain's authority and were willing to act according to his orders. This arrangement is but natural. India is a vast country and the means of communications were very poor in ancient time. Owing to this circumstance, the political writers of ancient India were generally in favour of continuing the existence of feudatory chiefs. It is important to note that even when an enemy or a king was defeated and conquered, the conqueror, according to Manu, was expected not to annex the kingdom of the vanquished king, but to crown him or any other member of his family, provided he agreed to behave in a loy al way.[1]

This principle of non-annexation was followed in India nearly by all the dynasties, as it permitted local culture, trading and political institutions to develop more or less unhampered. Even the Arab writer Sulaiman, who flourished during our period, observes, "When a king subdues a neighbouring state in India, he places over it a man belonging to the family of the fallen prince, who carries on the government in the name of the conqueror."[2] It is due to this principle that we find a number of feudatory states existing during our period of survey, as they did in the earlier period. The records of the Pālas, the Pratīhāras,

1. Sthāpayettatra tadvaṁśyaṁ kuryāccha samayakṛiyām.
Manu, VII, 22

2. Elliot and Dowson; *History of India*, Vol. I, p. 7.

the Senas, the Chandellas, the Chaulukyas, the Chāhamānas, the Paramāras and the Chedis clearly indicate that the rulers of the above houses had many feudatories under them. Some of them belonged to ancient royal families ruling for a long time, and others were kings of more recent origin. We propose to discuss the relations between the emperor and the feudatories in this chapter; epigraphical evidence and the data in works of writers on polity will both be of help to us.

As may be expected, the feudatories were of different grades. Śukra refers to two of them, the Sāmanta and the Māṇḍalika.[1] Contemporary inscriptions also refer to both these classes. Perhaps Mahāmaṇḍaleśvaras constituted a third and higher class. Our epigraphs refer to feudatories and their sub-feudatories. Thus *Rāṇaka* Śaṅkarasiṁha was a subordinate of the king Vāpanadeva, who in his turn was a feudatory of the Chaulukya emperor Jayasiṁha in 1146 A.D.[2] Yaśovarman, who was a feudatory of the Paramāra king Bhojadeva, had his own sub-feudatory chief *Rāṇaka* Āmam.[3] It is interesting to note that a similar practice prevailed in the South also during our period. The Raṭṭas of Saundatti, who were the feudatories, first of the Rāshṭrakūṭas and then of the latter Chālukyas, had their own sub-feudatories.[4] Govinda III, the Rāshṭrakūṭa king, had under him a feudatory called Karkka ruling over Southern Gujarāta in 813 A.D., who had in turn a sub-feudatory named Śrī Buddhavarsha of Salukika family, who was governing Siharika 12.[5] The feudatories could thus create their own sub-feudatories probably with the previous permission of the emperor.

It is important to note that during our period of survey, royal officers, ministers and provincial governors began to

1. According to Śukra I, 282-83, the income of the *sāmanta* was to be between one and three lakhs of silver karshas and that of the *māṇḍalika* between three and ten lakhs of the same coin. Karsha as a silver coin weighing 100 Raṭṭis was not in vogue in the Hindu period and we may therefore doubt whether the information holds good of our age.
2. *I.A.*, X, 159
3. *E.I.*, XIX, 73-7
4. *I.A.*, XIV, 24.
5. *E.I*, III, p. 53.

assume feudatory titles and hence sometimes it becomes difficult to state whether a particular Mahāmaṇḍaleśvara was really a feudatory king or whether he was a provincial governor with feudatory titles. This confusion becomes more confounded, when we find the defeated feudatory chiefs being appointed to important posts of administration. Śukra, however, gives a valuable clue for the solution of this riddle. He observes that a *Śāmanta* is a feudatory ruler over 100 villages, while *nṛisāmanta* is an officer in charge of the same number of villages.[1] This Nīti writer thus differentiates the two by giving them separate nomenclature; our inscriptions, however, do not do so.

Sometimes the feudatories were appointed to high posts in the Central Government. Thus the Vāghelā chief Vīradhavala, the feudatory of the Chaulukya king Kumārapāla, and Ratnapāla, the feudatory of the king Bhīma II of the same dynasty were both in charge of *Samastamudrāvyāpāra* (*E.I.* VIII, 219-22; *I.A.*, XVIII, 112). Māṇḍalike Malayasiṁha was a minister of Chandella king Trailokyavarman (*E.I. XXV* p. 2). Sometimes, they were even entrusted with the supervision of the entire kingdom of the overlord. The Ratnapur inscription of the Kalachūri year 915 informs us, how the Chedi king Pṛithvīdeva obtained great mental happiness after entrusting the government of Talahāri *maṇḍala* to his feudatory Brahmadeva (*E.I.*, XXVI, 257). All this evidence clearly indicates that the feudatory chiefs, when loyal, were well-treated by their overlords and were often appointed to high posts.

The status and titles of the feudatories naturally differed according to their grades. The Jain writer *Ravākopyachāra* informs us that 'important feudatories were entitled to the use of five musical instruments (*Pañchamahāśabdas*) namely *Śriṅga*, *Śaṅkha*, *Bherī*, *Ayaghaṇṭā* and *Tamaṭa*.[2] They were also allowed the use of a feudal throne, fly whisk, palanquin and elephants. They bore high sounding titles like *Mahāmaṇḍaleśvara*, *Mahāsāmanta*, and *Mahāmāṇḍalika*.

1. *Śukra*, I, 190.
2. *I.A.*, XII, 96; In Kashmir, however, the term Pañchmahāśabda denoted the five officers (1) Mahāpratihārapīda (2) Mahāsandhivigrahika (3) Mahāśvaśāla (4) Mahābhāṇḍāgāra and Mahāsādhanabhāga. *Rāja*; IV, 140-43.

Sometimes we find the feudatories even assuming the imperial title *Mahārājādhirāja*. It is difficult to understand the reason, which led the feudatories to assume the imperial title. In some cases, it is probably that the decline in the power of the central authority would have given them an opportunity to declare their independence and to assume the imperial titles. Thus during the decline of the Pratīhāra empire, a number of its feudatories quietly assumed the imperial title *Mahārājādhirāja Parameśvara*. The Rājor inscription shows that when Vijayapāladeva was unable to look after the administration, his feudatory Mathandeva declared himself as an independent ruler by assuming the imperial title *Mahārājādhirāja Parameśvara*.[1] Similarly when the power of the Chaulukyas was altogether weakened, the Vāghelā family, tracing descent from a sister of Kumārapāla, reaped a rich harvest out of this opportunity and leapt into prominence. Lavaṇa-prasāda, and his Vāghelā minister (the feudatory of Bholā Bhīma) and his son Vīradhavala carved out a principality round Dholka and thus established themselves in an almost independent position in Southern Gujarat. In the Mount Abu inscription of 1287 A.D., they are called merely *Rāṇaka* and *Mahāmaṇḍaleśvara* but in 1288 A.D., they assumed the imperial epithet *Mahārājādhirāja*.[2] During the decline of the Pratīhāra rule Dhūrmaṭa assumed the imperial title Mahārājādhirāja in *c.* 966 A.D. and Nishkalaṅka in 1025 A.D.[2] The position of these feudatories was perhaps similar to that of the provincial governors like the Vaziers of Oudh during the last days of Moghul rule, as observed by Dr. R.C. Majumdar.[3]

Feudatory chiefs had usually to entertain an officer from the imperial court, whose position was similar to that of the Political Agent or Resident under the British administration. He exercised general power of supervision and control over the feudatories and used to give full information to the king about the happenings in the feudatory states. He had a large number of spies under him to detect whether the

1. *E.I.* III, 266-67.
2. *E.I.*, I, 173.
3. R.C. Majumdar, *History of Bengal*, P. 275.

feudatory kings were contemplating sedition or revolt against the imperial power.

The 'Political Agent' considerably restricted the powers of the feudatory chiefs. We sometimes find him countersigning the grants of the feudatories on behalf of the king. Thus according to the Unā charter, Dhīika, who was probably such an officer under Mahendrapāla, gave his approval to a grant made by *Mahāsāmanta* Avanivarman II.[1] It was Tantrapāla Mādhava, who allowed Indrarāja, the Chāhamāna feudatory, to make an endowment for the upkeep of a temple.[2] It is thus clear that the 'Political Agent' occupied an important place of honour and power in the feudatory states. He was received, as merchant Sulaiman observes, "with profound respect that was naturally expected to be shown to the representative of the paramount power."

It will be convenient here to describe the relations between the imperial power and its feudatories. There is clear evidence to show that the paramount power did not exercise the same kind of control over all the feudatories. General obedience to the imperial power was expected in every case. All feudatories were also required to pay a regular tribute. This was sometimes sent directly to the capital, as was done by the feudatories of South Kośala in the case of their suzerain Jājalladeva I (*E.I.* I p. 53). Sometimes, however, it was collected by the emperor during his tour of inspection, as we find in the case of the Rāshṭrakūṭa king Govinda III, who is stated to have collected the tributes from his feudatories during his tour in the South.[3] Feudatories were expected to be present at the imperial court not only on ceremonial occasions,[4] but also at periodical intervals

1. *E.I.*, IX, I.
2. *E.I.*, XV, 182-8. These examples are no doubt few, but we cannot ignore their evidence. Usually the sanction of the emperor himself was taken and so there was no necessity of getting the permission of the Political Agent.
3. *I.A.*, XI, 126.
4. Mandalādhipati Chanda of Aṅga was present at Madanapāla's coronation and spread out the rich material for this ceremony (*Rāmacharita*, III-16 commentary). In Kashmir, vassals used to attend the coronation (Rt. VIII. 3303)

for offering personal homage to the king. They had apparently no right of issuing their own coins.

It is difficult to state whether the emperor had the right of interfering in the matter of the succession of feudatories, as the records of our period do not throw any satisfactory light upon the point. We do not know whether the permission of the sovereign was necessary at the time of succession, nor can we say with certainty whether the hereditary principle of crowning the eldest son was invariably followed. It may be noted that during the British rule, in the case of feudatory states, when a new prince was to be crowned the permission of the paramount power was required. The same probably would have been the case with the feudatories of our period also.

Under the Gupta administration, however, kings who had been reduced to the feudatory status after conquest, were apparently granted imperial charters, regranting them their territories under such conditions as were agreed or imposed. This claim is made in the Allahabad pillar inscription of Samudragupta, but we have so far discovered no such charters. It is very likely that the imperial overlord would be present in person at the time of crowning the new feudatory prince, as we find in the case of a Valabhi ruler Droṇasiṁha, who was a Gupta feudatory, whose installation was performed by the paramount master in person, the sole lord of the circumference of the territory of the whole earth.[1]

Very often, the feudatory chiefs in India had to participate with their forces in the military campaigns of their feudal lords. Thus Harsharāja Guhila, who was a feudatory of the Pratīhāra king Bhoja, is said to have assisted the emperor in one of his Northern campaigns.[2] Kakka, a feudatory of the king Nāgabhaṭṭa, also claims to have fought with the army of his overlord against the Gauḍas in battle at Mudgagiri.[3] Guṇāmbodhideva, another feudatory of Bhoja, had taken a prominent part in the campaign of the former

1. Majumdar and Altekar; *The Age of the Vākāṭakas*, p. 187.
2. *E.I.*, XII, 15.
3. *E.I.*, XVIII, 108, 112.

against the Pālas. The Kāhlā plates inform us, how Guṇāmbodhideva took away the fortune of the Gauḍas in his successful expedition.[1] Guhila, a chief of the Kalachūri family, accompanied his suzerain Mahendrapāla in his expedition against Magadha and Bengal with his cavalry recruited from the sea-coast.[2] Kalachūri prince Soḍhadeva is also known to have participated in the Bengal campaign of Bhoja.[3] Śaṅkaragaṇa, a feudatory of Nāgabhaṭṭa, is also said to have fought against the ruler of Bengal on his emperor's behalf. The Guhila king Bhaṭṭa, who was a feudatory of Mahīpāla, is said to have defeated the armies of the kings of the south at the behest of his overlord.[4] Balavarman, a feudatory of Mahendrapāla I, is stated to have 'freed the earth from the Hūṇa race' by slaying Jājappa and other kings.[5] The same practice was followed in the Gāhaḍavāla and other dynasties also. Kumārapāla and Vatsarāja accompanied the Gāhaḍavāla ruler Govindachandra, their feudal lord, in his military campaign.[6] Māṇḍalika, the feudatory of the Paramāra king Jayasiṁha, helped him in vanquishing the opposing force led by general Kaṇha.[7] Yaśodhavala, the Paramāra feudatory of Kumārapāla, assisted him in his campaign against Mallikārjuna, the ruler of Koṅkaṇa.[8] He also offered his services to Kumārapāla in his war against the Mālwā king.[9] Dhārāvarsha, a son of the feudatory chief Yaśodhavala, also followed the army of Kumārapāla in its march against Koṅkaṇa.[10] Prahlādanadeva, a son of Dhārāvarsha, also went to help the Gurjara king Ajayapāladeva, when the latter was attacked by Śāmantasiṁha of Mewar.[11] Lakshamaṇarāja, the Chedi

1. *E.I.*. VII, 85-93.
2. *E.I.*, XII, 15 Verse—23.
3. *Ibid.*,
4. *Ibid.*, IX, 12, 16.
5. *E.I.*, IX, 1-10.
6. *E.I.*, IV, 130-33.
7. *E.I.*, XXI, 47.
8. *E.I.*, VIII, 216.
9. *E.I.*, VIII, 216.
10. *E.I.*, VIII, 216.
11. *E.I.*, VIII, 202.

ruler, is also stated to have been accompanied in his march against the western region by the infantry of the tributary chiefs, whose names are unfortunately not mentioned in the records.

The contemporary south Indian records also show, how the feudatories had to supply a certain number of troops to their feudal lords and how they used to participate in the imperial campaigns. Thus Narasiṁha Chālukya, who was a feudatory of the Rāshṭrakūṭa king Indra III, is stated to have taken a prominent part in the latter's campaign against the Pratīhāra king Mahīpāla.[1] The Chālukyas of Veṅgi, the feudatories of the Rāshṭrakūṭas, had to support the latter in their wars against the Gaṅgas.[2] It may be noted that the practice of taking military help from the feudatories was followed in India also under the British rule. In both the World Wars, states like Bikaner, Gwalior, Mysore and Hydrabad had sent their forces to help the British in France, Northern Africa and Mesopotamia.

Whether the practice of allowing feudatories to maintain their own forces to be used by the emperor when necessary is a sound one, may well be doubted. Several instances, however, show that it was the root-cause of the weakness of Indian Polity, for very often, when an emperor was in great difficulties, the feudatory chiefs used to dictate their own terms, while giving him the military support. Thus Rāmapāla of Bengal had to pay a heavy price for getting the support of his feudatories to win the throne. Even when a strong emperor could keep the feudatories under control, the very presence of the latter was an influence, which disturbed the unity of administration. Feudatories were frequently intriguing against the emperor either covertly or openly.

The measure of internal autonomy, that was enjoyed by different feudatories, was not uniform in all the dynasties. It differed according to their power and prestige and also according to the circumstances. The bigger feudatories of course must have had enjoyed a large amount of internal autonomy. Subject to the payment of a certain amount of

1. A.S. Altekar, *Rāshṭrakūṭas*, 265.
2. *I.A.*, XII, 91-94.

tribute, they had full right over their revenues. They could even make land grants without taking the permission of the imperial power. Sometimes, they do not even refer to their suzerain in their records. Thus Mahāmaṇḍaleśvara Vaijalladeva, who was a feudatory of the king Ajayapāladeva in 1173 A.D. and was ruling in Narmadātaṭa-maṇḍala refers to a number of political officers such as *Daṇḍanāyaka*, *Deshaṭhakkura*, *Adhiśṭhānaka*, *Karaṇapurush*, *Shayyāpāla*, etc., while making a land grant.[1] It is, however, interesting to note that he is silent about the emperor's permission. Nor does the charter contain the signature of the emperor; it is signed by the feudatory alone. Similarly Mahāmaṇḍaleśvara Mahārājakula Somasiṁhadeva, the lord of Chandrāvati and the feudatory of the Chaulukya king Bhīmadeva, while granting the village of Davāṇī for the worship of Nemīnātha, did not take the permission of his sovereign.[2] Māṇḍalika, feudatory of Jayasiṁha, also enjoyed full powers over the revenues of his fief, for he is also stated to have made a land grant to the Maṇḍaleśvara, without taking the permission of his imperial over-lord.[3] Dhārāvarsha, feudatory of the Chaulukya king Kumārapāla, granted one *halavāhā* of land at the village of Śāvadā to the merchant named Ampā without taking consent of his imperial overlord[4]. Our epigraphs supply several other similar instances.[5]

1. *I.A.*, VI, II, 80-85.
2. *E.I.*, VIII, 204-07.
3. *E.I.*, XXI, 47.
4. *I.A.*, LVI, 51.

5 (a) *E.I.*, XIX, 80, for such a grant by Mahāmaṇḍaleśvara Pṛithvīdeva, a feudatory of a Tripuri king.
(b) *I.A.*, VI, 203-4, for such a grant by Sāmantaśiṁha, a feudatory of the king Vīsaladeva.
(c) *I.A.*, XVII, 230-234, for a grant by Mahārāṇaka Kumārapāla, a feudatory of the king Trailokyavarman.
(d) *I.A.*, XVII, 224-27, for a grant by Kīrtivarmā, a feudatory of the king Jayasiṁha.
(e) *A.S.I.W.C.*, for a grant by Rājyadeva, a feudatory of the king Naravarman.
(f) *I.A.*, XVI, 252-56, for a grant by Udayavarmadeva, a feudatory of the king Jayavarmadeva.
(j) *E.I.*, III, 266-67, for a grant by Mathanadeva, a feudatory of the king Vijayapāla.
(h) *E.I.* XIX, 178, for a grant by Mahāmāṇḍalika Sīyaka, a feudatory of the Rāshṭrakūṭa king Kṛishṇa III.

The bigger feudatories could create their own sub-feudatories and also could appoint their own officers to control them. They even could compel the sub-feudatories to take their permission at the time of issuing charters. Thus the sub-feudatory Rāṇā Śaṅkarasiṁha had to take permission of mahāmaṇḍaleśvara Vāpanadeva, when he wanted to alienate three ploughs of land to meet the expenses of a temple.[1] There is, however, an exceptional case, which refers to a sub-feudatory chief making a grant without taking consent of his feudal lord. The Kālāvān plates of Yaśovarman inform us that Rāṇaka Āmma, who, in his turn was a feudatory of Bhojadeva, granted certain pieces of land at Mahishābaddhika in the holy Tīrtha of Kālakeśvara without taking the consent of his feudal lord.[2] It is very likely that the plates would have been issued during the last days of the reign of Yaśovarman, when he was unable to control his kingdom, and his sub-feudatory gained power. It is also not unlikely that the non-mention of the consent of Yaśovarman might have been due to the negligence of the drafter of the grant.

Some of the feudatories of the Paramāras and the chedis though ruling over only ‹ 4 villages are seen referring to their Sandhivigrahikas and Mahāmātyas in their records[3] So bigger feudatories must have had a full-fledged ministry and all the paraphernalia of a royal court, if the smaller ones were having their foreign ministers and chief ministers.

It is clear that the control, which the emperor exercised over big feudatories was not strict. This is also evident from a letter of Akkam, the Lohāṇā chief of Brāhmaṇābāda, to Chacha, who had called upon him to recognise his sovereignty—"I have never shown you opposition or quarrelled with you. Your letter of friendship was received, and I was much exalted by it. Our friendship shall remain and no animosity shall arise. I will comply with your orders. You are at liberty to reside at any place within the territory of Brāhmaṇābāda. If you have resolved to go in any other direction,

1. *I.A.*, X, 159, Vāpanadeva was himself a feudatory of Jayasiṁha.
2. *E.I.*, XIX, 71-73.
3. *E.I.*. XIX, 10.

there is no body to prevent or molest you. I possess such power and influence and can render you aid."

The powers of small feudatories were limited. They had no full right over their fiefs. They were only allowed to enjoy their income. They could not alienate or sell villages and lands in their fiefs. Thus when Gāṅgeyadeva, who was a feudatory of the king Jayavarman, was making a grant, he had to supplicate the permission of his overlord.[1] Dharaṇivarāha, a feudatory of the king Mahīpāla, had to secure the consent of his overlord, before making a grant.[2] Rāṇaka Lavaṇapravāha, a feudatory of Madanapāla, had to take the permission of Govindachandra, while granting the village Rāmaitha in the Siguroḍha *pattalā* to Brāhmaṇa Guṇachandra.[3] Vatsarāja, a feudatory of Govindachandra, had to take his sovereign's permission, while granting the village of Ambavara to Brāhmaṇa Dalhuśarman.[4] The Pipliānagar plate of Mahakumara Harishchandra, the feudatory of the king Jayavarmadeva, not only bears his own signature, but also that of Rāmachandra, who was most probably his suzerain's representative.[5] In the Pratīhāra empire, even the feudatories in distant places like Kathiawar, had to take the imperial permission for such transactions; the officers of the Central Government had to sanction such alienations on behalf of their suzerain by authenticating the documents by their signatures. Thus when Balavarman and Avanivarman II of Kathiawar wanted to grant the villages of Jayapur and Amvulaka, in the Saurāshṭra *maṇḍala*, they had to take permission of Dhīika, who was a representative of the Central Government, and is seen signing the grant on its behalf.[6] The Chāhamāna records also show that their feudatories could make grants generally with the consent of the provincial representative of the suzerain.[7]

It is interesting to note that the same practice prevailed

1. *E.I.*, IX, 120-3.
2. *I.A.*, XII, 195.
3. *I.A.*, XVIII, 16.
4. *E.I.*, IV, 130-33.
5. *J.A.S.B.*, VII, 736-9.
6. *E.I.*, IX, 1.
7. *E.I.*, XIV, 176-86.

in the south also during our period of survey. Thus when Budhavarsha, a Chaulukya feudatory of Govinda III desired to give a village to a Jain sage, he had to supplicate for the permission of his feudal lord.[1] Vīrachola and Pṛithvīpati II, feudatories of the Cholas, had to take imperial sanction, before they could alienate villages in charity.[2] The early Kadambas also excercised a similar control over their feudatories.[3] All this evidence clearly indicates that the practice of getting imperial permission usually prevailed in most of the contemporary dynasties, both in the South and the North, with reference to smaller feudatories.

The position of the third-rate feudatories was very precarious. All their activities were strictly controlled either by the emperor or by his representative. They were not the masters of their fiefs and had no full control over their revenues. There are a number of cases to show the emperor giving away in charity villages situated within their jurisdiction. Thus the Godapura plate records a grant made by Gāṅgeyadeva at the dictate of his emperor Jayavarman.[4] The king Vijayachandra issued a charter in 1168 A.D., assigning two villages in the domain of his feudatory Śrī-Pratāpadhavala.[5] The Chaulukya queen Saubhāgyadevī alienated the village of Ajhāri, which was in the domain of her feudatory Yaśodhavala.[6] Naravarman granted on one occasion twenty ploughs of land from the village Kadambapadraka, which was under the jurisdiction of his feudatory Rājyadeva, and on another occasion he gifted away six ploughs of land from the same village.[7] The Gāhaḍavāla records also show that the Central Government could assign villages from the territories of its feudatories.

It would thus be seen that the smaller feudatories were not full masters of the entire revenues of their fiefs. It is also likely that their day-to-day administration was not

1. *I.A.*, XII, 15.
2. *E.I.*, IV, 82.
3. *I.A.*, VI, 32.
4. *E.I.*, IX, 120-3.
5. *J.A.S.B.*, VI, 547.
6. *I.A.*, LVI, 12.
7. *A.S.I.W.C.*, P.R., 84.

always free from imperial interference. The feudatories were subjected to a number of indignities, if they dared to rebel and were defeated in war. They were even deposed from the throne, if necessary. Thus the Ajhāri inscription of 1145 A.D. informs us that when Kumārapāla and Arṇoruṇa came into conflict, Vikramasiṁha, the feudatory of Kumārapāla, turned treacherous to his lord. Kumārapāla defeated and dethroned Vikramaśiṁha and put his nephew Yaśodhavala on the throne.[1] Sometimes the feudatories were compelled to do menial work. A verse in the Sanjan plates of Amoghavarsha I, which is incomplete and obscure, states that feudatories had to sweep the stables of horses (*virajasamabhitenuryasya vāhyālibhūmiṁ*) of his camp.[2] Feudatories were also forced to surrender their forces, elephants and treasury as a punishment for their disloyalty. Sometimes they had also to send their young princes as companions to the heir-apparent, as was done in the case of Mādhavasena and his brother in the time of Harsha. Even their wives were also sometimes put into prison, and the conqueror used to marry them forcibly as Chācha did in Sindh;[3] this would indicate that the less cultured princes used to subject them to further indignities and humiliations. The feudatories had also to offer their daughters in marriage to the emperor, if the latter was inclined to accept them. Thus under the Guptas, the Śaka feudatories of Samudragupta are said to have offered their daughters in marriage to the emperor. The records of our period, however, do not give us any such instances, though they were probably not unknown to it.

On the other hand, when the Imperial Government became weak, the feudatories could not only rebel with impunity but also assume independent status. Thus when the last few rulers of the Pāla dynasty were unable to carry on the administration properly, a number of feudatories

1. Ajhari Inscription of Yaśovarman.
2. Nikṛitivikṛita Gaṅgāśṛiṅkhalī baddhanishṭḥā (śṛinkhalābaddha) bṛitimayurankūla maṇḍleśā (maṇḍaleśāḥ) svabhṛitya. Virajasamīha temuryasya (mabhitena) *Vāhyālibhūmim* Parivṛiti (parivritimanu) vishṭyā Veṅgināthādayopi.
   E.I., XVIII, 246, V. 33.
   For *Bahyāli* as stables, see *Mānasollāsa*, Chap. III, p. 61-63.
3. A.S. Altekar, *Rāsṭrakūṭas*; 267.

asserted themselves and the authority of the Pālas was then confined to a portion of their kingdom, where they maintained a precarious hold for a short period, hemmed in the East by the Senas and in the West by the Gāhaḍavālas. The same was the case with the Chedis of Tripuri, for we learn that when the king Gayakarṇa was unable to exercise effective control, the Ratnapur branch of the Kalachūris asserted its independence in South Kośala. The feudatories of the Pratīhāras and Chaulukyas did the same during the decline of the power of their overlords. Even if the feudatories did not declare themselves independent, they practically exercised full sovereign authority. Thus the chiefs, who rallied to the cause of Rāmapāla, were all practically independent even though the *Rāmacharita* calls them Sāmantas. The charter issued by Vaijalladeva, a feudatory of the king Ajayapāladeva, is drawn up exactly in the style of independent kings.[1] It is further important to note that even when the emperor was a strong one, the feudatories were generally inclined to try to become independent by overthrowing the imperial yoke. Thus during the later years of Jayasiṁha's reign, his feudatory the Chāhamāna Āśarāja revolted against him and became independent. Under such circumstances, it was but natural for the kings not to get regular tributes from their feudatories.

The communications being what they were, kingdoms of considerable size could normally become possible in ancient India only by recognising local kings as feudatories, and inducing them to co-operate in the common venture of building up a strong state, which could, owing to its increased resources, secure a better and all-round progress of the country. This, for instance, happened under the Guptas, Harshavardhana and the Pratīhāras. The feudatories, however, introduced an element of instability in the imperial state; when there was no strong and tactful emperor at the centre, they would either fight among themselves or intrigue for overthrowing the imperial power. This stood in the way of the development of a strong centralised state in the country, so necessary for its defence from external foes. Possibly times were not favourable for such a development as a permanent feature of Hindu polity.

1. *I.A.*, XVIII, 80-85.

CHAPTER X

CONCLUSION

We have finished our survey and discussion of the different aspects of the administrative system during our period. It is hoped that the reader will find the account to be more vivid and comprehensive than that of most of the earlier periods of the Ancient Indian History. As regards the Mauryan period, we have valuable contemporary literary evidence, namely the *Arthaśāstra* of Kauṭilya, throwing a flood of light upon the Mauryan administration; but how far its picture is realistic and how far idealistic we do not know, for Aśokan inscriptions are not quite sufficient to check it. In the case of the Indo-Greek, the Scythian and the Kushana periods, the information that we get about their administration is admittedly fragmentary. As regards the Gupta Age, we have a large number of inscriptions of the Guptas as well as of their contemporaries, but the information supplied by them about the administrative structure is not quite copious. Further, we do not have the advantage of comparing the data supplied by the inscriptions with that supplied by any contemporary Nīti works.

During our period of survey, the epigraphical evidence is happily ample and it can be correlated with the data in the contemporary Nīti works, among which the *Śukranīti* of Śukra is the most important.[1] This work gives us a very vivid and comprehensive account of the administrative machinery. It is due to this reason that it has become possible to present a fairly detailed, comprehensive and realistic picture of the administration and political institutions of the period.

As regards the efficiency of the different governments of our period, it can well be claimed that they were usually able to maintain law and order and to develop the resources

1. It is probable that the work assumed its present form in *c.* 1400 A.D., but we have shown already how its data are substantially true of our period.

of the country by encouraging trade, industry and agriculture. The immense wealth consisting of pearls, gold and silver, carried away by Mahmud of Ghazna clearly indicates how prosperous the economic condition was during our period. Literature also prospered, especially in the branches of politics, Dharmaśāstra, poetics, astrology, chemistry and philosophy. In the realm of politics, a number of books like the *Nītivākyāmṛita* of Somadeva, the *Rājadharmakāṇḍa* of *Kṛityakalpataru* by Lakshmīdhara, the *Bārhaspatya Arthaśāstra* of Bṛihaspati, the *Yuktikalpataru* of Bhoja, and the *Mānasollāsa* of Someśvara were written during this period. The *Śukranīti* sums up the administrative condition of the age, though in its present form, it is about a couple of centuries later. The Dharmaśāstra works like the *Mitāksharā* of Vijñāneśvara, the *Dāyabhāga* of Jīmūtavāhana, the *Kalpataru* of *Lakshmīdhara*, the *Brāhmaṇasarvasva* of Halāyudha, were composed in our period. It may be pointed out that the first two of these are still regarded as authoritative in the law courts. In the realm of poetics, important authors like Ānandavardhana, Abhinavagupta, Kuntala and Rājaśekhara flourished in our period. In the sphere of chemistry also, our age made a fairly good progress. The chemical knowledge of the *Rasārṇava*, composed in this period is, according to P.C. Ray, distinctly in advance of that of the same period in Europe. Astrology attracted considerable attention. In the earlier period this 'science' hardly existed; in our period, almost every king began to engage a court-astrologer to ensure the prosperity of his kingdom and the success of his army. Some important works on history like the *Gauḍavaho*, the *Kumārapālacharita* and the *Rāmapālacharita* were composed during our period of survey. In the realm of philosophy also, great philosophers like Śaṅkara and Rāmānuja flourished during our period, though they belonged to South India. North India also had its own logicians and philosophers, among whom we may mention Vāchaspatimiśra, Udayana, Jayanta, Śāntarakshita, Jñānaśrī, Ratnākara, and Hemachandra.[1] Achievements in the realm of education were also striking. Our age produced some universities like Nālandā

1. Rahula Sankrityayana, *Pramāṇavārtikabhāshyam*. pp. *dha* and *na*.

and Vikramaśilā of international fame and we find them receiving donations from kings like Balaputradeva from distant Suvarṇadvīpa. Art and architecture also flourished remarkably during this period. Temples at Khajuraho. Bhuvaneśvara and Mt. Abu are remarkable for their architectural grandeur and sculptural beauty. The sculpture of Mathura was of such exquisite beauty that even Mahamud of Ghazna hesitated for sometime before ordering its destruction.

But on the debit side, we have to note that the ideal of India as one political unity could not yet be realised. India was divided into a number of states which were engaged in frequent feuds. An effort was no doubt made by the Pratīhāras to unite most of the states in Northern India and to establish there a strong empire, but that also did not last long. It functioned efficiently only about a century and the failure of the Muslims of Sindh to penetrate further into Rajputana and Central India may rightly be ascribed to the great barrier imposed by the Pratīhāra empire. But when it collapsed, a number of small states came into existence and Mahamud of Ghazna found it easy to gain victory over the different states in India. It may be further pointed out that even after the retirement of Mahamud of Ghazna, the states in Northern India did not unite and merge into a strong unitary state. Such a phenomenon occurred after the invasion of Alexander the Great, but it did not recur after the onslaughts of Mahamud of Ghazna.

Another great defect of the Indian polity of our period was that India did not recognise the importance of establishing mutual contacts with the neighbouring countries. In the Mauryan period, Greek ambassadors were staying at Pataliputra and Indian cultural missions were sent to the neighbouring kingdoms for the propagation of religion. We have some evidence to show, how in the Gupta age, Samudragupta seems to have received some embassies from adjacent islands like Ceylon[1] and probably from Java and Sumatra.

1. The evidence referred to above is the statement of the Allahabad Pillar Inscription of Samudragupta which states '*Daivaputra-Shāhi-Shāhānushāhi-Śaka-Murundaiḥ-Saimhalakādibhis'cha sarvadvīpavāsibhiḥ......... sevā-kṛita-bāhu-vīrya-prasara-dharaṇi-bandhasya*'' (*contd. on next page*)

But during our period, no such ambassadors were sent or received. Had the Chāhamānas and the Gāhaḍavālas kept regular missions in Kabul and Lahore, they would have realised how weak the successors of Mahamud of Ghazna had become by c. 1100 A.D. and could have taken steps to eliminate the foreign power from the Punjab. The advance of the Turks from Central Asia was hardly known in the Indian capitals. The invasion of Mahamud of Ghor therefore came as a great surprise to the states of Northern India, which could not unite together to give a joint resistance to the invader.

It is possible to argue that this statement may be a mere courtly exaggeration, hence we have guardedly stated that 'Samudragupta seems to have received some embassies'. It may however, be pointed out that the statement refers to diplomatic contacts with the Kushāṇas and Śakas as also the rulers of Ceylon and other islands. The diplomatic relations with the Śakas and Kushāṇas are generally taken to be sober historic facts; to doubt them in connection with the rulers of Ceylon and other islands would therefore be hardly fair. We know from Chinese sources that 'the Siṁhalese monarch sent envoys to the Indian potentate and obtained from him permission to build a convent at Buddha Gaya for the benefit of pilgrims from Ceylon to that holy place' (Majumdar and Altekar, *The Age of the Vākāṭakas*, p. 258).

If the embassy from Ceylon suggested by the Allahabad Pillar Inscription is thus very probable, there is no reason why we should distrust its statement, about other islands also doing the same.

BIBLIOGRAPHY

Original Works in Sanskrit

Ṛigveda	Vaidika Yantralaya edition, 1907
Atharvaveda	Vaidika Yantrālaya edition, 1907
Aitareya-Brāhmaṇa	Ānandāśrama Press edition. Edited by Haug, Bombay, 1863
Taittirīya-Brāhmaṇa	Ānandāśrama Press edition
Baudhāyana-Dharmasūtra	Anandāśrama Press edition, 1920
Mahābhārata	Chitraśālā Press edition, Poona, 1929-33
Manu-Smṛiti	Nirṇayasāgara Press edition, 1909
Nārada-Smṛiti	Edited by Dr. Jolly, Calcutta, 1885
Yājñavalkya-Smṛiti	Nirṇaya-sāgara Press edition, 1918
Agni-Purāṇa	Ānandāśrama Press edition, Poona, 1900
Matsya-Purāṇa	Ānandāśrama Press edition
Arthaśāstra of Kauṭilya	Edited by Dr. Shamsastri, Mysore, 1923
Bārhaspatya-Arthaśāstra	Edited by Thomas, Brussels, 1916
Kāmandakīya-Nītisāra	Published by Khemarāja Śri Krishnadas
Śukranīti	Edited by Jivananda Vidyasagara Bhattacharya, Calcutta, 1890
Yuktikalpataru	Edited by I.C. Sastri, Calcutta, 1917
Mānasollāsa	Edited by G.K. Shrigondekar; Gaekwad's Oriental Series, No. LXXXIV.
Rājadharma-kāṇḍa of Kṛityakalpataru	Edited by K.V. Rangasvami Aiyangar, Gaekwad's Oriental Series No. XI.
Kādambarī	Nirṇayasāgara Press edition, 1912
Rājataraṅgiṇī	Translation by R.S. Pandit, Allahabad, 1934.
Nītivākyāmṛita	Grantharatnamālā edition.

Modern Books on Polity and History

Aiyangar, K.V.	Ancient Indian Polity, 2nd ed., Madras, 1935.

Aiyangar, K.V. Rājadharma, Madras, 1951.

Altekar, A.S. State and Government in Ancient India, 3rd ed., Patna, 1955.

Altekar, A.S. Rāshṭrakūṭas and Their Times, Poona, 1934.

Altekar, A.S. Village Communities in Western India, Bombay, 1927.

Banerjee, P.N. Public Administration in Ancient India, London, 1916.

Beni Prasad The State in Ancient India, Allahabad, 1928.

Beni Prasad The Political Theory in Ancient India, Allahabad, 1927.

Bhat, B.V. Shivajichi Rājanīti, Rajawade Samśodhana Mandala, 1941.

Banerjee, R.D. The Pālas of Bengal, Calcutta, 1924.

Banerjee., R.D. History of Orissa, Calcutta, 1931.

Bandyopadhyaya, N.C. Development of Hindu Polity and Political Theories. Calcutta, 1927.

Chakraverty, P.C. The art of War in Ancient India, Dacca, 1941.

Dikshitar, V.R.R. Hindu Administrative Institutions, Madras, 1929.

Dikshitar, V.R.R. Mauryan Polity, Madras, 1932.

Dikshitar, V.R.R. Gupta Polity, Madras, 1952.

Gune, V.T. The Judicial System of the Marathas, Poona, 1953.

Ganguli, D.C. The Paramāras, Dacca, 1933.

Ghoshal, U.N. Hindu Revenue System, Calcutta, 1923.

Ghoshal, U.N. A History of Indian Political Theories, Calcutta, 1923.

Ghoshal, U.N. A History of Hindu Public Life, Vol. I, Calcutta, 1944.

Kane, P.V. History of Dharmaśāstra, Vol. III.

Keith, A.B. History of Sanskrit Literature, Oxford, 1928.

Jayaswal, K.P. Hindu Polity, Calcutta, 1924.

Law, N.N. Interstate Relations in Ancient India, Calcutta, 1920.

Law, N.N.	Aspects of Ancient Indian Polity, Oxford, 1921.
Majumdar, R.C.	History of Bengal, Vol. I, Calcutta, 1943.
Majumdar, R.C.	Ancient India, 2nd ed., Banaras, 1952.
Majumdar, R.C.	Corporate Life in Ancient India, Calcutta, 1920.
Majumdar, and Altekar	The Age of the Vākāṭakas, Ist. ed. Lahore, 1946.
Majumdar, and Pusalkar	The Age of Imperial Kanauj, Bharatiya Vidya Bhawan, 1955.
Mookerjee, R.K.	Local Self Government in Ancient India, Oxford, 1920.
Nāzim Muhammad	The Life and Times of Sultan Mahmud of Ghazena, Cambridge, 1931.
Ray, H.C.	Dynastic History of Northern India, Vol. I & II, Calcutta. 1936·
Sen, B.C.	Historical Aspects of Bengal Inscriptions, Calcutta, 1942.
Sarkar, B.K.	The Political Institutions and Theories of the Hindus, Calcutta, 1939.
Sarkar, B.K	The Positive Background of Hindu Sociology, The Sacred Books Series, Volume XVI.
Sarkar, B.K.	The Śukranīti, Allahabad, 1914.
Sinha, B.P.	The Decline of the Kingdom of Magadha, Patna, 1954.
Saletore, B.A.	Social and Political Life in the Vijayanagara Empire, Vol. I. and II, Madras, 1934.
Śastri, K.A.N.	The Cholas, Madras, 1935.
Tripathi, R.S.	History of Kanauj, Banaras, 1937.
Vaidya, C.V.	History of Medieval Hindu India, Vol. III, Poona, 1926.
Wright, H.N.	The Sultans of Delhi, Their Coinage and Metrology, Oxford 1936.

SUBJECT-INDEX

T

U

V

Corrigenda

P.	L.	Read	For
10.	33	should be	should not be
13.	39	sarvadā	sarvaād
18.	3	treasury	treasure
20.	17	than	thna
38.	12	impotence	importance
38.	34	shaṇḍha	shaṇḍa
40.	35	vāgraja	vāgra
40.	36	rājye	raje
41.	17	falling	failing
45.	31	covetousness	convetousness
51.	5	looked	look
51.	27	considerably	considerable
58.	21	principal	principle
59.	33	waning	waving
65.	2	brakes	breaks
66.	27	enjoying	enjoing
75.	20	describes	descrebes
75.	21	pondering	pondring
77.	13	probably	prabably
120.	17	It is	It it
142.	24	dependants	dependents
154.	18	predilections	predelictions
160.	5	records	recdrds
198.	2	councils	conncils
200.	16	fishermen	fisherman